BIBLES AND BAEDEKERS

Cross Cultural Theologies

Series Editors: Jione Havea and Clive Pearson, both at United Theological College, Sydney, and Charles Sturt University, Australia, and Anthony G. Reddie, Queen's Foundation for Ecumenical Theological Education, Birmingham

This series focuses on how the "cultural turn" in interdisciplinary studies has informed theology and biblical studies. It takes its leave from the experience of the flow of people from one part of the world to another.

It moves beyond the crossing of cultures in a narrow diasporic sense. It entertains perspectives that arise out of generational criticism, gender, sexual orientation, and the relationship of film to theology. It explores the sometimes competing rhetoric of multiculturalism and cross-culturalism and demonstrates a concern for the intersection of globalization and how those global flows of peoples and ideas are received and interpreted in localized settings. The series seeks to make use of a range of disciplines including the study of cross-cultural liturgy, travel, the practice of ministry and worship in multi-ethnic locations and how theologies that have arisen in one part of the world have migrated to a new location. It looks at the public nature of faith in complex, multicultural, multireligious societies and compare how diverse faiths and their theologies have responded to the same issues.

The series welcomes contributions by scholars from around the world. It will include both single authored and multi-authored volumes.

Published

Global Civilization
Leonardo Boff

Dramatizing Theologies: A Participative Approach to Black God-Talk
Anthony G. Reddie

Art as Theology: The Religious Transformation of Art from the Postmodern to the Medieval
Andreas Andreopoulos

Black Theology in Britain: A Reader
Edited by Michael N. Jagessar and Anthony G. Reddie

Home Away from Home: The Caribbean Diasporan Church in the Black Atlantic Tradition
Delroy A. Reid-Salmon

Forthcoming

Working Against the Grain: Black Theology in the 21st Century
Anthony G. Reddie

Another World is Possible: Spiritualities and Religions of Global Darker Peoples
Edited by Dwight N. Hopkins and Marjorie Lewis

Out of Place: Theologising at Crosscultural Brinks
Edited by Jione Havea and Clive Pearson

The Non-Western Jesus: Jesus as Bodhisattva, Avatara, Guru, Prophet, Ancestor and Healer
Martien Brinkman

BIBLES AND BAEDEKERS

TOURISM, TRAVEL, EXILE AND GOD

Mike Grimshaw

LONDON   OAKVILLE

Published by Equinox Publishing Ltd.
UK: Unit 6, The Village, 101 Amies St., London SW11 2JW
USA: DBBC, 28 Main Street, Oakville, CT 06779

www.equinoxpub.com

First published 2008

British Library Cataloguing-in-Publication Data

A catalogue record for this book is available from the British Library.

ISBN-13   978 1 84553 068 6 (hardback)
          978 1 84553 069 3 (paperback)

Library of Congress Cataloging-in-Publication Data

Grimshaw, Mike, 1967-
Bibles and Baedekers : tourism, travel, exile and God / Mike
Grimshaw.
     p. cm.—(Cross cultural theologies)
Includes bibliographical references and index.
ISBN 1-84553-068-3 (hb)—ISBN 1-84553-069-1 (pb)
1. Spiritual life. 2. Postmodern theology. 3. Christian pilgrims and
pilgrimages. 4. Tourism—Religious aspects—Christianity. 5.
Travel—Religious aspects—Christianity I. Title. II. Series.
BV4501.3.G745 2006
261.5—dc22
                    2006007974

Typeset by S.J.I. Services, New Delhi
Printed and bound in Great Britain by Lightning Source, Milton Keynes, UK.

Contents

Foreword

Mike Grimshaw has come at the business of constructing a cross-cultural theology from a very different angle. His provocative text is written out of an experience of self-confessed marginality. That is not especially unusual. It is not uncommon for those who construct a cross-cultural or diasporic theology to feel as if they are on the edge of the received mainline discourse and inhabit a position of liminality. Where Grimshaw differs is his interest in a cross-cultural dialectic that is western and secular.

Some of Grimshaw's language is familiar enough to the stock run of theologians: there is plenty of talk about God and Christology. There is reference to Karl Barth, Dietrich Bonhoeffer, to neo-orthodoxy and death of God theologians. But then there is a line of difference. For those of us who are familiar with various movements of theological modernism, Grimshaw's use of the term may well seem idiosyncratic and perhaps jar – until it is recognized that his use of modernism comes not from theology but from architecture. Here is a sign of an alternative method and concern. Grimshaw draws upon secular texts to explore what a secular theology might look like in a world variously described as pre-modern, modern, postmodern and modern again after postmodernity. For the sake of his cross-cultural theology there is no sideways glance to current scholars working in this territory – and part of the reason for this preference lies in his interesting strategy of making use of literature to do with art and travel.

The metaphor of travel is employed to describe what kind of theologies are on offer in this complex urban world. Are we tourists, travellers or exiles as we negotiate our way through the legacy of the Enlightenment and modernity? Grimshaw furnishes much food for thought in his guidebook suitably named *Bibles and Baedekers*. I found sections of this text most apposite when I was reading certain chapters while a guest of a Muslim network touring through Turkey. Who was I – and what was I doing in my own theology – as I made my way round the museum of the Hagia Sophia and to the ruins of Nicea, Assos and Ephesus? What kind of hermeneutic was I employing as I found myself to be a theologian crossing several cultures as, at least, hopefully an "intelligent tourist" with a *Lonely Planet* at hand?

This monograph by Mike Grimshaw is rather different from other texts on cross-cultural theology, then. Its hero is the *flaneur* who wanders through the secular western city looking for the presence and absence of

God in its architecture and sense of place. For those of us who live in highly hybridized cities where religiosity has made such a significant return, Grimshaw's writing reminds us to take into account the constructed secular city as part of the current theological agenda.

Clive Pearson, United Theological College, Sydney

Introduction

In 1844 Karl Marx stated, "the criticism of religion is the prerequisite of all criticism."[1] Over the following 150 years, the self-expressions of modernity seem to have been primarily engaged in carrying out Marx's injunction. It is important to note that this critique occurs both about religion and increasingly from within religion. The often overlooked self-critique occurs from within religious communities and thinkers seeking to locate a place for religion within the variations of modernity.[2]

In the light of these moves, it has become noticeable over the past decade that an inter-textual hermeneutic is developing between cultural criticism and what could be broadly termed religious studies. In particular, cultural criticism and religion are increasingly underpinning debates of the politics of location and the self.[3] These debates, however, have been primarily within the field of cultural criticism. It is fascinating and instructive to engage with secular critics using religious ideas, texts and metaphors (more specifically those from the Judeo-Christian narratives and tradition) to both underwrite and extrapolate their thesis.[4] Little, however, has been attempted to replicate this trend within the Judeo-Christian source. Partly this state of affairs has been due to the type of language used. Historians, philosophers and those working in religious studies are prone to refer to the need to integrate Christianity with culture. From their perspective, theology often appears wary of allowing itself to be remade and rearticulated with the same degree of openness that cultural criticism shows to theological/religious tropes.[5] Conversely, theologians are more likely to talk of the need to integrate gospel and culture, theology and culture, or Christ and culture. This difference can often result in the two general approaches, with theologians and those others writing on religion, effectively talking and writing at cross-purposes. Theologians often talk about a specific faith-based or confessional approach and analysis regarding culture. The non-theologian is more content to use the generic term Christianity in order to differentiate their approach as dealing with a hypothesized "Christian culture" (or its legacy) and cultural criticism. This difference means that the priority of the explicitly theological position serves to order any re-reading as occurring *only* through the lens of theology. Conversely, especially amongst more conservative Christians, there is often considerable resistance to theology being re-read through cultural criticism and still continuing to be able to be viewed *as* theology. For them, to re-read theology/the theological position through cultural criticism is viewed as stripping away the theological. Such a cultural re-reading is often viewed not only as an act of secularization, but also implicitly positing the efficacy of cultural criticism over the theological. In effect, it is the repeat of the old debate as to the efficacy of the sacred and the profane: is the sacred reduced by contact with the profane – or is the profane transformed?

One would assume that the priority of the theological means that no reduction can occur. That is, the theological as the sacred will always transform the profane, not be reduced and made profane in itself. It is acknowledged that a misreading may eventuate. Yet, in reality all theology is, to one degree or another, a form of misreading, undertaken as it is by fallible humanity. This necessary failing should be remembered by those claiming the need for a *literalist* theological reading. The attempt to read and believe in such a manner is an act of reductionism. Such an attempt limits the sacred and the Christian claim of revelation to that which can be *literally* represented, written and read *within* the world and limits of fallible humanity. What sits at the heart of any theological reading is the realization and acknowledgment that humanity is fallible. Any response, then, is only ever provisional and *can never be* literal. To acknowledge this element of provisionality is to recognize that all theology is a form of misreading, and is in constant need of divine correction. This necessity occurs because theology is an ongoing response to God in opposition to any literalist reading of theology or the Bible that seeks to freeze a certain period as normative.

In speaking of a theological reading that is frozen as normative, I am not just referring to the obvious example of the fundamentalist. Instead I wish to widen the scope to include such reading strategies as exist in many confessional and conservative theological writings and, especially, in a good deal of popular piety. At the risk of presenting a "straw man," I feel there is the need to recognize the reality of those forms of reading which take the biblical text and times as literally true as they are written and read in the Bible. Such a reading is often a form of looking to the presentation of the past in the biblical text as the location of what is true and normative for all humanity in every time and context.

The reality of any literal reading, however, is that the time (in the biblical text) that is frozen as normative is not actually the past that is literally read. Instead, what is frozen as normative are the particular beliefs of that current time and person who chooses to read that particular text as literally normative. This freezing is because the literalist reads the past as if it is the present and so demands a form of literal presentism. In such a reading, the text is radically dislocated by being literally rewritten for the reader as, for example, speaking specifically to my concerns here as I write in Christchurch, New Zealand on the afternoon of May 12, 2008. In doing so, I make my concerns and myself the focal point of the history of Judeo-Christian revelation. The biblical text and context become what is read as if written to address what I wish it to say here and now. If I were to partake in a literalist re-reading, I would (in the logic of the literalist) be able to claim that God *through* that particular text, that God *in* that particular text was speaking, actually, directly, intentionally, to me here and now.

What occurs in such particular reading strategies and piety is the confusion of the address of God to humanity in general with a self-affirmative belief in the address of God to humanity in particular. It ignores the conventional Judeo-Christian belief, especially the Protestant position, that the Bible is normative as the corrective to any attempts to freeze a literal reading. This is because the Christian belief in the Logos within the logos of text is actually the corrective encounter with all humanity and all texts. The Logos within the logos is the corrective encounter of revelation as rupture in opposition to attempts to limit literally the boundaries and expressions of that revelation and encounter. Too often we forget that to make God present or absent is the act of God; to read literally is seeking to act as God. To re-read theology from other perspectives cannot diminish theology. Rather, such readings always open us up to the rupture of revelation; they may actually serve as new forms of encounter and correction by the Logos behind all logos. The challenge is thus not to read theology in the light of other texts, but rather to take the risk of reading other texts as if they are theological. It is the challenge and the risk of reading non-theological texts while open to the possibility that the rupture of the Logos is present within them.

If we begin to read cultural criticism with the same strategy as cultural critics appear to read religious texts, then some important and interesting counter inter-textuality can occur. The *raison d'être* for approaching theology in this manner arises out of the current state of theology itself. This is especially so from an antipodean perspective. From such a post-Christian, postmodern environment[6] it is personally apparent there is a need to expand the limits of the theological endeavour to encompass the insights and articulations of other disciplines. Just as cultural criticism has made use of religion and theology to force a twist in perspective and a new way of seeing, theology likewise requires new approaches if it is not to position itself in a form of isolation. The need for such a re-orientation is especially true for those of us who locate ourselves on the margins of the theology and outside the institutional church. How might a re-reading strategy for secular theology as a form of cross-cultural theology be undertaken? How might a cross-cultural theology be a reading of rupture *between* the cultures of secular and theological western, urban modernity?

A starting point is to recognize that theological debates (and, in particular, those arising out of a Protestant tradition) most often seem to arise out of a textual dialectic. Of course, if one traces theology back through God-talk to a Logos/logos-centred approach,[7] then word is all it ever is – and ultimately can be. The result of such a reading is that word is both Logos and the expression of logos in the Word. So the first textual dialectic is the Logos as rupture within the words of the biblical text. In the Protestant tradition this encounter in the words of the Word is where God as Word is to be ultimately found – and is, therefore, freely available to all. This dialectic managed to survive, with increasing tension, into modernity. But, in a postmodern world (and, even more so, in a post-Christendom world) that secular–religious modernist divide has dissolved into a post-secular pluralistic negative[8] incarnation of word as words, text as texts, and ultimately word as wor(l)d. What we have here is the Marxian "melting of all that is solid" – read from the post-theological perspective.

The dissolution of theological solidity is the starting point for the reading strategy that underwrites[9] this particular attempt at cross-cultural theology. The rupture of the theological encounter that is distinct from the self-gnosticism of popular and pervasive spirituality is now engaged in a reapplied hermeneutic with the new sources of its own location and self-disclosure.[10] The challenge is one of rearticulating the theological endeavour in an environment where the traditional expressions and examples seem to have lost their relevance, potency and meaning. And yet conversely, this task must also be done in a manner which takes the theological endeavour seriously as theology, and not as a reduction to the self-(hip)gnosis[11] of much contemporary spirituality.

The following re-reading as cross-cultural theology arose out of two texts which, at first glance, have nothing at all to do with theology: Edward Said's 1993 Reith Lectures *Representations of the Intellectual*,[12] and Caren Kaplan's *Questions of Travel: Postmodern Discourses of Displacement*.[13] Reading them from a strategy of inter-textuality they became texts of rupture.[14] Their discussions on the implications of displacement and exile appeared to present a sense of what is involved and experienced in attempting to articulate theology in the postmodern world. With Said, in particular, it was his expression of the difficulties of the median state of exile: "neither completely at home with the new setting nor fully disencumbered of the old, best with half involvements and half detachments, nostalgic and sentimental on the one level, an adept mimic or a secret outcast on another."[15] For me this appeared to articulate the position of the postmodern theologian inhabiting the liminal state of the exile.

This, then, is the starting point: if the postmodern theologian is in exile, how might the modernist/orthodox theologian[16] be redefined? We will also need to re-think popular piety which is often read as being in tension with institutional and academic theology. The tension is a response from the position (from below) of popular piety and a rejection (from above) from institutional and academic theology. The re-reading I am proposing has three locations of possible rupture: the postmodern, the modernist/orthodox and popular piety. Such a re-reading is of crucial importance for the self-fractured world of contemporary theological endeavour. For while theology has been a forerunner in mapping out the issue of postmodernity,[17] it has also been one of the disciplines which, by virtue of its traditional orthodox and especially modernist concerns, has often also been at the forefront of opposition to postmodernity. Furthermore, popular piety has itself been an eclectic mix of modernist, postmodern and, indeed, pre-modern concerns.

This text argues for a fresh way of understanding what appears to be occurring in the self-fractured world of theology. It suggests a strategy of re-reading in a similar fashion to that undertaken by cultural criticism's use of theology and religion. To do so, Kaplan's text debating the differences between exile, traveller and tourist is of central importance. Her discussion situates a critique of the theories of displacement *as* a critical deconstruction of the terms and their implications in the continuing debates on modernity and postmodernity. As such it is intellectually provocative for theologians who may find themselves displaced academically. In considering the issues raised by both Kaplan and Said, an inter-textual reinterpretation of theology arises. If it is then proposed that the postmodern theologian is in a Saidian exile, can the case be made for the modernist/orthodox theologian being the traveller and explorer?[18] And does that make the belief and practice of popular piety analogous to that of the tourist? The implications of such a redefinition, re-reading and rethinking allows the differences between these positions to be investigated in a new way.

Having posited and examined what are three new theological tropes, those of tourist, traveller and exile, a problem arises. While all three mapped out many of the situations that theologians and writers on Christianity in contemporary post-Christian western culture find themselves, they do not actually offer a possible new way forward. All three tropes, while offering possible lines of interception with contemporary issues in Christianity, locate the encounter with what is deemed to be true, real, authentic elsewhere. Forcing this reassessment in my own thinking was the increasing centrality of the position of Bonhoeffer's call for a religionless Christianity. On the one hand, it is easy to reassign Bonhoeffer's call to a now-past modernity, speaking to a mid-century secularity arising as a form of modernist expectation out of a theology of crisis and a rapidly secularizing Europe. Now, on the other side of modernity,[19] Bonhoeffer's call comes afresh as a form of rupture.

This return to Bonhoeffer's challenge occurs out of the challenge of the return of religion in the past decade. Derrida, Vattimo, Bauman and Zizek[20] are but a few of the prominent theorists who turned to religion.

Out of this re-turn has arisen a new challenge: can we articulate what my colleague Paul Morris termed religionless religion?[21]

In my conclusion I begin to engage with what is involved in such a challenge. It is a provisional conclusion for it is a yet to be completed process. More work is needed on how it both intersects and deviates from what a rethought, reassessed religionless Christianity may entail.[22] It is provisional because until we re-think what a religionless Christianity entails, we cannot properly discuss religionless religion. The positioning of this text arises from my view that a religionless Christianity first needs to be articulated and engaged with as the post-Christian West embarks on a new form of modernity after the retraction from postmodernity. In this new turn to modernity, both secularization and desecularization continue apace (and in this are a rejection of both old modernity and postmodernity). Out of this re-turn a new challenge arises for those who exist still within Christianity, on its borders, or in its theological-cultural wake. Only by first re-engaging with a turn to modernity (whether in its mid-twentieth century or early twenty-first-century forms) as prophetically challenged by Bonhoeffer in his call for religionless Christianity, can we even begin to turn to a future engagement with what might turn out to be a religionless religion.

In this sense, I want to argue that for the post-Christian West, Christianity firstly has to be religionless before it can adequately engage with the challenge of religionless religion. Christianity also needs to do so if it wishes to offer an alternative that enables the West to be post-Christian. A post-Christian West is perhaps that culture that continues after the demise of Christendom, yet does not sink into sectarian relativism. Running throughout this text, then, is the continual challenge of how to articulate a religionless Christianity. How can we do this when popular Christianity so often seems to be turning back to religion, to piety, or to prosperity gospels of personal and communal self-affirmation that verge on Pelagianism?

It is also important, when undertaking such a radical critique – and especially when addressing the centrality of issues of identity and location in theology – to be up-front and locate oneself. This imperative is particularly important when writing theology in a way most people would not expect – or in a way that most probably consider unacceptable. My focus on the issues of religionless religion, religionless Christianity, and what could be termed secular theology, arise precisely because of where I find myself. Nevertheless, this work is, in the end, still very much a work of cross-cultural theology. It is a cross-cultural theology insofar as it occurs between (and within) western Christian and western post-Christian/secular cultures. I acknowledge that this project runs counter to the most common perceptions of what constitutes cross-cultural theology. It is a debate arising out of a position, globally speaking, of early twenty-first-century wealth and privilege. But a problem arises if I, and the millions like me who exist within this clash of cultures, are not allowed, or are not prepared, to express what cross-cultural theology means to and for us. If we do not speak, then we merely serve to perpetuate the claim that the real, the authentic – that grace – is only now, only ever now, to be located elsewhere: that is, in other times, other locations, and other cultures. Or, there is then the contrary claim made that in a western society grace is encountered only in locations and communities of sectarian, pietistic retreat. My position is that the corrective of theology, that rupture of Logos in logos, if addressed to all humanity, must also be allowed to rupture within and from within these western cross-cultural debates. Bonhoeffer's challenge is a clarion call, on this side of the return to modernity, to be aware that I, and those like me, must be open to the challenge and corrective as expressed within our own cultures.

I write this text as one who sits on the margins of Christianity – outside the institution but tied by culture, history and faithless faith to its theological challenges. I have moved from ordinand for the Presbyterian ministry, to licentiate, to one who has cut his institutional ties because I felt that I could no longer claim, with integrity, to be a member of the faith, and more particularly of the church, not believing as I did. I had and have too great a respect for those who do believe for me to claim that where I am falls within the same arena of belief as they would recognize. And yet, I have found a home of sorts in the discipline of Religious Studies, able to engage with, critique, discuss and write about Christianity in a manner that has enabled me to return to the margins of the faith. So I find myself in a position where I may not be able to say that I believe, but I can say that I "respond." This distance has also enabled me to re-engage with mid-century Protestant theology, with the claims of neo-orthodoxy, in a new way.

The challenge of Karl Barth and Bonhoeffer in particular, as theologians grappling with Christianity, modernity and secularity, suddenly spoke to me as I found myself on the other side of postmodernism. If I was to speak theologically, I could consider the use of the term rupture. For when I re-thought the background to secular Christianity I continually came up against the work of Barth and Bonhoeffer. To re-read them afresh, without the institutional demands or politics, was, it would be fair to say, to experience a type of dislocating rupture. This is not to say that I find myself suddenly relocated as neo-orthodox. I cannot exist as if the postmodern, non-realist challenge has not occurred. And yet I am increasingly aware of the limitations of locating oneself within a position and cultural shift that has, itself, now passed.

If, as I will argue, we are within a new type of modernity, then in a modern act of self-reflexivity, I will turn to that neo-orthodox past, in rupture with the postmodern recent past. In this text I seek a re-engagement with their twin provocations to a resurgent western, urban modernity. I seek to re-use them in this new type of modernity that is a secularizing modernity. We find ourselves in a new modernity that includes an increasingly sectarian Christianity turning more and more to pneumatic piety. And so in this modernity after postmodernity I wish to wrestle anew with the challenges laid down by Barth and Bonhoeffer in their particular critique of twentieth-century modern society. But I do so in a manner that acknowledges their context and my own are similar – but different.

This similar-but-different critique extends to my own situation in Aotearoa, New Zealand. Over the last decade there has been a neo-orthodox resurgence and dominance in our theologians and Protestant institutions. My re-engagement is, in this context, also internally cross-cultural. As a post-Christian outsider I often find myself engaging by necessity with neo-orthodox insiders. It has been fascinating to note the short-circuits that result when we find ourselves attempting to use (and re-use) common language and sources in different ways for different ends. These encounters for me are also underwritten by my continuing interest in the issues raised by the death of God theologians in the 1960s. For it was a provocative (I could say rupturing) experience to note that they had mainly been Barthians, who had turned to the death of God as a form of religionless Christianity.[23] The experience of re-reading their challenge and critique, allied with the provocation of Barth and especially Bonhoeffer (and in particular his *Christology*), severely challenged and disturbed me as I wrote this text. I realized that modernity itself included a form of theological response. While the postmodern turn to the spiritual was seen as allowing religion back into public discourse and theory, it was often, so it seems, predicated upon a false dialectic. Here the problem lay in how an intensely modernist form of theological thought (neo-orthodoxy) often presented itself as being in opposition to modernity, whereas it actually was (and is) intensely modernist – and indeed quite secular. In considering this problem, a nagging question arose: If we now find ourselves in a new type of soft modernism, then perhaps we need to re-encounter, re-read and re-use some of the claims and challenges from a neo-orthodox modernity?

The challenge of re-encountering Bonhoeffer forced this text on from the original tropes of tourist, traveller and exile into the new trope of the *flaneur*. The dislocation of the original tropes now demanded, in this new modernity, a form of relocation within the modern experience. The problem now is that postmodernity seemed to have all too uncritically embraced the dislocation of the tourist, the traveller and the exile. Postmodernity appeared to have taken these essentially modernist tropes and sought their resolution in the pursuit of the real now *only* to be found elsewhere. And yet if the real is only to be experienced or located where we are not, then is this not just the triumph of an atheistic, anti-theological modernity? In effect, the challenge to postmodernity from the newly emerging soft modernism is one of how can we regain that central modernist identity of self-reflexivity – that includes the theological? The question started to emerge: is the religionless Christian a type of theological *flaneur* amongst and within the modern, urban crowd?

The text, instead of ending with exile as the location and trope for the postmodern Christian, has taken a step onward into the new theological trope of the *flaneur*. To my surprise it also meant a move into the discussion of what a religionless Christology might possibly involve. It was the challenge of Bonhoeffer that forced this text out of its original agenda and idea, that of a more traditional, historical encounter of Christianity and location/dislocation. The results are to be especially found in the discussion on the *flaneur* in Chapter 4 and the possibilities of religionless Christology in Chapter 5. The reassessment of the attempt to undertake such a cross-cultural theology is discussed in greater detail in the conclusion.

So what has resulted is this work of secular theology, of secular cross-cultural (yet also inter/intra-cultural) theology written from the margins of faith. It is also written from a marginal physical location[24] and from within a discipline that, on one level, is antithetical to the claims made by theology. Such an attempt, however, is perhaps indicative of the space from which theology may increasingly be undertaken if it is not to be reduced to sectarian sentiment in a pluralist environment. It also is a work that takes very seriously the necessity of continuing to strive to write and think theologically even within the challenges of a secular discipline and a secular university. It is written from within a framework that takes as unavoidable the question posed by Bonhoeffer and, in effect, re-posed by the neo-modernist turn on from postmodernity[25] as we venture into this first decade of the twenty-first century.

The result is theology that many will not recognize as theology. In a sense, what we have here is theology by default and by dissent. It is theology that engages with the legacy of Christianity but refuses to limit theology to what occurs within explicitly theological texts and intentions. It is secular theology insofar as it rejects the desire, most often it seems expressed *by* Christianity, to locate theology and theological expression within quite self-consciously sectarian locations and expressions.

Perhaps the central methodology is that best articulated by Slavoj Zizek in his promotion of short-circuit readings. To understand his challenge it is worthwhile to reference his procedure in detail:

Is not one of the most effective critical procedures to cross wires that do not usually touch: to take a major classic (text, author, notion) and read it in a short-circuiting way, through the lens of a "minor" author, text, or conceptual apparatus ("minor" should be understood here in Deleuze's sense: not "of less quality", but marginalized, disavowed by the hegemonic ideology, or dealing with a "lower", less dignified topic)? If the minor reference is well chosen, such a procedure can lead to insights which completely shatter and undermine our common perceptions [which results in] ... the inherent decentering of the interpreted text, which brings to light its "unthought", its disavowed presuppositions and consequences.[26]

This text is thus a Zizekian-influenced deconstruction of minor texts on tourism, travel, exile – and *flanerie*. These have been short-circuited with the major texts of the Bible and selected traditions of theology. The short-circuits are ones that I observed, and sometimes caused by crossing the wires in particular ways. The aim of crossing the wires was to spark the challenge of re-thinking theology and what can be considered both a resource for, and as, a theological text. It is then a form of postmodern secular theology following Charles Winquist's statement:

A post-modern theology has had to rethink its warrant without authority from outside its own productive formulations. That is, theology is a *textual production* that is always in the middle of existing discourses...it makes a place of its own through strategies and tactics within a cacophony of diverse textual voices.[27] [emphasis added]

The short-circuiting is what occurs both *within* theology as a textual production and *as* theology as a textual production. This text takes a further step and includes postmodernity itself as another reading strategy and textual production that needs to be engaged with. Soft modern, post-postmodern, post-Christian theology such as this is theology that engages with modernity, postmodernity, secularity and Christianity in an inter-textual manner. As such, it is yet another return to that central modernist demand of self-reflexivity. For to be inter-textual, as Graham Ward states, is to note "that none of us write on a *tabula rasa*. We each stand within a tradition of some sort, with a legacy of some sort, and we are re-reading it."[28]

The central methodology and assumption of this text is the necessity of being inter-textual, of reading texts so they critique each other. It responds to what is in the short-circuits between texts in a reading strategy that holds open the possibility that perhaps grace may appear. The rupture of the Logos that sits behind Christianity, western secularity, western ontology and western ontotheology[29] is what is sought for in this inter-textual critique of texts. It is acknowledged that for most, such texts will be the last place to begin to think theologically. Nevertheless, I write out of the legacy of where I am inside both a western Christianity and western secularity. I am located more within the secular world than the overtly

Christian. And yet in fact I have made a (conscious) form of that very Protestant sectarian decision to move out of the tradition as it is – and yet continue to interact and challenge with that tradition I have reacted against. It is within the texts of the secular world in which I choose to live and read and think that I find I must textually search for the glimpses of grace.

This centrality of the search for grace is what Calasso noted as holding together the books, photographs and character of the travel writer Bruce Chatwin.[30] In my re-reading, the location of grace with the traveller is held up for critique. This text locates itself against such readings that seek to make grace variously sectarian, exotic, lost, or easily achieved. The critique is against all theologies of tourism, travel and exile. It is against all attempts to locate the rupture of grace anywhere but where we find ourselves.

The central re-reading strategy is to read texts on tourism, travel and exile as if they were theological writings because so often they seem to offer a possible location and experience of grace that is deeply attractive for a secular western modernity that locates the real, the authentic – or even grace – as that which has been lost, relocated or found only over there: anywhere but here.[31] In rejecting such a dislocation, I locate my attempt in the wake of two core challenges recently laid down. The first is that of Gabriel Vahanian's reminder that the *saeculum* is the only place we ever encounter God.[32] The second is that provocatively stated by Gianni Vattimo in his challenge to the West: either it retreats into an anti-modern Christianity that rejects modernity and rejects being a world and civilization and becomes a sect, or (as he and I wish) it needs to follow the alternative choice:

> To embrace the destiny of modernity and the West [which] means mainly to realise the profoundly Christian meaning of secularization.[33]

I also want to proceed with Charles Taylor's allied challenge for contemporary theologians in modern times: while "they may still think in theological terms...this is theology in quite a different register. They have to speak as theorists in a profane world."[34]

So this is unashamedly secular, profane theology and secular, profane theological theory. It has as its model that identified by Cunningham as lying at the heart of the Logos-derived Western theorist: Jacob wrestling with God (Genesis 32). Here the wrestling with God [Logos] – the location of truth – is a symbol of the act of interpretation, the symbol of the act of reading, and especially the symbol of the practice of deconstruction.[35] The theorist in a profane world, wrestling with the Logos in all its guises, needs to remember that Jacob may have received the blessing he sought after a long struggle, but he also carried a permanent wound as a reminder that, to mix theological metaphors, there is no such thing as cheap grace.

This is similar to the warning of Charles Winquist: deconstructive postmodern critique makes other texts unsafe.[36]

In a Protestant re-reading, it could be perhaps argued that all theology is to some extent textual deconstruction. For theology involves two types of deconstructive wrestling. It demands wrestling with texts where grace may be glimpsed and encountered, and a wrestling in texts that continually re-open an ongoing hermeneutic of challenge. It is, as such, the reminder that theology makes all texts unsafe. Such a lack of protection should be welcomed. Valentine Cunningham observes:

> Deconstructionism is not some awful spectre to be banished if possible from the Table of the Lord. Theology needs the reminders of deconstruction as much as deconstruction depends on theology.[37]

The challenge is laid down by Vattimo. The God of the post-metaphysical and postmodern epoch is the God of the book, who does not exist outside of it; nor does this God exist outside of "salvation's announcement" in the book, handed over "in historically changing forms offered, in the sacred Scriptures and in the living tradition of the Church, to the continuing reinterpretation of the community of believers. *It is not possible to believe in this God in the strong sense of the word.*"[38] [emphasis added]. This text takes the strategy of Vattimo's soft theology (what I will term response) and its textual location of God, extending it into the profoundly Logos/logos-centred, post-Christian (Christian derived) secularity of modernity. Here is a theology that wrestles with and for the textual God, the textual Christ, and the textual Logos encountered softly in texts. It does so in texts that exist outside of the self-chosen sectarianism of anti-modern Christianity and Christian reading.

This project, then, is theology that uses anything but traditional theological texts as its sources and reference points. It arises out of the limitations of such texts to discuss the theological endeavour in a way that has implications and resonance outside the very in-house jargon-filled and infatuated world of theological discourse. If, as theologians, we find ourselves and our discussions increasingly out-of-step with postmodern and resurgent late modern society, then perhaps we need to consider new ways of re-configuring theological approaches. For increasing numbers this way of expression has come to be the expression of a theology of disapora, of theology of and from postmodern exile. For me, a new wrestling emerges, however. I cannot be content with the backwards-looking dissatisfaction with the present that is indicative of the exile. My wrestling is that of how to be modern – in a new way, here and now. To get to modernity after postmodernity we need first to wrestle our way through and with those texts and approaches which seek to articulate the real with the tourist, the traveller and the exile. We should engage with those texts that arose as expressions of the loss of the real in that past modernity, and also those texts that seemed to offer a location of the real in and for postmodernity.

This text also arises out of my own response to the claims of tourism, travel, exile and *flanerie*. Living in the South Island of Aotearoa, New Zealand, tourism has always been part of my wider frame of experiences. As a child I lived for some years in the tourist mecca of Queenstown, where my father was the local Presbyterian minister. It was an idyllic place that every year had seasonal invasions of tourists. Even when we left I continued to journey back and noted the changes wrought by the increasing (and profitable) pursuit of the real experience. Later, at university, as a postgraduate student I studied Tourism for a year at Otago University. This experience arose out of a longstanding interest in how others viewed here (that is, New Zealand) – and what impact such perceptions had on both visitors and visited. My travel has been limited to journeys within my own country and yet they are travels that forced the recognition that countries and nations are, as Benedict Anderson reminds us, only ever "imagined communities." By this observation I mean that travelling, primarily by road in big old cars (most notably a 1968 Pontiac) throughout my own country, has made me aware that difference is encountered most often where we seek similarity. The two islands of this small country may as well be two different countries. Within them, the regions are themselves quite different when one spends time moving slowly, watchfully, through them. My overseas travel is limited, by finances and family circumstances, to a singular trip from small town South Island New Zealand to Sydney Australia for a month when I was twelve (that is almost thirty years ago). I have always voraciously devoured travel books, sought out foreign films, visited galleries and museums, indeed purposively read, listened and watched widely. As for exile, both my paternal and maternal grandfathers were British immigrants to New Zealand in the first thirty years of the twentieth century. They were economic exiles seeking a better life. Both died well before I was born. Yet their children and grandchildren are the beneficiaries of their act of self-exile from Bolton and Edinburgh. As a child in provincial New Zealand I remember feeling a sense of exile that my parents did not. Maybe this dislocation was due to the way in which all adolescents seem to feel that the real is happening elsewhere. But provincial, rural South Canterbury seemed a more cruel exile than most in the early 1980s. Somewhat ironically I am probably one of the very, very few of my age, and especially of my education, in Aotearoa, New Zealand who has never had what is called the "O.E." (Overseas Experience). Traditionally this meant a trip to Britain in your early twenties, living with other antipodeans, working at menial and/or temporary jobs, brief forays to the continent and then returning home to "settle down" by your mid-twenties. I kept choosing education and eventually reached the stage whereby I am happy to be a *pakeha* New Zealander who travels overseas in his head, in his reading, in his viewing and in his mind. One day I hope to visit, but I also know that many who have gone to find the real, return to say only on return that "it" was here all the time. I do not want to fall into either trap; that is, that the real is to be pursued over there – or that it is actually here all along. Rather I prefer a cosmopolitan real that is where people are in all their difference. As for *flanerie*, I have spent most of the past twenty years wandering city streets: to get to university, to get to work, and to just get around. I have never walked with a walkman or an iPod. Rather I prefer to walk and think and watch and listen; I like to be open to what may be the everyday, minimal, secular ruptures and short-circuits. It is out of these various experiences and reflections that the central question of this text arose: do we need to discover a new land, a new way(s) of writing, debating, questioning theology?

1   The Tourist: Popular Piety and Practice as a Package Deal

Introducing Tourists

For thousands of years the combination of shrines, relics and pilgrimage have created a symbiotic relationship between religion and what could, in modern terminology, be termed tourism. People have travelled to partake in the supposed efficacy of sacred sites (places) and sacred sights (relics) as both a substitution and augmentation for what was available at home. The history of the world's religions is often presented as a history of travel to "the sacred," "the transcendent," "the holy" and such catchphrases of "the numinous" – itself another catchphrase. In a similar fashion, travel has often been justified as undertaken in the pursuit of such intangibles as wisdom or enlightenment.

Over the past two hundred years, following the Romantic reaction to the Enlightenment, these experiences have been coalesced by the Western seeker. Following the turn against religion in the West, a new form of religious travel has occurred. The experiences dismissed and marginalized in the modern West are viewed as still located and experienced in other religious traditions. The aim of the Western seeker is to relocate and participate in what has been lost. This relocation takes two forms. She can experience by her participation in a religious tradition that has relocated to the West. Alternatively, rather than participating in 'the exotic' in her home location her relocation is often a physical one from the West to what is viewed as the host culture. Both relocations occur as part of what could be termed the traditional reading of religion and tourism. This approach studies relocations and movement within a traditional view of religion, often focusing on pilgrimage sites. A belief in religious efficacy is viewed as the primary motivation.

The publication in 1976 of Dean MacCannell's *The Tourist* challenged this traditional historical and anthropological reading of tourism. MacCannell linked tourism and religion as a political act worthy of examination by radical geographers influenced by Marxist analysis. A new reading was offered of "Tourism as religion." Tourism was presented as the *de facto* new opiate of the masses in a reading combining the Marxist critique and disdain of both religion and capitalism. Early in his text, MacCannell locates his position as that of the Enlightenment-derived, rational social scientist. In examining his data he deduces an unplanned (i.e. irrational) typology that "provides direct access to the modern consciousness" where "tourist attractions are *precisely* analogous to the religious symbolism of *primitive* people"[1] (emphasis added[2]). He then defines tourism as a form of pietistic behaviour undertaken now that God is dead. Tourism as religion exists in both the modern secular capitalist form of "appearing holier" and as an expression of "the religious impulse to go beyond one's fellow men." In MacCannell's view, this religious impulse is not just expressed in Weber's work ethic. It is now infiltrating and corrupting "some of our leisure acts as well."[3] MacCannell continues his attack by raising the spectre of (false) "staged authenticity," undertaking a subsequent discussion of the sacralization of "the Tourist gaze." Sightseeing now becomes something staged and undertaken to reinforce societal differentiation. We sightsee as part of a collective attempt to transcend the totality of modernity. But MacCannell claims this act is doomed to fail. For in its attempt "to construct totalities, it celebrates differentiation." Furthermore "[t]he middle class…has a transcendent consciousness."[4] To achieve meaning, the tourist (and by implication this is the capitalist middle class who partake in and enforce tourism) undertakes a process of site and sight sacralization. The site is firstly marked off as different and worthy of preservation. It is then presented or displayed (elevation) and delineated by an official boundary (framing). This action is followed by enshrinement. Once this is done, the site is set aside and commodified where mechanical reproduction[5] occurs in the mass media. The tourist sets off in response to this action (that is, images of the site, the event, the attraction appearing in magazines, newspapers, books, brochures, television and cinema). Having seen copies, the tourist now seeks "The Real Thing" and "the true object." Such activity is, in effect, a secular, modern version of the religious pilgrimage and quest narratives. The final stage is social reproduction. Here the local and the copy become renamed after famous real attractions,[6] as for example within theme parks and, most famously, the fake real of Las Vegas where capitalism and tourism in pursuit of the fake real meet.[7]

MacCannell's move to relocate tourism as a new form of capitalist opiate for the post-institutional-religious masses (that is, secular Western society) became quite influential for those wishing to make easy connections between tourism and religious practice. Such a re-reading is attractive in providing an obvious argument for those who wish to follow a Marxist-derived critique. It is killing two birds with one stone, namely both the false beliefs of capitalism and the new opiate of tourism combined in the worship of capitalist globalization. Yet MacCannell's argument is too simplistic. For in dismissing the religion of tourism he seeks also to dismiss the importance of religion in general. To attack the religion of tourism is merely just another form of attacking the existence and continuation of religion, religious practice and belief in a world where religion is an opiate and, therefore, needs to be critiqued and dismissed. In other words, tourism is actually critiqued more for its perpetuation of the opiate of religion than for anything else.

An alternative presentation of MacCannell's thesis occurred in David Lodge's *Paradise News*.[8] This novel is his typical mix of dislocated, questioning academics attempting to engage with the real world. Its protagonist is Bernard Walsh, an agnostic theologian, on holiday in Hawaii. A variety of encounters force him to re-evaluate his life. If Walsh the theologian is unsure of his faith, then his contrast is with Roger Sheldrake, an anthropologist from the South-West London Polytechnic. Sheldrake is researching a thesis on "Tourism as religious ritual" that verges on plagiarism of MacCannell:

> The thesis of my book is that sightseeing is a substitute for religious ritual. The sightseeing tour as secular pilgrimage. Accumulation of grace by visiting the shrines of high culture. Souvenirs as relics, guidebooks as devotional aids. You get the picture...it suddenly struck me: tourism is the new world religion. Catholics, Protestants, Hindus, Muslims, Buddhists, atheists – the one thing they have in common is they all believe in the importance of seeing the Parthenon. Or the Sistine Chapel, or the Eiffel Tower... It's no coincidence that tourism arose just as religion went into decline. It's the new opium of the people, and must be exposed as such.[9]

The move from academic text to academic novel signals that such a reading of tourism is now rather commonplace. Lodge satirizes it as often involving a form of academic elitism against the activities and enjoyment of the masses. As such, it is often part of an ongoing project of reductionism cocking a sneer at the pleasures and experiences of a non-elite market for partaking in secular religion or being part of the worship of global capitalism. There is also, however, a strong line of argument where mass tourism is seen as part of a search for authenticity. The tourist becomes a modern-day pilgrim seeking a lost authenticity in other times and other places.

This evocation of the trope of pilgrim and the act of pilgrimage operates by linking tourism back into a sacred narrative of the search and the quest. It thus enables a linking and a rereading to occur. In such a thesis, tourism is merely secularized and commodified religion. It is the modern equivalent of the traditional religious experience involving the commercialized pursuit of a secularized incarnation (and a form of cheap grace) that is theoretically available to all (with the available time and capital). Such cross-referencing has become commonplace with links made applying Durkheim's classification of religion into *Sacred and Profane* (1912) to modern tourism. Tourism becomes the realm of the sacred. It is a non-ordinary state where the marvellous happens, in opposition to everyday work life that is the realm of the profane. The resultant claim is that the movement between the two is where our new rituals and ceremonies marking the beginning and end of life now occur.[10]

The cross-over point between pilgrimage and tourism was signalled to a general audience with the rise of the package tour in the nineteenth century. Mark Twain's acerbic anti-tourist report, *The Innocents Abroad*, records the passage of a group of American tourists back to the authentic world of the Mediterranean. He notes how in the 1860s the secular tourist trip was displaying elements of the religious pilgrimage. This cross-over was especially true of Palestine where the varying denominational church backgrounds of the tourists had both prepared them and yet blinded them to the real Palestine they encountered. Twain's pilgrims found their own particular creedal Palestine (whether that be Presbyterian, Baptist, Catholic, Methodist and Episcopalian). Their pilgrimage actually occurred in advance. This indoctrination and expectation meant that what they saw, felt and experienced was actually a combination. Their creedal Palestine was perceived as primary, whereby the real Palestine was always mediated through and by their creedal expectations.[11] And yet, once there, the real kept intruding and disconcerting the travellers:

> It seems curious enough to us to be standing on ground that was once actually pressed by the feet of the saviour. The situation is suggestive of a reality and a tangibility that seems at variance with the vagueness and mystery and ghostliness that one naturally attaches to the character of a god.[12]

Twain's book has become a central text in discussing the rise of tourism as secular pilgrimage and secular religion. Here, it could be argued, in the nineteenth century, in the midst of a time of evangelical up-welling, even the pietistic find tourism and religion coalescing into something new, strange, maybe modern. That very modern, self-reflexive just now experience of standing in Palestine creates a formidable challenge. All those traditions, expectations, beliefs and desires that led tourists to this place are now under scrutiny. This challenge raises the question of whether they reject or refract the real. Do they privilege their expectations over the reality? Or, do they re-read the reality through their expectations and make some accommodations, while still privileging their expectations? It is, of course, a matter of degree. But the alternative – to reject their expectations in favour of trusting their own experience of "the real" – is to hold up for question all those beliefs and expectations that have brought them to this place. Similarly, it is noted that the dissenting Protestant clergy who travelled to the Holy Land on the early Thomas Cook tours were often offended by ritual and "monkish practices" (that is, Catholic and Orthodox activities) at the Holy sites they viewed, rejecting them as expressions of superstition and obvious fakery. In response, these early Protestant evangelical tourists either transferred their emotions "from sites to scenery"[13] or, when confronted by the claims and expressions of Judaism and Islam at sites shared between the Abrahamic faiths, sought "depending on one's point of view – to consecrate them or desecrate them by engaging in Christian worship."[14]

While tours to the Holy Land continued,[15] a shift in focus occurred from religious tours to tourism as religion. Anthropology in particular has been keen to continue the association. Victor Turner has led the chorus: tourism is a form of secular religion, especially so because it invokes a variety of pilgrimage. The tourist is then "half a pilgrim" and a pilgrim is "half a tourist," with the sunbathing, anonymous tourist seeking "an almost sacred, often symbolic form of *communitas*."[16] Such a take on tourism finds parallels in popular journalism like that by John Casey, writing in *The Spectator*. Here, sunbathing tourists on the Mediterranean beaches are a secular form of medieval pilgrims seeking indulgences so as "to acquire a merit that will last them through winter."[17] Even Laurence Durrell in his travelogue of joining a tourist charter around Sicily falls into the simplistic analysis:

> Binoculars, scarves, thermos flasks, picnic baskets and cameras; we carried all the lumber with us like all modern pilgrims do.[18]

This view relocates tourism as a modern, secular pilgrimage, a search perhaps for transcendence now only fleetingly available.[19] It is a "sacred journey" in which "the whole point" is "re-creation" and "renewal," a type of re-birth.[20] David Brown argues that pilgrims and tourists can turn into each other. Pilgrims who are fake tourists can become real tourists by "enjoying the joke" of what they encounter. Tourists "who enjoy the joke" (i.e. the fakeness [21]) of what they encounter can also "try to penetrate the mystery" and so become pilgrims. All of this is, of course, another expression of the difficulty of successfully negotiating the authentic and its fakes in the contemporary world.[22]

However, I do not wish to focus on the claims of tourism as either a modern sacred journey or as secular pilgrimage. Too often such discussions quickly become just another version of MacCannell's thesis. In this analysis the survival of religion and religious impulses occurs in tourism. Or, alternatively, for most people the sacred journey and the search for the transcendent occurs now only in the tourist experience. Yet they are unaware of the real nature of their participation. That critique just continues the Marxist-derived line linking tourism and religion as forms of opiate that the masses are either deluded or oppressed into accepting.

Donald Horne provides a more sympathetic reading of the tourist experience.[23] He presents his own reading of the tourist experience derived from MacCannell and continues and develops the 'tourism as modern religion' thesis. Tourism is described as involving four elements. The first is myth, expressed in the "possibility of regeneration through travel." The second is ritual through physical proximity to magic places and items. The third are legends encountered through guidebooks, stories and brochures. Finally there are relics that the tourist purchases to bring home.[24] Yet Horne, while re-presenting MacCannell's Marxist-derived critique, still wishes to justify and self-differentiate those, like himself, who find pleasure in tourism in the modern world. He is keen to state the case for intelligent tourism. The intelligent tourist participates in the outward signs of the traditional ritual and pilgrimage thesis. Yet he or she has the self-knowledge to remake these images and experiences. This remaking is undertaken in a manner that not only proves satisfactory to the tourist but also (implicitly) will set them apart from the crowd.

In other words, Horne is the equivalent to the educated laity who view themselves as amateur theologians and so closer in ethos and (implied) intelligence to the theologian than to the ritualistic, acquisitive and uncritical piety of the mass(es). At heart it is a romantic belief in the persistence of the authentic in the modern world, available to those of a sympathetic (and educated) perspective. There is still a disdain for the masses deceived by the spectacle of mass tourism, but this position holds onto the possibility of a form of redemption, available to those who in the midst of deception can discover the deeper, hidden truth. In effect, Horne's intelligent tourist is a form of secular Gnostic locating himself within the self-reflexivity of modernity. Doing so also positions the un-reflexive tourist of the mass package deal as non/anti-modern in a strongly Protestant-derived antipathy to the Catholic mass(es).

This ability to read the sites and sights sits at the centre of the guidebook, which I want to argue has developed as a type of mediating text of the other in a manner that could be seen to echo the Protestant reliance on the revelatory, authoritative, and mediating text of the Bible.

Re-reading the Guidebook

The history of the guidebook is linked to the origins of organized travel and mass tourism. Various claims have been made as to when and where the modern guidebook originated. James Buzard notes that the term "guidebook" was first used in Byron's epic poem *Don Juan*,[25] while the "handbook" (as precursor of the modern guide) was invented in 1836 by John Murray II of the publishing firm of the same name.[26] Alternatively, John Julius Norwich claims that in 1820 the elder John Murray commissioned Mariana Starke to write a handbook on travel on the continent, which soon developed into a series of handbooks.[27] In Germany,

Karl Baedeker published a guide to the city of Cologne in 1829[28]; then, in 1832 he reprinted *Journey along the Rhine*, previously printed by a competitor who then went bankrupt. The revised and edited second edition, published in 1835 is, according to Whitman, "widely considered the first real *Baedeker*"[29] of what became the definitive set of guidebooks for the discerning traveller for the next century. Between 1832 and 1943 some 1,100 *Baedeker* guides in English, French and German were issued; they were bound in red cloth and designed for practicality in the size of a traveller's hand.[30] The guidebook was literally a handbook. These guidebooks of John Murray and Karl Baedeker became the entry point for the tourist, preparing his way, directing her steps, their gaze and their responses.[31]

Of course the easiest comparison and reading to make is with the Bible. This is nothing new. Elsner and Rubies, in discussing the cultural history of travel writing, observe that:

> In the case of the Holy Land, the Christians possessed a guidebook which they used to redefine the actual places and landmarks they found on the terrain in relation to their dominant mythology, namely the Old and New Testament.[32]

Here they were building on established custom. John Murray writes in the preface to his *Holy Land* guide of 1868 that: "The Bible is the best Hand-book for Palestine; the present work is only intended to be a companion to it."[33] More recently, Bruce Feiler attempted a re-walking of the "footsteps of Abraham," which meant, in effect, an attempt to navigate a way through the Middle East using the Torah. At one point he exclaims: "It's almost as if the Bible's a *Baedeker*… It's certainly better than my guidebooks."[34]

What I want to do is not use the Bible as a form of *Baedeker*, but rather consider what we can learn if we view the *Baedeker*,[35] and the responses to it, as a type of *de facto* Bible. In the popular mind such cross-textual identification became easier when, after 1872, *Baedeker* began to use "the extra-thin paper used for Bibles (*Dunndruckpapier*)" for its handbooks.[36] The comparison would not have been lost on the traveller. What they held in their hand was a secular version of the Bible, a form of handbook that operated along the already-established lines of reading an authoritative text to "prepare their way, direct their steps, their gaze and their responses." Furthermore, the *Baedeker* ethos and experience was extremely Protestant, focusing on the individual reader of the text who ventured (at least to some degree) on their tour, on their travel alone. Authority and authenticity was ultimately that which was described, defined and delineated by the text and consumed by the individual who was independent of the mass experience.[37] This mass experience was at one level the communal package tour, yet it was also very clearly a northern

European Protestant suspicion[38] of southern European Catholicism and middle eastern Orthodox Christianity,[39] Judaism and Islam. In an almost liturgical sense, the singular Protestant was independent of the "Mass experience" of Catholicism – and also the mass experience of the rituals, worship and practices of other faiths encountered. The singularity coalesced in the guidebooks. For the northern European Protestant individual,[40] the guidebooks were mediators, definers and directors that could act to define, discuss and ultimately dismiss that deemed surpassed. In Italy and Spain the churches were redefined as religious museums and the art, beauty and aesthetical experience was divorced from the reality of southern Catholicism. The implication was that the Catholic practitioners did not fully understand or appreciate what they encountered everyday. Indeed, if they did note their surroundings, they were liable (from the northern guidebook ethos) to misread and corrupt it. The location of true vision and knowledge was, therefore, re-located from the culture and people who had created and participated in what was under observation to those who stood at a critical cultural and religious distance. This practice again sits as part of an emerging modern self-reflexivity: only those who were modern could really understand. Those who were seen by the modern tourist were deemed incapable of true vision because, on one level, they did not possess the guidebook.

Sitting at the heart of the guidebook – and its use – is the question of authenticity. The guidebook itself was the result of previous tours and texts that, in their selection and rewriting by the compiler, in effect became codified and canonized into the authoritative experience. The guidebook was thus actually a guide to a series of events. Firstly, it was a guide to those previous tours and books deemed normative by the compiler. Secondly, it was a guide to the subsequent trip undertaken by the compiler to verify what had been noted. Thirdly, it was a guide to what the compiler, in his trip, had noticed for himself, and subsequently deemed normative for those who chose to follow in his footsteps. The user of the guidebook thus set out to encounter what had *already* been deemed authentic, real and of note – and so had their experience prescribed for them.

As Allen notes, with the guidebook two things occur. Firstly, the reader/ traveller/tourist has their identity supplanted by the identity of the compiler. This is because, through the use of the guidebook, they see through the eyes of another. Secondly, the identity of what they are encountering is supplanted not only by what the text prescribes should be seen but also by the textual description. In the guidebook, textual presence takes precedence; in fact, material presence is converted into a textual presence that is the authoritative encounter.[41] The guidebook becomes a form of secularized *sola scriptura*, the privileged text and the definer of experience. In effect, the guidebook is that which makes an experience or a place more authentic[42] precisely because in the text, knowledge, expectation, a directed gaze and material place all meet. Allen argues that what we have here is a reductionist approach that seeks to eliminate the distance "between the word and its object, and so it denies the prophetic power of language."[43]

This tendency raises the issue of how such texts should be read. If a literal reading is taken as providing *prior* authentic validation (and so is read as the guide to the authentic encounter with what is sought), then the language of the guidebook is only ever referential to that which is encountered. This encounter has *already* been delineated and defined first in words. That is, what is read in the guidebook prescribes the authentic encounter, and yet what is read is *itself* based on *prior* texts defining "authentic encounters." Penny Travlou notes something similar in guidebooks of Athens:

> In general, the guidebooks draw a textual map which describes the few recognizable landmarks and reinforces the pre-existing mythology of the Athenian landscape. The writing of the travel narratives is a form of inter-textuality, where the text is dependent on previous texts.[44]

What should be emphasized is the degree to what is presented and read is pre-defined and codified *as* authentic and normative. To what extent does a heavy reliance on the guidebook then limit the interaction with what is there? How far is the mediated account actually the representation of the experiences of *other* mediated accounts? Travelou describes this encounter primarily through the text in terms of responding to "the pre-existing mythology."

In *A Room with a View* E. M. Forster has Miss Lavish offer this advice to Lucy Honeychurch:

> …I hope we shall soon emancipate you from *Baedeker*. He does but touch on the surface of things. As to the true Italy he does not even dream of it. The true Italy is only to be found by patient observation.[45]

And yet, as James Buzard discusses with reference to Forster's writing on travel, even Forster was aware that any attempt to "sweep away all previous texts" itself "finds utterance in only another text."[46] Aldous Huxley offers a variation, claiming:

> For every traveller who has any taste of his own, the only useful guidebook will be the one which he himself has written. All others are an exasperation.[47]

Huxley adds a note of caution, however, warning "[t]he personal guidebook must be the fruit of bitter personal experience."[48] This linking of travel and *travail* with a self-didactic focus again puts the self-reflexivity of the modern traveller/intelligent tourist in opposition to those who participate in the mass experience. And yet even Huxley unwittingly links his elitist view back to the ethos of the guidebook whereby tourism was undertaken for an educative purpose: the *Baedeker* was a compendium of knowledge written and read so as to allow personal knowledge to occur.

If not prepared to strike out alone as Huxley desires, then perhaps the best alternative is to customize the guidebook. Laurence Durrell, in *A Sicilian Carousel*, recognizing "the difficulty of disentangling what is historically important from what is artistically essential,"[49] notes with approval the actions of his fellow tourist Deedes who annotates his guidebook with what he decides, perceives and discovers. In a sense he secularizes the text by making it a part of his world, rather than accepting it as normative. Deedes' action is not the expectation of those who produce the guides, for their content is presented "to be followed, mainly to be read and rarely to be analysed."[50] Of course the aim of the guidebook is to provide a security of evidence that, as Terry Caesar notes, acts as if it were "proof of selfhood itself."[51] The security offered is a security not only of what is encountered, but more so that it "will" be encountered. Lydia Wevers comments: "Once a guidebook is available, travel becomes the domain of tourists, schooled to react and evaluate."[52]

In reaction to this discussion, I wish to raise the issue of how our religious texts, including the Bible, may (potentially) make tourists out of us through how we approach and read them. Do we use them as what will define, describe and order that which we seek to encounter, because we have already read that this is how we should respond – and that this is what we should encounter if we are to encounter the authentic? Do we actually seek to encounter a world, a truth, an authenticity that are so because we have read and heard that they are indeed "so"? According to Donald Horne this framing allows the guidebook to isolate what is under observation from the rest of the world.[53] Our meditation is actually a form of mediation[54] that defines and delineates the experience for us. For Christianity the issue becomes one of asking the question: do words limit and domesticate access to the Word (logos limiting access to the Logos)? If we engage with the Bible or theological texts as forms of *Baedeker*, then what do we encounter? To what degree do we encounter not the God they write with reference of and to, but rather merely a "written God"? To refine this point, does the Word (Logos) become limited to words? Is there now a limitation to the words of others? And is this a reduction to an inter-textual reference that forgets its pre-existing mythology? Is the "God" that is approached now "not the object but its image," a construction to fit the expectation of the "Tourist"?[55] Because the guide has told the tourist that what she gazes upon *is* authentic, the tourist reaffirms what frames her gaze *as* authentic. The tourist and text (believer and pietistic sentiment and belief) become a closed system whereby any alternative can be rejected as transgressive.

Such an approach will only take us so far in our attempts to inter-textualize religion. I wish to turn their way of doing things on its head. Rather than re-reading tourism as a religious experience, it is my intention instead to consider the possibility of religion as analogous to the tourist experience. David Lodge, once again, provides an insight in *Paradise News*. His disgruntled theologian Bernard Walsh reconsiders his experience as a parish priest:

> The appeal of the Gospel message, though, remains essentially the same. The Good News is news of eternal life, Paradise news. For my parishioners, I was a kind of travel agent, issuing tickets, insurance, brochures, guaranteeing them ultimate happiness.[56]

I want to raise the question of what follows if popular religion *is* a form of spiritual tourism? What follows if it is, in effect, a weekly package deal which takes the participants on a journey to encounter the expected exotic Other that is then experienced in a non-confrontational way and, in due course, transports them back to their embarkation point? Lawrence Durrell offers a comparison in his observation of the Sicilian package tour, noting:

> ...the twenty or so captives of tourism tip-toeing around monuments they do not comprehend with a grave piety they do not feel.[57]

Of course it would be easy to use such attacks on mass tourism to make slights on the piety of those who attend church for camaraderie, for a time out of normal daily routine, or those who use the weekly attendance at church as a way to provide a form of piety that frames their life and their expectations of God. Here is to be found what Taylor refers to as "the tourist's goals of reassurance" and that "characteristic tourist anxiety of missing the essential experience of a treasured landscape or site."[58] It is in response to this anxiety that the central stress on repetition occurs; it is that focus of the tourist gaze seeking "reassurance through familiarity." This repetition is "crucial since it returns to tourists whatever they were looking for."[59] The reassurance extends to those with whom one travels. Together you are experiencing that which is not like you (i.e. the exotic location and experience), but you are doing so alongside people who are like you. As a group you not only share the experience but, just as importantly, you are able to "comment on the oddity of the new in a familiar vocabulary."[60] This complex, constructed experience is what Buzard calls "the beaten track" of mass tourism[61] along which, Risse notes, tourists follow someone else's agenda: "there is no need to get

lost socially, physically or linguistically as they have a structure in place to
do the interpreting, arranging or decoding for them."[62]

While this state of affairs could be easily deconstructed into being re-
read as indicative of the mass piety of the church-going tourist/Christian,
others are not so sure that no decoding goes on. It is too glib to state that
a structured liturgy stops any questioning or thinking or that all church-
goers are merely passive instruments of clerical tour guides. Nevertheless
the mediated experience does occur within a certain set of expectations.

Paul Fussell, a stringent and influential critic of mass tourism, has
continually, unfavourably contrasted the mass aspect of tourism with the
solitary, modern(ist) traveller. Tourism, in Fussell's reading, is a form of
the expression of convention and the conventional. It is a form of opiate,
an escape from the challenges of the world; it is, in effect, a retreat into
the comforts of prescribed piety:

> Tourism soothes you by comfort and familiarity and shields you from the shocks of
> novelty and oddity. It confirms your prior view of the world instead of shaking it up.
> Tourism requires that you see conventional things, and that you see them in a
> conventional way.[63]

Underlying such a reading is the expected challenge from the solitary
elite traveller with their (self-justifying) belief in lone travel as better,
more uplifting and worthy. In such a reading of tourism, there is the
challenge to and dismissal of any embrace of the spiritual equivalent of
the Cruise Liner, the Club Med, the Costa la Sol, the Gold Coast, Acapulco,
Las Vegas or Disneyland. Its worth is second rate and ultimately of little
real value or meaning. The question then arises: does there exist an
ascetic, puritan chic? Does it take the form of whereby "good = pain,
struggle, torment, independence and uncomfortable surroundings" and
"bad = comfort, relaxation, being supported and communal"? Daniel
Boorstin famously delineated between travel and tourism, retracing the
etymology of travel back to *travail* and hence to active work, whereas the
tourist "was a pleasure seeker."[64] Such challenges to both popular tourism
and to popular piety represent the return of a body/spirit dualism that
privileges the spiritual over the body and so (in traditional theological
language) "makes a mockery of the reality of the incarnation and bodily
resurrection." Is not popular piety an embodied, corporeal experience? Is
it not a basking in the warmth of the love of God, of being part of a tour
party seeking the authentic experience, the communal experience of
feasts and festivals? Is the desire to enjoy the trip enough, not only to
wish to repeat it but to convince others that they too should go because
"it's just what you need"?

When we start to excavate the notion of tourist/ism a strange slippage
occurs. Caren Kaplan's debates on the nature of the tourist experience

begin to send out a certain resonance towards questions that are traditionally the realm of religion and metaphysics. With respect to a touristic reality she writes: "Tourism, as a manifestation of a crisis in reality, insists upon proof of the authentic."[65] This insistence results in the photograph, the souvenir, the travel diary – and the use of guide books and tour guides to reassure us that what is seen (and recollected) is the real thing. We are aware that we exist in a (fallen) world of the fake and inauthentic. We know that the world is a snare and trap for the naïve, the innocent, the believer. We live in an age that seems determined to shatter illusions. This awareness means the question of the real and the authentic has come to play a central part in discussions on tourism.

Tourism and the Issue of the Real

To consider this central issue I want to examine two statements (one by Evelyn Waugh and the other by Mark Twain) that appear to locate this crisis as part of the issue of the "reality" of religion in the modern world.

Statement One

Evelyn Waugh's Catholicism did not prohibit a scepticism concerning religious relics, or rather, the presentation of relics to fit a modern gullibility for the expected appearance of the "authentic." Writing of a trip to Palestine, he notes:

> We went to Cana of Galilee, where a little girl was offering wine jars for sale. They were the authentic ones used in the miracle. If they were too big she had a smaller size indoors; yes, the smaller ones were authentic too.[66]

It would be a trap to fall into reading Waugh's comments through an Orientalist lens whereby the little girl as non-European "other" becomes a stereotype of Orientalist cunning, fakery and wide-eyed false gullibility. Rather, I want to suggest that something else is occurring here. This is the recognition, by both the tourist (Waugh) and presenter of the inauthentic (the girl), that the authentic may be sought but can never be recovered. What is presented is real in the sense that it confirms both assumptions. For the tourist, the fake is purchased as real because the real (that is the original, that which is not fake) is inaccessible. The symbolic real is also, at the same time, a symbolic fake. We collaborate in a play of the faked authentic knowing that, if what is presented does not suit, there is the possibility of another faked authentic readily available to suit our expectations and our desires. It is easy to move from this reading to the claim that this is what the weekly piety of church attendance involves.

Here there is an interplay between clergy and congregation whereby both implicitly recognize that the experience and presence both sought and presented are, actually, what could be termed an authentic fake (presence) and the faked authentic (experience). Both clergy and congregation realize that, if what this particular clergy/church present does not fit with congregational expectations and needs, there is somewhere a religious product that will.

All of this makes piety and worship little more than a game where both refuse to speak the truth: (which is) that the authentic is unavailable in such materialistic, commodified terms. So we go along and purchase the fake and keep it as a reminder that it is a fake, but also as a reminder that it symbolizes a real(ity) that is no longer accessible. To critique properly such a move, we need to be aware that it is not the products that are fake. The whole experience that brought us to encounter the fake products is, itself, fake. To understand this claim, we should return to the issue of tourism.

The provocative French writer, Michel Houellebecq, in a series of brilliantly satirical novels, directly confronts what he perceives to be the nihilism of modern existence. In his books, the twin "faked consumptions" of what are meant to be real – sex and tourism – are exposed as delusions and fake attempts to desperately regain any type of ontology in an atomized world. In *Platform*, a novel critiquing sex tourism in Asia, his narrator restates the opiate thesis of tourism:

> I behaved like a typical, average tourist: I rented a sun-lounger with a fitted mattress, a parasol; I consumed a number of bottles of Sprite; I went for a dip, in moderation. The waves were gentle. I went back to my hotel at about five o'clock, averagely satisfied with my free day but intent nonetheless with carrying on. *I was attached to a delusive existence.*[67] [emphasis original]

Houellebecq's cynicism extends to the transaction between the tourist and the tour operator. The delusion we enter into revolves around a belief that the tour agent, the travel agent, will offer us something authentic that can be (re)arranged to suit us as individuals. We participate in a delusion that, after a type of commercial confessional, they can "discover your expectations, your desires, perhaps even your secret hopes."[68]

Yet all of these delusions, and what we seek are, according to Houellebecq, "confirmation of what they've already read in their guide books."[69] Julian Barnes, in a considered critique of Houellebecq, links him to Flaubert, especially to Flaubert's hedonistic journey of (self and sexual) discovery in Egypt.[70] Barnes identifies what he terms:

> the central, Flaubertian irony [of tourism's psychology] whereby anticipation and remembrance (the brochure's false promise of happiness, the holiday snap's grinning lie) often prove more vivid and reliable than the moment itself.[71]

Waugh's tourist self is remembering the moment of being offered the faked authenticity – and its possibility of replacement by other, more acceptable true fakes. The anticipation is that in the Holy Land, the land of the expected true and real, what actually occurs is the presentation of the fake. It is only to be expected that the real and the authentic will no longer be present. The remembrance has turned this encounter into an anecdote that makes it a real experience, even though what it involved was the inauthentic.

More recently, Bruner claims that tourists are quite happy to participate in the delusion, knowing that it is so. Tourists are actually not seeking the authentic elsewhere, but rather are happy to encounter the "theatrical suspension of disbelief," as long as it is not presented to them as "an outright fake":

> Tourists are willing to accept a reproduction, as long as it is a good one, or as one tourist brochure put it, as long as it is an "authentic" reproduction.[72]

This statement is, of course, a reference to Walter Benjamin's critique of lost aura and modernist technology: "The Work of Art in the Age of Mechanical Reproduction" (1936). It is referenced, though, in such a way that misreads Benjamin. Benjamin's concern was with what constitutes the authentic when technology has enabled a form of reproduction (the photograph) that is not a fake but a copy that replicates the original. His interest lies in with what makes the original special, which is this aura of the original. This aura constitutes a one-offedness that can never be replicated even though it can be mass reproduced by technology. To apply Benjamin's critique to the discussion of the tourist, we could claim that the tourist goes in search of what is communally inauthentic yet, paradoxically, is authentic for them as individuals. However, that which has facilitated their pursuit of this lost authenticity is, always, inauthentic. Boorstin (in elitist mode) claims that this inauthenticity is actually what the tourist desires:

> The tourist seldom likes the authentic (to him often unintelligible) product of the foreign culture; he prefers his own provincial expectations.[73]

Waugh and Bruner, in different ways, undercut this dismissal. Their perspective is that there is no recoverable authenticity available to the tourist. That this should be the case is of no concern because the tourist does not actually seek authenticity in the manner the academic critic might desire of them (so that they might be dismissed). Bruner archly notes:

> Authenticity is a concept more in the mind of the Western social theorist than in the mind of most tourists or natives.[74]

Jonathan Culler makes an alternative claim that the tourist is actually a semiotician, reading "everything as a sign of itself."[75] For him, tourism becomes a quest for signs of the authentic, an authenticity that has been lost in modernity and can only be found in signs we preserve of the past (antiques, restored buildings, imitations of old interiors) or outside of the modern, urbanized West "in other regions or countries."[76] Over the past twenty years this turn discerned by Culler has led to changes where types of tourism are now privileged as morally superior to the package holiday. Examples of such are ecotourism, sustainable tourism, green tourism, alternative tourism and community tourism.[77] Most of these types are located (for the western consumer) in the realm of the other – and are also (or perhaps rather because of this) viewed as true and authentic. It is illuminating to note how closely these morally superior forms of new tourism correlate to new (and self-articulated morally superior) forms of Christian piety offered as the new authentic location of Christianity. Butcher discerns a new moral tourism, its key features being "a search for enlightenment in other places, and a desire to preserve these places in the name of cultural diversity and environmental conservation."[78] Or, as Houellebecq observes:

> Completely insensible to the splendour of his surroundings, the native generally sets about destroying it, to the anguish of the tourist, a sensitive creature in pursuit of happiness. Once the tourist has pointed out this beauty, the native becomes capable of perceiving it, preserving it, and systematizing its exploitation in the form of *excursions*.[79] [emphasis original]

All of this relativizes the semiotic tourist as one who reads the signs that she wants to read. Waugh reads the fake as fake. The package tourist, confronted by the authentic fake as spectacle, reads it as fake authentic spectacle. Culler's tourist is really more so the theoretician attempting to recast himself as tourist.

McKenzie Wark claims:

> All intellectuals are tourists, apprehending only the surface of the experience and taking it home as souvenir. *Souvenirs d'egotisme*. It takes a certain idiocy to make sense of the world.[80]

Another critic, Georges van den Abbeele, tracing theory back to the Greek *theoria* ("a sight, a spectacle"), claims "the theorist is as much a 'sightseer' as the tourist."[81] And yet, over and against such a trivializing of the tourist – and the theorist – stands the second statement I want to examine. It is one that confronts the fake in a different way. This statement, while articulating a semiotics of tourism, is not so quick to dismiss what occurs, or to make it quite so simple.

Statement Two

An alternative fake relic occurs in Mark Twain's *The Innocents Abroad*, this time in Paris:

> We went to see the cathedral of Notre Dame. We had heard of it before. It surprises me, sometimes, to think how much we *do* know, and how intelligent we are. We recognized the brown, old Gothic pile in a moment; it was like the pictures.[82]

This observation raises the issue of what exactly is real in the tourist experience, and more so, what is "real" in the tourist's expectation. In other words, to what degree does expectation frame what is encountered – and define how it is encountered?

Bell and Lyall make an important point concerning the non-visibility of the tourist event in their discussion of the Jungfrau railway in Switzerland. Tourists travel up a mountain to a railway station where, even if there is a white-out, they can have their pictures taken in front of a "huge backlit indoor photographic mural of *what they would have seen.*"[83] As Bell and Lyall note, the tourists come prepared for what they may or may not see, having both "foreknowledge" and constant pictorial reminders (on murals, postcards, menus and tickets) which means: "Not seeing the mountain does not really matter. One knows it is up there."[84] And, following on from Twain, if it is encountered, it is experienced according to these expectations and representations. The analogy with church is perhaps too easy to make. If church is a form of package tour, then how quickly and to what degree does it frame and delineate the God that is encountered there? Is God, more often than not, a Jungfrau God hidden in the white-out? With liturgies, ritual, biblical texts, sermons, church architecture and decoration (especially stained-glass windows) do we effectively have our pictures taken in front of the God mural and know that God is there?

Mark Twain confronts this kind of issue when, in *The Innocents Abroad*, his (nineteenth-century) tour party travels to view the faded glory of Leonardo da Vinci's *Last Supper* and he hears:

> ...men apostrophizing wonders, beauties and perfections, which had faded out of the picture and gone, a hundred years before they were born.[85]

In the post-Enlightenment world, in a world post-Darwin, post-Nietzsche, post-Freud, post-Barthes (a world of the triumph of science and rationality, evolution, the death of God, the rise of psychoanalysis, the death of the author...to name but a few – let alone biblical criticism and the perpetual challenge of the Shoah and the gulags), is this not perhaps the position of most churchly piety and belief?

Twain's response places him in the position of the modern secular person who is confronted by claims of belief. He notes he believes that "the eye of a practised artist"[86] might be able to see what is now no longer there, "But *I* can not work this miracle. Can those other uninspired visitors do it or do they only happily imagine they do?"[87] It could be asked, is the experience of God that which has already been seen in expectation, doctrine and church piety? Is the gaze of church piety just another form of what has been termed the "tourist gaze"?

John Urry's book *The Tourist Gaze* is a discussion not only on what a Tourist sees, but more importantly on how a Tourist sees – and how what Tourists see is constructed by how Tourists see and what they may expect to see. What defines the tourist gaze is what non-tourist experience it is contrasted with.[88] Urry sees this tourist gaze as "a core component of Western modernity" in the way in which it combines both the desire for and collective experience of travel and "the techniques of photographic reproduction."[89] In this the collective experience and treatment of the mass tourist "as similar to each other with common tastes and characteristics"[90] also results in the construction of tourist events and tours in which that which is distinct from everyday life is experienced, but in a way that provides a communal experience that meets expectations. Urry's stress on "pleasures which involve different senses or on a different scale"[91] from everyday life as signs of a successful tourist experience can perhaps provide some understanding as to why it is the more experiential forms of Christianity – Pentecostal, born again, fundamentalist, and highly ritualistic Catholicism and Orthodoxy – that are on the increase, and why the liberal/mainstream forms of Christianity (especially liberal Protestant) are on the decrease. Who wants to go on a tour, a holiday, where everything is basically like home, like your everyday life? The tourist gaze and the church piety gaze are perhaps not that different. Both seek the containable, communal different experience that is mediated and controlled.

The souvenir – and especially the photograph as the record of the real – becomes important. The tourist's expectation is that she will encounter the real, and by photographing it, or more importantly, having herself photographed in front of it, she includes herself into the framing of the real – and hence also confirms her own reality. The world becomes captured in images and experiences, many of which occur out of a pre-travel framed expectation: "I will go there and see this and do that. Once there I will participate in the capture of the image and of the experience. I will then relive that experience and image when, back home, I look at that photograph." (Or, in plain language: I take photos to record I've been there and when I return home I look at them to relive the trip and to show others where I went and what I saw.) Having captured or experienced the real there, the tourist will now often seek it elsewhere. On one level this is indicative of a crisis of the real and the authentic in the modern world. "[T]ravel becomes a means of appropriating the world through images."[92] So the images and the expectation they frame actually structure our experience.[93] What we seek to encounter has, as Twain notes, already been encountered beforehand. We expect it to match our expectations. The photograph becomes our capturing of the presence of the real, which is why we still prefer to take photographs for and of ourselves rather than just rely on postcards. We cannot frame the postcard, nor can we be framed within it. All that can happen is the annotation, the textualizing of the image, the "this is our room" with an arrow. The postcard calls for a message on its back that signifies a meaning *behind* the image – yet, in the photograph, the meaning *is in* the image.

Geoff Dyer observes with bemusement that those not capturing the scene by photographic (mechanical) means, those not seeking to frame or be framed with "the real, the authentic" are "the lowest possible caste of tourists: the unseeables." To participate in the authentic as an individual, seeking to be *with* the scene (by walking, sitting or looking) without the intent to capture it, makes you into a "second-class citizen."[94] Yet this is exactly what the postcard represents: the scene, the image, without a record of your presence. Perhaps that is why we prefer to take photographs, because in our attempts to capture what is deemed authentic, we make ourselves real and authentic by mechanical participation.

If we consider the postcard, we come to the realization that it is paradoxically the recognition that the authentic is not readily available. What we photograph is most often not "what it is believed tourists want to see: the attraction at its most sublime, the sky a clear post-card blue, and tourists absent from the images."[95] If it were, then there would be no need for our individual mass-photographing of what is readily available, in picture-perfect form, in the postcard. We actually recognize that the authentic cannot be truly presented or experienced in such a mediated, commercialized, sanitized way. Maybe there is another lesson here for those churches that attempt to present experiences as controlled, ordered and replicable as the postcard. We instead seek what the individual captures. We are seeking the jostle, the pursuit and, most importantly, the individual framing of the authentic and our encounter with it. The disdain for the mass tourist experience is perhaps similar to the elitist liberal Protestants' disdain for sweaty, emotive, communal "package Christianity." As one critic of the postcard notes, their problem is that "they suffer from a propagandistic tendency to show that all is well under a heavenly, eternally blue sky."[96] The tourist gaze of the photograph is a reaction against such piety. It acknowledges that the sky is not always blue, the reality is not that which is pre-determined, that the scene cannot be encountered without the distractions and intrusions of others, that propaganda is no substitute for the individual response and experience. We may send postcards to others to enable the "necessary lie" of "ideal communal experience" to be perpetuated – and yet we often de-mythologize it with the truth of our experience in what we write on the reverse. The photograph is our attempt to overcome and dismiss the enforced communal experience. We may venture because of the pre-existent images and texts of the real – indeed seek to encounter the expected real for ourselves. But we want to participate in and with it. We seek to include ourselves in the experience and so capture it and reproduce it for ourselves. The authentic is thus acknowledged as both authentic and inauthentic.

It is perhaps this near-illusion that is most real in the modern world. The recognition that the authentic may be delineated, pre-determined and even kitsch, but that by framing it ourselves – and more so, by putting ourselves in the frame with it – the authentic is first and foremost experiential and communal. As Osborne perceives:

> Tourists and their sites exist in order to be photographed; indeed are photographed in order to attain their existence.[97]

The tourist gaze is something, then, that creates both the tourist and that which is gazed upon. The gaze is a way of encountering that which has been sought, and in looking, what is encountered is therefore "there." In other words, the gaze creates that which is sought. The reality of what is there/is not there is secondary to that which is expected and seen. The existence is captured because in the capture (in the experience, in the photograph) the tourist affirms her own existence. She has encountered that which is sought. The reality of it has already been mediated, created, defined and expected. Even if what is sought is not visible, the disappointment is mediated by the fact that she is/was in the presence of that which was/was not there – the Jungfrau railway experience. What is important is not so much the site/sight itself, but rather that the tourist found herself in the presence of that which was sought. What becomes central is the encounter with the authentic which is seen to be exotic. Feifer describes

> …the curious process that tourism brings into play: set up by the travel writer and framed by the camera, other people's ordinary lives are transformed into exotic entertainment, history into myth.[98]

Angus Wilson asks: "…would the tourists welcome Sri Lankan women into *their* homes to take the photos of *them* having a bath?"[99]

Wilson's question is central to the mythologizing of the tourist experience in that it enables a form of transgression to occur. The transgression is that it enables the participants to act in ways that in normal, domestic life they would not. This occurs in a variety of forms, from what is looked at and recorded (i.e. people bathing), to participation in rituals and activities that would not be countenanced at home because here they are detailed as exotic, primitive, authentic. In effect, the tourist enters a zone of mediated experience whereby what is perceived and experienced is that which is primarily expected, and therefore controllable. The transgression is that of mediated transgression. It is a world where one participates in what one *does not do* at home because one knows that this is not a permanent state. So the transgression is the suspension of the everyday world, of everyday life in which one goes in search of the authentic which is located anywhere but where we usually exist. The tourist gaze is then directed in two ways. It frames that which is encountered and, perhaps most importantly, it frames that which has been left behind. In this manner, domestic tourism offers a challenge in that the gaze and the authentic are of what is here yet not here, other yet the same. That which is familiar is yet strange[100] – or sought to be seen as different. The exotic is localized, perhaps even domesticated – yet still perceived as different enough to undertake and facilitate the experience.

Perhaps domestic tourism is the best analogy for mainstream Christian church worship and piety. It is like going on a restorative holiday to the seaside or the countryside within your own country. The locals are the same as you, yet different. You can still participate in transgression, but that exercise is then limited by the cultural mores of your shared home society. You share a common expectation that what is encountered will be familiar. It will be something that will only undergo a certain degree of change. The transition between home life and tourist life will be different enough to make it worthwhile, but similar enough not to cause dislocation. The expectation is that the authentic encountered is that which confirms your identity, not challenges it. The tour and tour guides will be composed of people like you, undertaking this particular trip for similar purposes. Disruptive elements on the domestic tour are perhaps less forgiven and more transgressive because they do not have the excuse of the locale and disorientation of the exotic. The gaze is, therefore, even more communal and yet also more iconoclastic on the domestic front. In the domestic sphere, what may be acceptable in another location, in another experience is, in the constraints of the more familiar, not so acceptable. The introduction of the faked spectacle, the intrusion of the exotic as authentic, has to occur within prescribed limits. What occurs is what can be termed the reaffirmation of touristic travel. In this experience (*pace* Osborne[101]) touristic travel acts as a reaffirmation of both the participating tourists and of the tourist culture's view of "the legitimacy of its central axioms"[102] whereby the otherness of the place and of the sight/site encountered is confirmed by one's own presence.

The tourist event is acceptable to the degree in which it affirms the tourist and the culture he represents. This process may operate in a way in which the tourist gaze confirms what the tourist and the culture see as normative. Or, it may operate, by way of an alternative, in a way in which what is encountered affirms what the tourist sees as problematic with/in his own culture. In this way the transgressive gaze is transgressive to the tourist's home culture but affirmative of the tourist's feelings of dislocation. However, these feelings are not enough to force a permanent shift into the transgressive location. Rather, the transgressive gaze is brought back and remains as a normative way to encounter the home society. On the one hand this could be seen as a romanticist search for what Lippard notes is "the illusion or remnants of so-called primitivism. The notion of authenticity is largely applied to other's lives, not to our own."[103] At its extreme, it can manifest itself into the search for primitivism that is desired as a site/sight but not as a relocatable home experience. As Geoff Dyer dryly observes:

> All visitors to the developing world, if they are honest, will confess that they are actually quite keen on seeing a bit of squalor; people living on garbage dumps, shanty towns, that kind of thing.[104]

This encounter with squalor is to see, as Bauman sees, a world where "the strange is tamed, domesticated, and no longer frightens; shocks come in a package deal with safety."[105] It is an experience where, as Richardson comments, in respect of the exotic in Zanzibar:

> A tourist can't really expect to get anything but the taste of difference itself. Is that the point – the whiff of a different world? To relieve us of the burden of our own?[106]

Butcher discerns a similar approach in discussing what he terms "the new moral tourist." This participant "morally elevates tradition above development" and acts from a romanticized, New Age perspective seeking "enlightenment from the experience" with the aim of learning "profound truths, absent in developed societies that are considered superficial."[107] Inglis further refines: "Tourism becomes a way of experimenting with feelings without having to live them too fully."[108]

This temporary encounter with the exotic, with the other, with the authentic is perhaps what most clearly defines the tourist. All of these encounters are mediated, controlled, and commodified. The encounter is purchased specifically as a controlled experience. The change of the event is temporary and may or may not continue to influence the tourist's life outside of the event. The aim is actually for events that do not radically disrupt life outside the event. For the emotions encountered, the changes engendered, the perspectives gained or developed must be ones that not only can be accommodated back in the non-tourist world, but also must whet the appetite for more; they should form a habit that in many ways becomes seen as something this person does. Osborne wryly states:

> The advertiser's ideal tourists see what they expect to see and expect to see what the advertiser has intended. Tourists are positioned as both consumers and producers.[109]

Out of this arises what can be described as tourist hope. This is a hope "that pleasure will outweigh anxiety." Such a hope results in the seeking of "reassurance through familiarity: repetition is crucial, since it returns tourists to whatever they were looking for."[110] In this world of tourist hope, what is experienced must correlate to what is expected and transgression is, therefore, a mediated and controlled (and controllable) experience and event. In this way the repetition of transgression is what domesticates: it becomes a sought-for, looked-for, repetitive event:

> Repetition not only smothers the unexpected but also reliably re-presents the already known. It guarantees a high level of group solidarity and satisfaction.[111]

(If we want to explicitly slip over into a discussion of church worship, here is the controlled, repetitive transgression of the mediated experience of the divine, the sacred, the Spirit – from liturgies and Eucharists right through to weekly faith healings and speaking in tongues. These soon become repetitive transgressions, limited to the event of the worship service. They are only truly transgressive when occurring in public spaces outside of the church package.)

The tourist gaze may be constructed out of expectations, hopes and fears, but the tourist experience is the seeking of a manageable, controllable experience of sought-for authenticity. Kaplan sees this quest as linked into the situation of exile:

> …both exile and tourism construct authenticities. For the exile, the site of the authentic is continually displaced, located in another country. For the tourist, authenticity is elsewhere as well, and the present is inauthentic. The figure of exile represents a single break with the past, while the tourist negotiates numerous rifts and fragmentations of experience. Both figures, when mystified into primary subject positions, represent melancholic seekers after a lost substance or unity that can never be attained.[112]

We will turn to consider exile later on in this book (Chapter 3); for now I only wish to consider Kaplan's description of the tourist. Under my schema of the tourist as representative of popular piety, the authentic experience sought by the pietistic tourist is primarily a constructed and mediated one. The expectations have been underwritten by that religious *Baedeker* of the Bible telling you what you should look at/for, and why. It explains the "strange customs and natives" of this authentic world of biblical times where the authentic is primarily located. Yet the pietistic tourist can seek an authentic experience of their own by a ceremonial and spiritual holiday away from the mundane concerns and claims of their everyday, real world by participating in a service of worship. The value for money guarantee occurs when the present participatory experience of the tourist is judged not only with primary reference to the textual authenticity of the *Baedeker* Bible and their own memories of other trips (memories of participation in services). It is also viewed with reference to other tourist tales of similar experiences, both in the past and the present (family and cultural tradition and also an experience of church). In much the same manner as Lodge's Bernard Walsh comes to realize, the clergy are primarily tour guides who weekly shepherd the tourists through a spiritual quickstop tour, a "greatest hits/snapshot/souvenir/tick the boxes" experience that contains enough difference and exotica hopefully to excite, yet enough support and comfort so as not to upset. The intention is not to create an all-inclusive total package for that would be to undermine the operator's aim of continued patronage. The intention is to put in place a deliberately incomplete authenticity that seeks to hook and develop a taste for more. To alter the tour is to risk upset and a change to either another operator or a stay at home attitude. The aim is to have repeat customers. These are those tourists who seek to return again and again because they enjoy the experience as a manageable excursion towards an expected and controllable authenticity.

The situation is one of a complicit delusion on both sides: there is the creation and controlled mediation of the experience by the clerical guides and the acceptance and patronage of that experience by the pietistic tourist. Even to venture further afield into the realm of adventure tourism and the backpacker is to still exist with a constructed tourist gaze and expectation. For this relocation is to exist on the margins of the tourist, seeking the experience of the domesticated traveller, the autodidactic traveller. Here is the tourist who classifies herself as spiritual as opposed to the derided popular pietist. This one is not quite an autonomous traveller/theologian, yet self-consciously self-set-apart from the popular mass piety and tourist experience.[113] The difference in the end is one of structured education. The tourist is the amateur, a gifted amateur perhaps, an insightful amateur maybe, but always in the end an amateur. His intent and experience, his expectation and, crucially, his account of what was seen, encountered, experienced and understood, will be different from that of the traveller. The traveller is expected to possess the ability to construct a coherent and critical evaluation, as opposed to the touristic descriptive report of what is seen and encountered (and created?).

Paul Fussell delineates the difference in an interesting manner that is useful for this schema. In order to match the differentiation made in his text, we now undertake a deconstructive re-reading outlined in the introduction. Let us read orthodox theologian for traveller, modernist theologian for explorer[114] and popular piety for tourist:

All three make journeys, but the explorer [Modernist theologian] seeks the undiscovered, the traveller [orthodox theologian] that which has been discovered by the mind working in history, the tourist [popular piety] that which has been discovered by entrepreneurship and prepared for him by the arts of mass publicity. The genuine traveller [orthodox theologian] is, or used to be, in the middle ground between the two extremes. If the explorer [Modernist theologian] moves towards the risks of the formless and the unknown, the tourist [popular piety] moves toward the security of pure cliché. It is between these two poles that the traveller [orthodox theologian] mediates, retaining all he can of the excitement of the unpredictable pertaining to exploration, and fusing with the pleasure of "knowing where one is" belonging to tourism.[115]

The tourist outlook includes a predominance of expectation and location. It is the venture, with an itinerary within confined and constructed boundaries, conducted with the expectations arising out of a tourist gaze. The journey is expected to include the manageably different, the accomplishable challenge and experience to be found and located within a controlled and demarcated tourist zone. Even those who attempt to achieve a degree of self-knowledge through excursion off the beaten track still rely upon authoritative guides and guide books[116] to ensure a safe return. In other words, the package is the experience.

This point forces a reassessment of what is the traditionally anthropological use of the trope of pilgrimage and tourism. In much contemporary Marxist-derived discussion, there is a form of what I term post-Protestant hostility which views and dismisses tourists pursuing experience, relics and locations of encounter as but the latter-day versions of an indulgence-seeking, saint-worshipping Catholicism that is beneath the modern, secularized (post) Protestant. But this is not to say that Protestantism does not involve pilgrimage. As Bauman (*pace* Weber) argues, Protestantism is itself a form of inner-worldly pilgrimage in which the daily world is seen to resemble the desolate desert into which the hermits of the early church retreated to encounter God.[117] The daily world for Protestants became desert-like: it is a place of impermanence and placelessness, a world impersonal, cold and empty. It is a world that is on the one hand a place of encounter and, on the other, a negation on the attractions and trappings of everyday sensual experience. In this world the act of pilgrimage across the desert is that which gives the desert meaning – and conversely gives the act of existence the meaning of pilgrimage. The pilgrimage was given meaning and purpose by the pursuit of a point of fixed arrival, the desert given meaning as the location through which this systematic journey was to occur. The result is the pursuit of systematic theology, which is the guiding purpose of so much Protestant thought and endeavour. Yet the crisis of contemporary Protestant theology, that of how to do systematic theology in a postmodern, pluralist world, arises directly out of this Protestant pilgrimage experience. Bauman observes:

> The world is not hospitable to the pilgrims any more. The pilgrims lost their battle by winning it. They strove to make the world solid by making it pliable, so that identity could be *built at will*, but built *systematically*, floor by floor and brick by brick. They proceeded by turning the place in which identity was to be built into a desert. They found out that the desert, though comfortingly featureless for those who seek to make their mark, does not hold features well. The easier it is to emboss a footprint, the easier it is to efface it. A gust of wind will do. And deserts are windy places.[118] [emphasis original]

It is in the face of such experience that the everyday, carnivalistic, sensual, immanent, commodified pilgrimage of popular piety comes under attack. In its revelling, perusal and accumulation of all that is experientially lush and communal, the lonely desert pilgrimage of the Protestant is held up for comparison and seen (by most) to be lacking. For our society has become a post-Protestant world in its search for sacred places, holy relics and communal assertion of identity by group participation in the experiential. The inner-pilgrimage is replaced by the return of the outer pilgrimage; the journeying is now multi-directional and repeatable. The desire is to experience the world as personal not impersonal, hot not cold, vibrantly full not empty.

Conclusion

Such a reading is a challenge to those who long for a distant past of dignified, elite (i.e. Protestant) travel. Paul Fussell embodies this sense in *Abroad*,[119] his influential examination of travel writing between the wars. He backhandedly disparages the tourist experience, stating somewhat loftily, "Tourism is egalitarian or it is nothing…it is difficult to be a snob and a tourist at the same time…the tourist moves towards the security of the pure cliché."[120] In a similar vein that self-titled "real travel snob" Evelyn Waugh remarked:

> Every Englishman abroad, until it is proved to the contrary, likes to consider himself a traveller and not a tourist.[121]

He also claimed:

> The word "tourist" seems naturally to suggest haste and compulsion…pitiable droves of Middle West schoolteachers…haggard [and with] uncomprehending eyes…these poor scraps of humanity thus trapped and mangled in the machinery of uplift.[122]

Aldous Huxley made the difference more one of belief. For him, in a secular modernist view, tourists seek "fables and fantastical hopes… mythology" because they lack a proper "interest in the real and actual." Whatever they do encounter "however curious, beautiful and varied, are a disappointment." In comparison, "the genuine traveller…is so interested in real things that he does not find it necessary to believe in fables."[123]

Out of this legacy, and in this egalitarian age, perhaps today's issue when seeking to define and discuss tourists is to not "reflect the worst qualities of country club denizens deciding on new members."[124] To disparage the tourist in that matter is the inverse of the disparagement of popular piety and popular and communal forms of religion: tourism becomes the opiate of the masses in a secular age. Yet perhaps the final word is that from the semiotician Paul Culler. He is more sanguine regarding such attacks on the tourist, locating them as rather part of what I could term piety:

> Ferocious denigration of tourists is in part an attempt to convince oneself that one is not a tourist. The desire to distinguish between tourists and real travellers is a part of tourism – integral to it rather than outside it or beyond it.[125]

This is why I wish to link travel and tourism as both modern(ist) tropes to be re-read as attempts to grapple with the question of faith, theology, piety – and God. The traveller may define himself in opposition to the tourist. And yet travellers are the ones who prepare the expectations of whatever encounter and gaze may occur. They exist as the claimants (in Huxley's terms) of the real that may be turned by the piety of tourists into fables and mythologies. But what is this claim of the real that the traveller goes in search of and claims that she encounters? What can it mean – both theologically and non-theologically – in the contemporary age? This is what we must next consider. For, is it true, as Jan Morris wants to claim, that:

> …the best guide books, like the best travel books, are generally written by resolute outsiders – observers who preserve the integrity of detachment, and write first and foremost to their own satisfaction [?][126]

2 The Traveller: Modernist and Orthodox Theology as Interpretative Experience

At the end of the previous chapter an important question was raised, concerning the pursuit of the real, or rather, the pursuit of what is perceived and deemed to be the real. This chapter examines whether the pursuit of the real is the central question raised by the traveller. In other words, does the traveller, in an act of self-definition against the tourist, pursue what is claimed to be the real?

Jan Morris' claims for the traveller combine the superiority of the outsider with the necessity of writing first and foremost for herself. Such a claim serves to position the pursuit, encounter and observation of the real as that which can only be truly undertaken by modern, atomized individuals. Such individuals will locate themselves as outsiders not only to where they venture, but also, more implicitly, as outsiders to their home location. Such dispositioning occurs as part of the self-reflexivity that is one of the central, base standards of modernity and the modern person (as individual). Self-reflexivity is here directed not only against the new context viewed by the traveller, but also against the home society that forced the move away towards the new, "other other."

This move can be seen as part of the secularization of modernity and identity. Traditionally the individual's identity was located in relation(ship) to the other who is God. In this case, we could say that the relationship was traditionally perceived as a vertical one (where God is traditionally located in the heavens). Who and how one is was considered and reflected upon in relation to this vertical claim and vertical relationship. With the modern, secular turn, this vertical relationship with other is dismissed, however. The vertical relationship is negated and overturned. Now the other is encountered in this world, as other person. It could be claimed that the incarnation has already secularized the vertical relationship. For did not the other now become other person, able to be encountered in this world? Yet Christian popular piety tends to follow more of an ascensionist than an incarnational model. The modern, secular move is also, perhaps primarily, against Christian popular piety. The move against the vertical other (God) is also a move against the incarnated other (Christ) – who is ascended. Such piety makes the incarnation an historical event and not an ongoing theological reality.

Locating itself against such popular piety, an incarnational model of God in Christ encountered in this world is the basis of secular Christianity. Yet such a move tends to be a re-iteration from within Christian margins after the dismissal of the vertical relationship. Secular Christians agree with the dismissal of the vertical relationship, but do not agree that it signals the end of relationship. The secular Christian model of relationship in this world is the return to the incarnational model of encounter and relationship. Such a theology is, understandably, most strongly repudiated by popular Christian piety.

Before we can move to a secular Christian model of relationship, however, we need to first encounter the modern, secular model. This relationship could be seen to be an horizontal one: it is a relationship with the human other that occurs because of the end of the primacy of the claim of the vertical other of God. We turn from God as primary other because the real is now presumed to be no longer located in God. Such a turn means our identity has to be re-negotiated. Who, and what we are, is now no longer to be found in the vertical relationship with God. The secular turn means identity is now a negotiation with other humanity. The self-reflexive modern is self-reflexive not only to and of herself, but is so because of the self-reflexivity occasioned by the relationship of identity with those who are like-but-not-like oneself.

The change instigated by the traveller is the relocation of where the real as other humanity is to be experienced. The traveller as self-reflexive modern is one who seeks the other "other" elsewhere. The traveller believes that the other who is the real cannot be experienced where and how the traveller originates. For self-reflexivity has meant that the traveller himself does not feel that the real is to be found in the society or the people in which they live. The traveller is, therefore, one who is an outsider to both their home society and people and also an outsider to the society and people to whom they venture and observe. This observation is also, therefore, often an observation of themselves: they can only truly be self-reflexive in and with the other who is the real. It could be said that travel is then an attempt to restore the vertical relationship of other within a horizontal location. This is why travellers often pursue the experience of festivals, rituals and religions located with the other who is real. They perceive that the traditional Christian vertical relationship has been negated in their home, secular society. They believe what has been negated at home may yet be re-encountered elsewhere in and as the other who is real. In other words, the new horizontal relationship over there may yet provide access back to the lost vertical relationship.

With this cultural turn as background, in this chapter I want to continue to develop the challenges of re-thinking theology if we follow the tropes of tourist, traveller and exile as deconstructive theological positions. Just as there is often a self-delineation between the tourist and the traveller (admittedly usually by the traveller as a form of self-elitism), there is often also a distinction made between lay/clerical piety and those who undertake the academic pursuit of modernist and orthodox[1] theology. (I note that in theology the disdain is often directed from both sides – the laity and clergy often dismissing academic theology as ivory-tower and academic theologians prone to dismissing laity and clergy as naive and simplistic.) In this chapter I want to ask: what happens if we re-read both texts on travel and travel texts[2] as forms of modernist and orthodox theology?

To ask this question is to reassert the centrality of hermeneutics as crucial to any discussion on the theologian as traveller. It is, in effect, to continue the self-reflexive turn of modernity, which is why the traveller is such a quintessential modern figure. In this reassertion of interpretation, the delineation includes an acknowledgment of the traveller's possession of (self) knowledge and critical skills, and the ability, attitude and desire to differentiate himself against the tourist of the package-deal popular piety. The traveller here is also the explorer of Fussell's schema; he is one of those who stand within the general frame of realist theology from either an orthodox, traditional viewpoint (traveller) or modernist re-articulation (explorer). The difference is that the traveller sets out to (re)discover that which *is* already there, while the explorer sets out in pursuit of what they believe to be there. Both the traveller and the explorer involve a journey to the realm of the other that is sought, expected, experienced and articulated as the real. Crucially, both expect to return to their starting point/land of origin. As a consequence both traveller and explorer fall under the general designation of traveller – as does their theological output (modernist and orthodox) under my inclusive terminology and (re)definition of travel literature.

What, then, is involved in this desire to re-read writing about travel and travel writing as if it were writing about theology?

At one level it is the return of the centrality of the inter-textual claim which sits under this whole attempt. One possibility is to consider how an insight of Walter Benjamin has been linked to Dietrich Bonhoffer. This linking forces a reconsideration of the relationship of critical theory and theology. Scott Holland notes that, while Bonhoeffer and Benjamin both lived in Berlin at the same time, they never met. But this does not stop Holland linking the two in a fascinating way:

> If they had [met], Benjamin would have likely told Bonhoeffer, "In the fields with which we are concerned, knowledge exists only in lightening [sic] flashes. The text is thunder rolled along afterwards."[3] Like Benjamin, Bonhoeffer would later see that it is the literary fragment – the letter, the paper, the poem, the story, not the systematic manuscript – that best reflected traces of the lightening [sic] flash.[4]

I want to claim that, in my procedure of re-reading, the lightening flash is what occurs when reading travel writing as if it includes within it the possibility of the lightening flash of theology. It is to read travel writing as if it could be/can be/is(?) theology – or at least theological writing. This claim can be read as another version of the Zizekian short-circuit. Following Bonhoeffer and Benjamin, the fragments I choose to use are not systematic manuscripts but rather writings that are created out of fragments. These are the images, thoughts, jottings, readings and experiences that are given a narrative structure afterwards, in the times of imaginative reflection undertaken by the travel writer. Seen from this perspective, travel writing is, like the lightening flashes, an inter-textual affair. I want to claim that this hermeneutic is similar to the pursuit of traces undertaken by Benjamin and Bonhoeffer. It is thus similar to both the process of writing theology and to the attempt to think theologically. To deconstruct the lightening flashes of travel texts and texts on travel is to open up the possibility of re-encountering theology in a short-circuit flash precisely because of its fragmentary nature and the turn away from the systematic manuscript. Yet, also central to my claim is the recognition that, like travellers, modernist theologians visit or go in search of that experience which has already been visited, sought and experienced:

> The place has already been named and preconceived. There is a referentiality of places and their texts that each new voyager relies on and denies simultaneously.[5]

Jacques Rancière makes even more explicit the theological–travel dialectic. Discussing the post-resurrection journey of Jesus to Galilee in the Gospel according to John (John 21:1–25) he makes it an issue of incarnation, presence and trace:

> [This is] what is theoretically at stake in traveling; not discovering far countries and exotic habits, but making the slight move which shapes the mapping of a 'there' to 'here'. The mapping is the additional way, that is to say the human way of making flesh with words and sense with flesh.[6]

Perhaps even more explicit still is Siegfried Kracauer's linking travel and dance as forms of "excesses of a theological sort and predecessors of a profane sort" in a society in which technology and mechanization have taken hold. Both forms of movement are disruptive and excessive because they provide an alternative meaning and possibility of movement (even if it is inauthentic). For Kracauer they have "theological significance" as the "liberation from *earthly woes*, the possibility of an *aesthetic* relation to organized toil." [emphasis original]. This occurs in modernity (Kracauer was writing of Weimar Germany) in a manner which might allow the type of elevation that might/might not have occurred "within people's existence in the relation to the eternal and the absolute."[7] The possibility opened up by travel, as Kracauer sees it, is the feeling "as if the Beyond (for which they have no words) is already announcing itself within this life here."[8] Yet, he warns, this is a false feeling of redemption and encounter because "the infinite and the eternal" "can never be contained in any life here."[9] His conclusion follows my observation that the original vertical relationship with/of other has now been secularized by the horizontal relationship. And yet, being this-worldly, there is the sense of it being inauthentic, that is, not real compared with the prior, vertical one.

What Rancière's return to the post-resurrected Christ's travel signifies is the incarnational challenge to any rejection of the continuation of that perception of the vertical relationship. That is, Christ's post-resurrection travel means the vertical relationship continues – but in a new way. Travel signifies that what was seen as lost can still be experienced in the horizontal, modern world. But crucially, this challenge is a challenge because it is incarnational. The vertical relationship has been relocated as horizontal-yet-vertical; that is, the other who is God is now to be found as the other who is God with us. Travel is, first and foremost, theological because the other who is God, the other who is real, has already travelled to be with us. This is the journey behind all journeys. What we have done is invert it: instead of the real travelling to be with us, now, in a secular, horizontal world, we seek to travel to be with that which we perceive to be the real. What travel involves is a mimicking yet secular repudiation of the incarnation. Travel is the relocation of flesh through space and time, of "making flesh with words and sense with flesh," in encounters with the beyond, with the other, with the sought for; yet in ways which are always excesses and transgressions.

Such a situation is what Hassan terms the radical nature of travel writing, a form of literature where "as in key moments of our lives too, a proposition need not be either logically true or false to achieve the highest intensity, and so alter our lives."[10] Out of this ambivalence arises a challenge of re-reading travel as "a dialectical metaphor of unmargined realities" – but which "assumes borders, if only to transgress them."[11]

Is travel, as Simon Raven stated, then, real when it is "independence in action, and as such is detested by the authorities"?[12] If so, the travel–theology dialectic is only real when theology is a form of transgression and independence. Theology thus involves a form of movement in excess of the expectations and needs of the authorities – whether they be religious institutions, theological colleges or, more so, popular piety. Here the transgression is to leave home, to move into an encounter with the other, to undertake a journey "into whatever we can't explain, or explain away."[13] And yet, just as Bauman reminds us that the Protestant-derived desert of modernity now starts outside our front door, so Pico Iyer states, "the Other is everywhere today, not least on our front doorsteps."[14]

Traditionally, the desert was the place travelled *into* to encounter the other; it was a place often endowed "with redemptive and purifying powers which 'cleanse' the suffering individual."[15] Even when Bauman's Protestant-made desert came right up to the front door of the modern individual, a particular dialectic of meaning occurred. The lone Protestant pilgrim made meaning for himself and for/out of the empty desert of the world by wandering through it to the place where "the meaning resides."[16] In other words, travel through the empty space of the world always still had a meaning, a sense of pursuit, and, in short, ontology. Travel was the encounter of self and space (the modern self-reflexive horizontal turn) in that "non-space" where meaning was seen to reside. Thus the traveller sought an encounter with what was believed to be attainable and with that which was believed to be an encounterable entity. The central point is that wherever or whatever the travel, what occurs is the following of a known route, the pursuit of the known and the expected. Whether speaking of the real desert or the desert of modernity, we remythologized the desert by our tracking across it in pursuit and expectation of an encounter with the real.

What, Then, Can We Term the Ontology of Travel?

Trinh T. Minh-ha states that: "in traveling, one is a being-for-other, but also a being-*with*-other." The other is that which is seen – and sees us; the other is a "presence to oneself [that] is at once impossible and immediate."[17] It is this sought-for presence that I would claim lies at the heart of the ontology of travel and of the travel–theology dialectic. Robert Dessaix boldly states that the issue of identity is what makes travel "travel" – any other reason to "move around the globe" is "merely displacement."[18] And yet perhaps displacement is what sets us off on travel. We move in search of self, in search of other, in search of self in encounter with other, because of the displacement we feel, are told we feel – or told we should feel – "at home." Dessaix explicitly relates travel as a form of "saving our souls," yet claims that "[n]ot believing very strongly in souls anymore we call it self-discovery."[19] Out of such a delineation of the purpose of travel, it could be further argued that the being of the traveller is expressed in two ways. The traveller is one whose being is not only discovered in the encounter with the other (that secondary, modern, secular horizontal other) – but crucially, is one whose being is sought and discovered (as a self-reflexive modern) as one who is not a tourist. This is because (*pace* Fussell etc.) travel is perceived as authentic and the tourist is seen as an inauthentic follower. So, reading both ways in the traveller/ theologian dialectic, to either find oneself on a package tour, or to encounter really "the other" in the mass event of weekly piety, is deemed an impossibility by the traveller/theologian.

The important factor for self-identity is the intention of the movement. Travel is not ultimately undertaken for the souveniristic piety of the tourist. In fact, travellers are often at pains to differentiate themselves from the tourists. And yet, it is often the traveller who opens the way for the tourist. She does so not only in venturing to and encountering the other, but also by most importantly returning and recounting her experiences. For, in many ways, the tourist only knows where to go, what to see, what to expect and what to souvenir because of the prior experience of the traveller.[20] The traveller is thus the one who is the thin end of the wedge in both the encounter and the domestication of the other. In his never-ending pursuit of the new and the authentic (or the related rediscovery of the lost and the exotic) the traveller is the one who says to the potential tourist: "Now I have been, so can you. Let me show you the way and what to expect." Of course, some of the traveller's independence is accessible as mediated tourism to the semi-independent tourist we call the backpacker. These are tourists who see themselves as travellers. The backpacker most often follows a prescribed route already travelled by the traveller, however. They are, like the traveller, at pains to locate themselves in opposition to the tourist. Yet, in the end, they are merely sectarian tourists – in effect, partakers in dissenting piety. In theological terms, backpackers are those seekers who only sporadically attend the weekly church service, often renaming themselves as Christian in opposition and repudiation of denominational identities. They may move from church to church, from denomination to denomination, seeking the new and the novel within certain controllable boundaries. However, while a simulacrum of the traveller's experience may become open to the backpacker, for the tourist to participate, the (clerical) tour guides and package operators have to be willing to add a series of containable and repeatable locations and experiences to their map.

Travel literature (and thus in this schema, theology) tends to operate in the pursuit of the fulfilment of two criteria: a new vision and a new persona/life. As Mark Cocker notes: "The central unifying principle in travel books is that abroad is always a metaphysical blank sheet on which the traveller could rewrite the story, as he or she would wish it to be."[21] Or, as Chris Rojek states: "Spatially speaking then, travel experience involves mobility through an internal landscape which is sculptured by personal experience and cultural experiences as well as a journey through space."[22]

The travel text is, therefore, an exercise in both autobiography and re-biography,[23] and is often read as if it is fact, not faction.[24] But, as Fussell notes, the traveller's text is often read (and written) as if it were something else:

> Travel books are a subspecies of memoir in which the autobiographical narrative arises from the speaker's encounter with distant or unfamiliar data, and in which the narrative – unlike that in a novel or a romance – claims literal validity by constant reference to actuality.[25]

Now two important qualifiers need to be made. We do not want to fall into modernist/orthodox assumptions, taking the traveller/theologian as the scribe of encounter. For a memoir relies not only on that faulty faculty of human memory, but also on the (willing) reader's belief and expectation that this is a factual account that describes *real* events, personalities and occurrences. Both a word of warning, and a question that needs to be asked, is to be found in Geoffrey Moorhouse's *The Fearful Void*.

Moorhouse's book details his trek through the Sahara. Before setting off, he visits a Russian Orthodox church. Considering his faith, he ruminates on the existence of a navigational tool called the Point of Aries. This is where the sun's path intersects the celestial equator on March 21 each year. Moorhouse notes that, while all zodiacal bodies are related to this point, there is no actual entity called Aries; rather it has been invented by astronomers and navigators. It is Moorhouse's reflections upon this conundrum that are, I believe, crucial to understanding the modernist(ic) theological endeavour:

> It is because Aries exists that the navigator is able to make his calculations, and so fix his position on earth. This is the focal point of activity for all those millions of light specks we call stars. It regulates their relationships. It also gives man, trying to find his way across the wilderness of the earth, a security that he can find it, if only he learns the secret of using Aries correctly. Perhaps…God should be thought of as a spiritual Point of Aries… Without an awareness of this God, without a sense of common relationship with God and with each other through God, without being able to refer to God, we are quite lost; people spinning helplessly and hopelessly through a fearful void of the spirit.[26]

Is theology an account of this sort of traveller and navigator, exploring the realm of the other, taking as read a guide which in reality is nonexistent – except in the form of a created and imagined necessitated existence?

A more recent discussion of a similar occurrence occurs in McKenzie Wark's ruminations of life with a Global Positioning Satellite. Each meditation is headlined by his GPS data-life location lived under the eye of a technological god/Point of Aries:

29 Jan 2001 3:55pm EST

To leak into the cracks in a perfect world and flee along them. That might be what home is now. A home that could be anywhere. Not elsewhere; anywhere. Life need not be elsewhere, always pressing nose to glass. Home can be here. But here is anywhere. This where, now: Homing. *It is part of morality not to be at home in one's home.*[27] [emphasis Wark's]. It is the ethos of the ethical to embrace anywhere as part of another home.[28]

Wark's issue is that of the authentic location of home in a dislocated world; a world where, under a GPS system, you are permanently located yet dislocated. The Point of Aries was fixed – if imaginary – and a collective belief gave it permanence. With the GPS things have changed. If the Point of Aries was real but non-existent, now with the GPS we have a new axis that is real but artificial. The distinction is an important one. For in the twenty years between Moorhouse's and Wark's texts, the question of the real seems to have changed. Moorhouse seeks refuge in a faith he orientates around a God who is necessary – but not real. God is the focal point that links and positions us, ensuring we are not lost. By the mid-1990s, the traveller can guarantee *they will not be lost*: not by investing in faith but by investing in human technology. Now while the turn to the security offered by modern technology ensures the traveller is no longer lost, what *is* lost is the location of home. For, claims Wark (reading from Adorno), to be able to be located anywhere is, in fact, to be dislocated from any authentic, real home. This claim may initially be read as an ethical statement in that it discourages partisanship and stresses the universality of humanity. Yet, perhaps fundamentally overlooked by Wark's re-reading, is the point that such ethical purity comes with a real-world price. That is, only those with access to money and technology can actually afford to be dislocated in such a sense.

Deconstructing the Nomad

Such claims for the superiority of the ethics of dislocation occur in what can be named the nomad turn.[29] Central to this re-positioning are the writings of Bruce Chatwin. His approach was diffused with what could be termed a nomadic ethos where movement in itself is perceived as revelatory, no more so than in an early piece "It's a nomad nomad world" (1970). Here, in a counter-counter-cultural turn, he contrasts the settler's naive identification of God "with the vine, hashish or a hallucinatory mushroom" while "true wanderers rarely fell prey to this illusion. Drugs are vehicles for people who have forgotten how to walk."[30] This challenge to the then-prevalent psychedelic mysticism of the counter-culture is underscored by a puritan ethic: "Actual journeys are more effective, economic and instructive than faked ones."[31]

Both Moorhouse and Wark challenge this perception from different angles. To travel under the Point of Aries is, in effect, a faked journey: you are travelling under the guidance and direction of what you know is not there, but continue to believe in because of the security offered by the illusion. In Wark's case the journey is one where you are constantly under the gaze of the artificial Aries, a point physically created by humanity to locate and direct themselves under and against. But, under the GPS you are always in a journey where you can never get lost, or indeed just wander. On one level, home, for Wark and the GPS world, is like the nomad and wherever one finds oneself. The difference, however, is that even the nomad wanders within a certain boundary, often to an itinerary – even, one could say, in a type of ritualized liturgy. The practice of movement within boundaries provides the home. Under the permanent gaze of the GPS, home is, of course, wherever – and yet never – where you are. Wark's Adorno-derived ethical dislocation is a counter to Chatwin's illusion-free nomad.

Chatwin's western nomad is himself, nevertheless, an echo of the counter-cultural drugs and vehicular-non-walkers of the Beats. Jack Kerouac, in *On the Road*, himself echoes unwittingly the futurist ontology of the worship of speed and movement.[32] Perceiving that freedom is encountered in the car traversing open spaces, Kerouac's alter-ego, Sal Paradise, proclaims:

> We were all delighted, we all realized we were leaving confusion and nonsense behind and performing our one and noble function of the time, *move*.[33]

This is very similar to Marinetti's proclamation that "running at high speed is a prayer."[34] Maybe a link can then be traced in western counter-cultural expressions over the past century of the transcendent experience of dislocation. Pico Iyer discusses what he terms the newly emergent dislocated self in *The Global Soul*. He explicitly links technology and travel as the "two great engines of our age" which force humanity into continual longing to explore the potentials of both through greater and greater speed.[35] There is in this a direct line from Marinetti and Kerouac – yet the heritage is unacknowledged. For the global soul is a member of the counter-cultural elite. Marinetti and Kerouac are the disreputable counter-culture with links to Fascism and failure. All three acknowledge the pursuit of speed, freedom and transcendence through technology in the modern world. But perhaps the end point is indeed the GPS, as Wark found. We can never travel fast enough to escape the dislocated no-place of the GPS artificial home.

William Dalrymple, in *From the Holy Mountain*, discusses an interesting example of the failure of travel in the modern world to encounter the sought-for real. He set off from London throughout the Middle East in search of the survival of ancient forms of Christianity. His journey is one of encountering exotic Christianity in exotic locales. Yet, he wryly notes, in searching for the exotic elsewhere he missed the location of the exotic in the local. While he searched for remnants of Nestorian Christianity in Syria, he returned to England to find that the Nestorian Patriarch has been recently crowned in Ealing in London. In fact, Ealing is home to the largest Nestorian community in Europe:

> Such are the humiliations of the travel writer in the late twentieth century: go to the ends of the earth to search for the most exotic heretics in the world, and you find they have cornered the kebab business at the end of your street in London.[36]

The relocation of the exotic into your everyday mundane reality is a challenge to the traveller. What could only once be experienced and located over there is now readily available here. This relocation in turn forces a re-orientation for the traveller. If your identity has been constructed on the search for the other elsewhere, how do you reconstruct your identity when the other is now here? Do you have to search for new exotic others who are not yet here? In other words, is inaccessibility the true mark of authenticity for the traveller? To slip over into overt theological questioning: if God is readily accessible in our everyday mundane world is this actually a disappointment for the modernist theologian?

An alternative possibility is that offered by Wark's GPS dislocated traveller. She has the possibility of being a foreigner everywhere. She can, as Iyer notes, find "oneself discerning Edens where the locals see only Purgatory."[37] This is a challenge to the Chatwinesque school which can only see purgatory in the western societies in which they live. Their response is to seek to repudiate their society in favour of a sought-for authenticity. Such an act of repudiation, however, seeks not so much to affirm the other which is actually beyond encounter (for it is not static as the romantic wishes). Rather, as Cowley archly notes, "they seek not to discover but to celebrate – themselves."[38] The self-mythologizing of such travellers, their affirmation of a romantic mythology of the disappearing, static (as in never-changing) but often mobile, nomadic truth, free from the illusions of a declining and decadent West, form a potent mythology. As Inglis notes:

> Romantic journeys are always on the point of vanishing and the way of life the travelers encounter is always on the edge of extinction.[39]

While Chatwin may seek to walk away from the illusion created by "vine, hashish or mushroom," away from drugs or vehicles, his ambulatory revelation was not as illusion-free as he may have desired. Michel de

Certeau, in his discussion of the practice of walking in everyday life, locates travel and walking as substitutes for the legends and superstitions of the past, which "used to open up space to something else."[40] Chatwin's false claim of the illusion-free nomad, in fact, merely substitutes one form of illusion for another – in his case the romanticized myth of the revelatory individual traveller:

> The nomad renounces; he reflects in his solitude; he abandons collective rituals, and cares little for the rational processes of learning or literacy. He is a man of faith.[41]

The nomad as intellectual outsider also influences another romanticized use of the nomadic metaphor. Deleuze and Guattari, in *A Thousand Plateaus: Capitalism and Schizophrenia*, base a central section around what could be termed nomadic claims. The result is what I call nomad chic amongst theorists anxious to prove their otherness credentials. The nomad became an essential reference point in any critique of modern western society. In effect, the nomad became a source and trope of anti-western essentialism – albeit used primarily by western intellectuals. It could be argued that such a reference to the essential nomad becomes a form of the intellectual's Point of Aries.

Deleuze and Guattari's central concern was with the nomadic encounter and the delineation of territory. More specifically, they were concerned with the identification within that of what points (water, dwelling, assembly, etc.) occur "as principle" and what is "only a consequence."[42] In other words, why does movement occur, and what is its cause?

The contrast here is with the migrant who, unlike the nomad, travels neither as a consequence and nor on a trajectory.[43] For the nomad follows a path. In a sense he follows an itinerary, even a type of ritual liturgy, that keeps him on the move and, by choice, dislocated yet located within the trajectory. The appeal for cultural theorists of the nomad within late modern life arises out of what is termed nomadic deterritorialization. Unlike the migrant, nomads do not seek to shift from one territory to another. Nor do nomads seek to remake where they are as is the custom and practice of the sedentary.[44] Rather, the nomad is (as later presented by Wark's GPS dislocated traveller) "in a *local absolute*, an absolute that is manifested locally."[45] Deleuze and Guattari thereupon theorize the possibility that monotheism arises out of the nomadic life by "making the absolute appear in a particular place" – especially in "smooth spaces (desert, steppe, or ocean)." It leads into the conclusion that: "in short, religion converts the absolute."[46]

This claim as to the appearance of the absolute in the midst of nothingness means that out of the nomadic experience, the absolute can now be experienced as universal absolute, and not as one tied to a particular locality. The travelling God is one who is experienced wherever the traveller is. In Deleuze and Guattari's terms, it is a "nonlimited locality" experienced "in an infinite succession of local operations."[47] The nomadic encounter is opposed to the institutionalization of religion with its attempts to fix and delineate both the absolute and access to it – whether it is "the priest or the god." Rather, the nomadic encounter prefers a monotheistic absolute which is "a singularly atheistic one."[48]

And yet in the modern world we are – and are not – nomads. The GPS-located traveller is actually always fixed and delineated in relationship to the new technological absolute. The traveller fixing herself to the imaginary Point of Aries is likewise seeking a stability that (reading out of Deleuze and Guattari) the nomad would reject. Furthermore, the fixed stability is, I would claim, inimical to monotheism, which is not tied to any particular location.[49] The rejection of locatedness inherent in monotheism is also, therefore, a critique of religion as cultural embodiment. Slavoj Zizek raises the issue as to whether the separation of religion from culture is where and when modernity occurs:

> One possible definition of modernity is: the social order in which religion is no longer fully integrated into and identified with a particular cultural life-form, but acquires autonomy, so that it can survive as the same religion in different cultures.[50]

Such a reading raises the intriguing issue as to whether western modernity first occurs with the proclamation of Pauline Christianity. Modernity so often then gets rejected with the institutionalized culture of Christendom. This means modernity and Christianity in particular become irreparably linked. At times Christianity institutes modernity and, at others, it acts to reject it. The moves to a pre-modern and/or post-modern culture occurs when Christianity becomes a culture (pre-modern) or becomes a cultural expression (postmodern), rather than an intra-cultural and counter-cultural critique. From this arises the further question that perhaps Christianity (as opposed to Christendom) becomes the monotheism that rejects cultural locatedness. The rise of religion (and Christendom was the building of a culture of religion) as an attempt to fix the absolute within a particular location, to build locations of encounter and worship, to institutionalize the encounter of the absolute, is seen as that which is in opposition to monotheism and the absolute. This is therefore a challenge to the establishment and located expression of Judeo-Christian culture and belief. Richard Sennett notes this challenge in his study of cities in western culture. A culture that is situated and metropolitan paradoxically arises out of a tradition arising out of and celebrating the "experiences of human dislocation and homelessness... Our faith began at odds with place."[51]

The Judeo-Christian Traveller

In tracing the basis of Judeo-Christianity back to Abraham (noting that the exile from Eden [Genesis 3:23–24] will be included in the discussion on exile), within these traditions the encounter with the absolute is primarily to be experienced in a dislocated experience. Dislocated by the call of God, in response Abraham becomes a traveller who in the process undergoes the transition to a new identity (Genesis 12:1–3). Edmond Jabes locates Abraham as one who seeks the other, in which is found his identity:

> The man who leaves – Abram – where does he go? Sets out in search of his identity and discovers the *other*. He knows from the start that he will perish of this *otherness*, in the unfathomable distance separating him from himself, out of which rises the face of his solitude.[52] [emphasis original]

If the call of God to Abraham is of the non-located God calling on Abraham to dislocate himself, then this sense of distance is further expressed in the call of Moses. It is traditionally taken that the God of the burning bush, when asked his name, replies: "I AM WHO I AM" (Exodus 3:14). It is often overlooked, though, that an alternative reading is more provocative. A challenge to Christian locatedness occurs when we remember that the self-disclosure of God, EHIE ASHER EHIE, is in Hebrew actually/potentially: "I WILL BE/BECOME WHAT I WILL BE/BECOME."[53] We too often forget that the name refers not to God's being but rather to his action and presence.[54] This latter reading (actually the return to the original Hebraic meaning) is, in effect, a nomadic self-declaration compared with a settled, located, institutionalized one of the usual "I AM" reading. Consider what occurs in a reappraisal of the event when Moses is instructed to say to the people of Israel "I AM has sent me" (Exodus 3:14). If what he says is actually "I WILL BE has sent me," then this indicates a God who is never fully encountered, located or indeed finished Divine action or presence. Here, "the God of your fathers" (Exodus 3:15) is the One who is not only of the past, but of the present and of the future – a God that exists on divine and not human terms and expectations. The reading of God as I AM "is precisely what the name EHIE eliminates." This God (I WILL BE/BECOME) written out by settled society is rather a God appearing at "the onset of nomadism and inverted exile. He also appears in a place which is a kind of *no place*."[55] In contrast, our modern world is a world where I AM is directed by the GPS; likewise as Moorhouse stated, I AM was located in reference as a type of mythological Point of Aries. In both cases the settled, domesticated I AM who appears on human terms and expectations is replicated. This way of thinking causes problems for the traveller who may venture out under a created God so as to locate himself in the midst of dislocation. And yet the claim of the traveller has also been that of a search for identity located in what he will be/become. Can one really be a traveller under a created past-tense located God when the aim is actually a search for dis-located future tense possibility of God – and self?

This transformative search for a new/emergent/developing self is what lies at the heart of the travel narrative. The travel text exists on two levels. While we might read it as the report of an experience that has been undertaken by the traveller, in fact, it is actually an experience transformed in order to be retold for the reader. It is this that takes the experience out of the personal travail and into its relocation as travel text. It is in the text that the reader participates in the retelling of what the author wishes to tell of their travel. An important point is that made by the doyen of modern travel writers, Patrick Leigh Fermor:

> You can't be a travel writer…you can only be a writer who needs to travel in order to further your inquiries… The whole point of writing is to learn through your inquiries and then pass it on to others.[56]

This way of understanding sits in conversation with Krist's delineation of contemporary travel writers as either those who use the world as backgrounds for their expressions of the self – or those who outwardly project their investigation of the world.[57]

When discussing the purpose of travel books, the challenge for a realist narrative comes from Paul Theroux. In his view, the travel writer and their text should "tell the truth" in a manner that is "prescient without making predictions."[58] To retract and retreat into (what is claimed as) reportage is too often to become just another tourist seeking to exist without or despite the mass rituals and carnival occurring around them. Theroux is also prepared, however, to make claims for the prophetic activity of the travel writer – or, rather, to claim "that the truth is prophetic." Recounting his reassessment of China following the Tiananmen Square revolt of 1989 and, in turn, reassessing his Chinese travel text *Riding the Iron Rooster* (1988), Theroux locates truth whereby:

> if you describe precisely what you see and give it life with your imagination, then what you write ought to have lasting value, no matter what the mood of your prose.[59]

And yet, somewhat strangely, his aim of prophetic truth-telling is received as a form of demythologizing – but only in the sense that he was a form of intelligent tourist, a "journeying Everyman, concentrating on what all tourists notice but then overlook."[60] This attitude makes him not so much a travel writer as rather a "tourist with [a] typewriter."[61] Can Theroux's model of "reportage and imagination" actually be prophetic when what is sought is the participation in the mass experience but undertaken with a disruptive "angle of vision" and, then later, "given life with the imagination"? In other words, can prophetic truth occur in retelling and retrospect? Can one really be a prophet after the event? Is there actually a difference between the prophetic voice and the retrospective analysis? The issue here is concerned with what is seen and experienced is only ever partial and, as a consequence, a double movement occurs. Firstly, the traveller moves through what is encountered. Secondly, that which is sought or viewed is caught only in partial glimpses which are then recomposed with a new sequencing and commentary afterwards. In this case, travel "constructs a fictional relationship between gaze and landscape."[62] Jonathan Raban, himself a travel writer of note, is well aware of this relationship – and the gap that is needed before the relationship can emerge. The journey is not the narrative that emerges; rather "[i]t is a shapeless, unsifted, endlessly shifting accumulation of experience."[63] This result is because of the huge difference between what is experienced and how it is presented:

> For traveling is inherently a plotless, disordered, chaotic affair, where writing insists on connection, order, plot, signification.[64]

So we return to the question as to whether the prophetic event occurs in the act of participation and observation – or, in the act of imagination that re-orders, re-presents and re-edits what has and has not occurred? There is, of course, the possibility that what occurs is indeed the lightening flashes that link Benjamin and Bonhoeffer; but where do these lightening flashes occur – in the glimpses of what is observed and encountered, or in the attempt to review and order them afterwards? Perhaps each informs the other: what is glimpsed and experienced exists in dialectic with what is reconsidered. The prophetic event is that which is glimpsed and then re-told and re-expressed. In effect, the prophetic event is that which moves from the personal experience to the public expression. The truth is not only what is told but also, crucially, how it is told.

Theroux's well-known grumpy, misanthropic persona makes his truth telling an activity of little grace or joy. This sober estimate is in keeping with the statement put in the mouth of Roberto, the guide for Lawrence Durrell's coach tour around Sicily:

> Traveling isn't honest. Everyone is trying to get away from something or else they would stay at home.[65]

Yet there is more than just the getting away from home which could be seen as the location and expression of I AM. For there is also the movement towards, in pursuit, in search of something else that will provide the alternative, the antidote, the explanation for that which caused one to leave. Here the call of I WILL BE/BECOME acts as challenge to I AM. As such it sits within Zizek's positioning of modernity as the rupture of settled religion within culture. Of course, from the settled location of tradition there is the rebuke that it (travel writing) "is specifically about disconnection" being written out of an "adolescent" frame of mind, unsure whether to be "accepted" or to be "something special."[66] Such a response is like a return to the sureties of reportage, the sureties of a world readily explained and delineated, an encounter that can be easily controlled, codified and ultimately domesticated. That is, the world that seeks the self-limitation and enculturation of I AM. What needs to be remembered is that the traveller as modern is an outsider;[67] one who writes into and out of a "perennially marginal position" which allows both "idiosyncratic formal innovation" and "the production of a self in the course of writing."[68]

The self that is produced in and by the act of travel is one that is "processed, preserved, understood and given meaning" in "the centrality of print" through "the leaking categories of Travel writing."[69] Hassan links this to the theological task, as a genre "defying any comfortable distinction between fiction and fact," addressing "fundamental issues of human existence, problems personal, social, metaphysical."[70] (In this way, the lightening flashes, the Zizekian short-circuits are also forms of leakage, locating insight in the inter-textual encounter.) Yet it is also an "act of control,"[71] a transformation of meaning for those "possessed...by the *wayward* (pun intended) vitality of an irrational logos"[72] which is expressed in a genre that "also hints at its own abolition – in death, in silence, in extreme spiritual risk."[73]

It is here we need to remember again the claim, the challenge and provocation of the divine name: EHIE ASHER EHIE ..."I WILL BE/BECOME WHAT I WILL BE/BECOME." The God who travels with Abraham, who travels in Sinai, who travels in the diaspora, who travels, Jews and Christians claim, to the ends of the earth, is a travel writer whose text is possessed by an irrational logos. This travel-writing God is in a constant battle for control with wayward humanity. This travel-writing God is, by human reason and reckoning, necessarily irrational. This is a travel-writing God who, in the kenotic offering, perhaps does more than hint at abolition, death, silence, extreme spiritual risk. The theological traveller and the travelling theologian (and here are the leaking categories) are those who end up providing the end of that guidebook (whether Bible or *Baedeker*) which guides the tourist – and perhaps lured them into this encounter with "the irrational logos":

> Theirs is the guidebook in its final debasement: scoured of all claims to objectivity, deprived of italics, reduced to the power of the inner vision and the creative pen.[74]

Far too often the text written is that of the God who has travelled, the one who is, the now past event of I AM rather than the future challenge and provocation of I WILL BE/BECOME. In effect, again using Zizek's definition, modern theology too often attempts to dismiss the rupture of modernity. This effect is also true of attempts to enculturate the Gospel or theology as culturally normative. The rupture of the travelling God is too often re-domesticated in where it travels to. As Colin Thubron notes the "mutability" of many travelogues:

> The traveler moves in the past tense (probably), not the present of the guidebook or academic study – recording not what necessarily is, but what for an instant was.[75]

Furthermore, that "instant was" is often itself the product of a textual encounter; it is that which has been prepared for, that which has been anticipated and expected. It is, in Wever's terms, "deeply textual"[76] and this is what enables it to be more easily the "I AM *as was as* I AM" than the I WILL BE/BECOME. By this formulation I mean that by our travelling to and focusing on the I AM who is declared and located in the past text and event, the dislocated and dislocating I WILL BE/BECOME can be dismissed, overlooked or relegated to the textual footnote. For the I AM displays a formidable certainty. The I AM is an *IS* that is located and locatable, yet the I WILL BE/BECOME is harder to locate and is more sought than encountered. What is at issue is perhaps the issue of a trace. Is what is sought a trace of the located I AM no longer available? Or is it the trace of the passing (and therefore future) of the I WILL BE/BECOME?

> The route is basically a trace left in geographical space and chronological time, but the imaginative continuity and quality of this trace can vary.[77]

The challenge is the reminder that no trace is ever pure:

> …we are all belated travelers. There have always been too many before us and they have left their inescapable marks… Nobody gets there early enough. The delusion of unthinking travel writers is that they can somehow see the place pure, free from intrusions from the outside or the preconceptions that come from reading earlier accounts.[78]

The trace is therefore a palimpsest of traces – and of those seeking the trace before the present attempt. Yet the difference in time between the search, the travel, the exploration and then its textual expression means what is presented as immediate, as of the present, is always, by necessity of that which already was.

The pilgrim is perhaps the traveller in search of the trace of the I AM *par excellence*. He follows a route that is already pre-ordained, that has expectation built into every footstep. Pilgrimage operates on the I WILL BE/BECOME being subsumed, on arrival, into the location of the trace of the I AM. For the pilgrim, resolution is achieved following her participation in the trace of the trace; the pilgrim path following what is, yet is not there. And yet the pilgrim is also the tourist, the participant in the commodification, the commercialization, the rupturing perhaps of the trace into that which can be taken back. The pilgrim as tourist purchases evidence of what was/was not there. It could be ventured that the purchase of the souvenir is actually perhaps to assuage the disappointment of the reality that I WILL BE/BECOME is not the same as the locatable, stable I AM.

Elsner and Rubies see this as characteristic of the modern(ist) dilemma confronting the traveller (and by my extension, the theologian). They perceive travel as:

> a dialectic of dominant paradigms between two poles, which we might define as the transcendental vision of pilgrimage and the open-ended process which typically characterizes modernity [as such] modern travel writing is a literature of disappointment.[79]

This underlying disappointment occurs because in a post-Renaissance, post-Enlightenment age, one is not only open to, but culturally required to, self-question and self-critique. The result is the modern intellectual landscape characterized by relentless progress and questioning which, in turn, results in an acceptance of a necessitated deferred resolution and attainability. As they go on to state:

> authenticity emerges as incompatible with modern historical consciousness. What is lost to the modern traveler is the 'stupendous spectacle' of the full vision, a reality once available but now vanished.[80]

This loss is a constant problem for the modern traveller. Not only is now where they came from a non-place and the (non)location of the non-event – but where they seek the real place and event is increasingly far-off or difficult to reach. Even more so, what may be experienced there is, on reflection, not what they actually sought. As Robert Byron lamented in "The Problems of Modern Travel":

> It is often remarked that the Twentieth Century is an age of easy travel. In fact, there is scarcely any more traveling to be done. The most ingenious brain must find it hard to contrive a novelty.[81]

Byron did, of course, contrive some degree of novelty by firstly venturing into the closed world of the Orthodox monasteries on Mount Athos in *The Station* (1927), and then traveling overland in what has become a classic event (and text) in *The Road to Oxiana* (1937). But it needs to be remembered that the novelty had as much to do with Byron and his retelling of his travels as with the travels themselves. They are, as Evelyn Waugh comments, indicative of a turn in travel writing, being the work "not of travellers who feel compelled to write, but writers who feel compelled to travel."[82] Waugh's comment is a crucial one for it raises the necessary question of what drives this compulsion. One answer could be the inherent self-reflexivity of modernity directed with critical gaze upon its own context. Helen Carr claims that many of the tropes of these modern travel writers are given expression in T. S. Eliot's *The Wasteland*:

> [These tropes are a] sordid metropolis, fragmentation, tawdry present, jumbled cultures, the flotsam and jetsam of a decayed civilization, nostalgia for an earlier, lovelier world, fear of the past and future horrors.[83]

While it needs to be noted that many of these fears and nostalgias are, in fact, causes for carnivalistic celebration in postmodernity (even if the carnival is one of nihilistic despair), in modernity there was the sense that that relocation could provide an antidote to the decay of modern life. There was indeed a sense that writers were a form of secular priest and prophet, the ones who could encounter the other on our behalf and enable us to experience it (whatever "it" was) in a mediated experience. This experience could lead to perceived distinctions whereby the traveller is located in opposition to the tourist, with the articulation of a "sacred (freedom) [traveller] versus profane (constraint) [tourist] distinction."[84] The traveller is one who "requires a crowd in order to shun it. There is a privileging of solitude, of role distancing in need of an audience."[85]

What becomes the novelty is not so much the travel itself as the recounting of it by the traveller. What becomes the *travail* of travel, therefore, is not so much the journey itself (as we know that it has been accomplished) but rather the narration of the *travail* of the traveller. We are actually aware, even if we do not want to acknowledge it, that we can no longer find refuge in "an especially conceited form of romanticism," by which Clive James warns:

> you imagine yourself in the curled shoes and flowing robes of Sir Richard Burton or T.E. Lawrence. Such adventures were already beyond recapture when they were first heard about, since new ground can only be broken once.[86]

And yet again, as Carr notes of modern travel writers, they "wanted to write of areas for which guide books could not be purchased."[87] What occurs is an intermediary event: modern travel writers are those who follow the explorers of the past. Modern travel writers follow in the footsteps and texts of those who first ventured. The modern travel writer is, therefore, not an original in himself, but rather the follower of the trace of others. What is then offered by way of originality is either the way the trace is travelled (by bicycle, with a handcart, etc.), or in whatever they, as individuals, can offer in what and how they see and experience. The distinction put forward is therefore between the travel text and the guidebook. Those who write the travel text write not for the tourist but rather write, first and foremost, to recount the change and challenge of the event upon themselves. They write, in effect, aware that what they seek to encounter is already under threat and challenge. It is already passing away into an unattainable past. (Here the analogy with modern theology becomes explicit. The modernist theologian writes of that which is continuously assailed and challenged by modernity.) What occurs is an act of cultural recollection. It is in practice a form of nostalgic self-reflexivity. Mather comments:

> The very best traveling is all in the mind. Travel books should not make you want to go to a place, but make you feel as if you have been there… Travel books are not guides.[88]

The self-reflexive reader of travel books is someone who acknowledges that what is experienced by the traveller is already unrecoverable. There are two (often implicit) acknowledgments that create the distance of the trace. Firstly, she reads acknowledging that the traveller's experience and encounter are beyond replication by the reader (for it is the traveller's singular encounter). Secondly, she reads acknowledging that, by the time the reader encounters the text, no longer is there an "as it was" – if, indeed, it ever "was." Yet she reads with the expectation that there *is* something to be encountered in the text, that there is "a certain necessariness," otherwise it is "no more than a marketing contrivance" with "all the intrigue of someone else's holiday snaps."[89] So, in response, there is a Romantic dialectic between travel writer and their reader, of "an equation between exterior landscape and an interior, subjective state which is supremely individual."[90] In effect, the reader travels with, and encounters with, the travel writer – yet with(in) the textualized account of the travel and traveller's encounter. The other is relocated in the textual encounter of the individual reader, mediated through the text. Both the traveller and reader participate in an expectation of danger and challenge which is the Romantic expectation of the risk of "insanity, the disintegration or total transformation of the self."[91] We read that we too may participate in this risk.

This is perhaps the central claim of the theology–travel dialectic. We do not want theological texts to be a guidebook nor a series of holiday snaps. We seek the prophetic, romantic challenge of disintegration, a perpetual textual experience of wrestling with God (Genesis 32). With Jacob as our example, we camp on the side of the river, seeking the name, the blessing, and yet also participating in risking (hoping for) the wound that is a reminder of the blessing. Not only does the traveller wrestle for themselves, they wrestle for us, on our behalf. And then we, as readers, wrestle with their texts, seeking the encounter within their texts that we perceive is there:

> If there is an art to travel writing, perhaps it consists in conjuring up ever more ingenious ways of stripping the self so it can be cracked open. This alone lets the writer understand new people and places, not to mention the old self, the old world

of home. In all traveling there is a constant two-way tug, a constant reference to a life, a readership, left behind.[92]

An issue that arises out of this tension is that of any claim to total novelty. As Duncan and Gregory remind us, travellers themselves undertake a form of inter-textual preparation, reading the texts of other travellers and noting their recommendations. Of course we have here a "Catch-22" situation: how then does the inter-textual traveller describe their own re-visiting and re-noting of the familiar in a novel and interesting way?[93] In response, I want to raise the issue of whether the theologian as Traveller journeys to the other of God *via* the texts of the Bible and other theologians? Here the encounter is already written – and re-read – into being. For Protestants, such logocentric theology sits (often unacknowledged) at the heart of a post-Reformation hermeneutic. To understand this self-reflexive reading strategy we need to firstly consider how, in logocentric theology, we read the incarnation.

Reading the Incarnation

In this articulation of the incarnation as itself being a reading strategy I am aware that I am pushing the boundaries of what may be considered acceptable theological critique. My intention in this section is to force a re-reading from the position of a re-thought logocentric position. It is just possible that here, in a deliberate mis-reading of Barth on the incarnation, I too can claim:

> If we think that this is impossible, it is because it is [*sic*] our concept of God is too narrow, too arbitrary, too human – far too human.[94]

In short, what happens when we read the logos-incarnation as a text?

My starting point is inherently orthodox. The incarnation is the ultimate challenge to the Gnostic for, in this doctrine, God seeks to be embodied in order to overcome the separation between Godself and humanity. The body, the expression of our humanity, becomes the location of the ultimate divine–human encounter. For in the incarnation, humanity as *imago dei* is reaffirmed in both the particular and in the universal. This occurs because God becomes particular humanity, the man Jesus. In the incarnation, God becomes a particular body, sharing in our full humanity in order that the universal onto-theological body of humanity may be reaffirmed – for here is the new Adam (1 Corinthians 15:45–47).

The incarnation declares that, it is through (but not in) the body that God is known. The incarnation is not an indwelling of the divine within a human shell – that is, it is not God as spirit residing within a human, fleshly shell. Such attempts to delineate the incarnation make it a form of possession, not incarnation. Rather, we need to return to the classical, orthodox statement of incarnational mystery of "fully human and fully divine." It is through this particular incarnation of the embodied God that we know God can be known. It is also through this embodiment of God that true humanity is re-learnt: we have no meaning, no existence without God.

Zizek, in his re-reading of the incarnation, claims that it is precisely this incarnational action that makes the Christianity of the Trinitarian God the only true monotheism:

> the lesson of the Trinity is that God fully coincides with the gap between God and man, that God *is* this gap – this is Christ, not the God of beyond separated from man by a gap, but the gap as such, the gap that simultaneously separates God from God and man from man.[95]

Reading on from Zizek in a short-circuit manner, the incarnation is a reading strategy that acknowledges that the gap continues and yet is overcome – even while it continues. The embodiment of God is an embodiment simultaneously within God and between humanity. This embodiment as gap holds not only the separated God together. It also holds separated humanity together. That which is separated within itself, whether God or humanity, and that separated from each other, which is God and humanity, are held together by the gap which is where God in Christ as incarnation occurs.

The logocentric reading strategy arises out of how we read the incarnation – in effect, how we read the gap of presence and trace. In the incarnation, Logos – the Word of God – does two things. Firstly, the Word of God enters the world to be transcribed as a human body. Word as Logos becomes embodiment so that the truth of God and of humanity can be read within the embodied text of Christ. In Christ the embodied Logos, we can read both of true God and of true humanity. But secondly, we also secularize the Logos as text. Just as in Eden, death is essential for divine and human self-knowledge:[96] a relationship that has its ontology in death as the location of the revelation of truth. Without the death of the incarnation there is no salvation. All we have is presence that has no meaning in itself. That presence is misread, because as presence it is Logos as word, as text, that is not yet read. It is the absence of the presence (even within Godself: God truly dies) that is overcome which forces the realization of presence with meaning. The presence of Logos as Word becomes a text not only read but proclaimed. Without the crucifixion there can be no bodily resurrection. In the death and bodily resurrection of the Logos Christ, the body of humanity in Christ becomes reaffirmed as both the sight and site of salvation. The text has to be fully no longer present (to God and to humanity) in order for the re-presentation to occur. What was mis-read before the resurrection now becomes able to be read – and understood, namely God and humanity reaffirmed – and God as truth, humanity as onto-theological. To claim otherwise is to venture into a spiritualized Gnosticism.

Re-embodiment as Reading

Such a reading strategy, however – even one so orthodox as to stress the central necessity of a bodily resurrection – here forces a challenge to traditional orthodox expression. The disembodiment of God following the incarnation, crucifixion and resurrection requires a new embodiment so that God can be known within the world of the body. For the world of humanity, post-incarnation, has the secular confirmed as the location for the divine–human encounter. This disembodiment is the paradox of the Logos Christ incarnation in that the resurrection is bodily, yet the ascension is the withdrawal of the Christological body into the non-body of the Triune God. That which was and is – is yet not what it was. This raises the question of how does the disembodied God, the resultant disembodied incarnation, the resultant disembodied Logos become known? The answer is by re-embodying itself.

The reading strategy here follows on from the centrality of proclamation. The incarnation was a proclamation of God that was not heard – until the resurrection. The proclamation of humanity of this prior proclamation of God in Christ in turn facilitates the new proclamation of God and humanity together. In this new proclamation, God-in-Christ and humanity combine to enable the continued proclamation and presence in the world. What occurs is the return of the continued presence of the Logos.

The Logos, the Word of God, becomes re-embodied and, as it were, re-incarnated in the body of text: that is, the Word (Logos) becomes words (the logos of the Bible). The incarnation of the Logos Christ confirmed a new humanity known by the self-revelation of God into and as that which is not God: humanity. We know God by what God has done by revealing Godself in a new form of what is, yet is not, us. The non-human and the human join together to confirm *who* is God – and *what* humanity is.

This confirmation, reading on from Zizek, involves both the confirmation of God to Godself and the confirmation of God to humanity. It is also the reminder to humanity of just what humanity is: *imago dei* as separated yet relational. This confirmation (which is to be read in all three ways by humanity) now needs to be proclaimed. In order for this to occur, post the Logos Christ incarnation, the Logos is re-incarnated as logos-text, in the body of text which is now the location of the divine–human encounter. In the text we read God and read ourselves.

The question of how do we come to know God and recognize ourselves as *imago dei* is answered. The response of Protestant Christianity is that, in the end, it is a reading strategy enabled – one could say demanded – by the self-limitation of Logos as logos-text. In reading the words of God (Bible-logos) we read the Word of God (Logos). In the act of reading, the human and non-human become reaffirmed.

It is the logos-text that sits behind our reading of the incarnation. We read of what has occurred by that which still occurs. This means that the logos-text is the reminder of the presence of the Logos. The reading strategy we undertake now, by necessity (the particular underwrites the universal) underwrites all our reading strategies.

The incarnation confirmed humanity as a text in which the truth of God can be read. That humanity comprises both the particular humanity of Christ and also in universal humanity as the embodiment of the particular as *imago dei*. Yet this notion of humanity as both a text for God to inscribe, and as the inscribed text in which God in Christ was revealed, needs to be read through the new incarnation of God. In this new incarnation of proclamation, it is the body of text (logos-text in the Bible) that allows the embodiment of the knowledge of God (that is, humanity as embodied *imago dei*) to read of the truth of its onto-theology. As Laurence Paul Hemming reminds us: "Self-reflection lies at the heart of Faith."[97] Our knowledge of text as location of truth arises because it is in the inscription of Logos as logos-words that we read of salvation through the body, which is represented through the body of the text. That is, we read the textualized body of Logos Christ (the incarnation) through the body of the textualized body of truth (the logos-Bible) that acts as truth because God in Logos Christ is now God in Logos Christ in logos-text. Faith is therefore a reading strategy of self-reflection in response to what has been proclaimed by the Logos that has now become logos-text.

In the wake of the ascension, the Bible becomes the re-embodiment of Christ as proclamation. The Bible is a Logos revelation repeated now as a post-bodily-specific incarnation. This new Logos revelation occurs as a universal textual incarnation linking the pre-incarnated (Old Testament), incarnated (Gospels) and post-incarnated (non-Gospel New Testament writings) Triune God into a new body of text. The reading strategy of self-reflexive faith occurs when we, as the universal condition, yet singular experience of *imago dei*, read the narrative of encounter and salvation and, in responding, make the universal particular once more.

Too often we read not to be confronted but rather to be confirmed in what we consider correct. This resolution is easier to accomplish if what we read is considered to have occurred and not to be occurring. We need to be aware that too often the God encountered in the text is read and encountered as the I AM, not the I WILL BE/BECOME. Just as the particular and the universal are in relationship in Christ, so too are the Logos and logos-text in relationship as particular and universal. The logos-text is the reminder that the Logos (word) is the word behind all words. If God is limited to I AM, then what has occurred is normative. Yet if God is I WILL BE/BECOME, then self-reflexivity occurs first in God and then, as response, in *imago dei*. If Christ is the self-reflexivity of God, where in the Trinitarian relationship God encounters and is challenged by Godself, then Logos becomes, in logos, where *imago dei* encounters and is challenged by the self-reflexivity of God.

For the traveller/theologian this self-reflexivity often occurs in a sense of autobiography. In the journey to the other, they (and we) learn more about themselves (ourselves). In their referral and meditations upon those who had gone before, whether they travel to Oxiana with Byron in their pocket, to Patagonia with Chatwin, to Cyprus with Durrell or back even further with earlier texts, we learn not so much that the destination itself has changed (though it might have in a manner that upsets Romantic notions[98]), but also how human society and its attendant self-perception transforms itself over time. This shift is most readily apparent when we attempt to encounter that which is not here. And yet, when it is searched for in the manner of the past, it is found to be no longer there either. For example, attempting to rediscover or recover a belief or sense of God which the theologian feels is lacking in contemporary existence, she references past texts and beliefs as the location of an authentic authority which is held up as a critique of the present day, conveniently forgetting the massive cultural change that has occurred. This imaginative leap means texts and beliefs of the past are read and referenced as if they were/could be written in the present. There are, of course, those travellers/theologians who manage to seemingly overcome this impasse. This occurs in a self-reflexive turn with the rupture of the short-circuit quotation. That is, texts from the past source are radically dislocated and re-appropriated in a re-presentation in order to cause a dissonant rupture in text and reader. The rupture occurs not because that being short-circuited was/could be written in the present day, but precisely because of the awareness that they were/could not. And yet the underlying rupture of Logos-logos continually asks: "what if they were?" As Dennis Porter notes: "The most rewarding kind of travel writing is often that which manages to surprise its reader with *images* that are startlingly new or with the extravagance of an idea *that can no longer be thought*."[99] [emphasis original]. As Porter implies, it is not so much discovery but rather the re-articulation or attempted recovery of a discarded and dissonant past. In this sense travel writing becomes not so much about the journey or attempted encounter as it is to do with the *Sitz im Leben* of the author-traveller and what encouraged the attempt in the first place. The attempt to leave home becomes, in many ways, either an attempt to remake home and self-(images), or a rejection of home and the contextual self in pursuit of what is felt as having been lost in the transition to modernity.[100]

There is yet another, more challenging, critique also to be offered against the modernist(ic) theologians. From the perspective of being on this side of the Enlightenment, do they ever actually leave home and travel like they say they do? In short, do they cite a short-circuit without reference and acknowledgment?

Retelling the Past: I AM as "I Was There"?

In Anthony Powell's 1939 novel *What's Become of Waring?*,[101] the title question is one asked concerning a celebrated travel writer, T. T. Waring[102] whom few have ever met. The "Waringness" of modernist(ic) theology is related to the fact that Waring is a fraud: while he writes of great adventures in foreign climes, he actually never ventures past his bolt-hole on the French Riviera. Rather, he plagiarizes and expands forgotten travel books[103] and passes them off as new adventures and truthful works of actual travel. His methodology is explained as: "he just told the story in his own words, with the philosophic stuff added."[104] A little later on in the book a defence is raised of this approach and deceit:

> "But the books were all written by other people."

> "Even so, he had to adapt them and write in the uplift."[105]

How does all this relate to modern(ist) and orthodox theology? The answer is in the type of sources used as a basis to write theology. In a way they are both navigators of Aries and theological Warings. Modern(ist) and orthodox theology is both the practice of rewriting the past experiences of others and (predominantly) attempting to write of a pre-Enlightenment experience in a post-Enlightenment existence. In other words, their writing of and about a God that does not exist in the manner (once) stated. On the one hand, they navigate their travels using as their guide the nonexistent Arian[106] God that is deemed necessary to fix the heavens and guide their journeys. On the other, they write of a God encountered and written of within a pre-Enlightenment world, yet rewrite their non-travels reusing texts of the past as if they describe the post-Enlightenment traveller-theologian's own journey.

The point at which they differ from both the Arian navigators and the Warings is that of knowledgeable intent. They do not set out to deceive. Their aim is the opposite. The intent is usually twofold. The first, especially of popular theologians,[107] is to provide a *Baedeker* of the exotic and of the other. They are writing guidebooks for the tourist who wants to be an amateur traveller. Edwin Dobb observes, with respect to this interface between "worldly traveler, sophisticated tourist":

> Each distinguishes himself from the next inline by claiming to be on special terms with the exotic – unknown facts, undiscovered country, uncommon pleasures. All seem to agree that the ideal trip delivers one into a foreign set of circumstances, eliciting unprecedented behaviour or new modes of thought, and perhaps inducing lasting change, a scar, a change of heart, a more nuanced view of the human condition. To travel well, the consensus seems to be, one must court difference.[108]

The important point is that, as travellers, they expect to and do return. They venture in search of difference and the other; they then find it, explore it and come back to where they left. Of course, as Mark Cocker notes, such travel produces a "literature of change and of transformation":

> The self that set out is never quite the one that returns. Equally, the insights and revelations inspired by a journey were unique to it. They can never be repeated identically on a second visit, nor inherited by the next generation of travelers. They are a deeply private, life-limited category of wealth.[109]

Cocker's insight is one of the historian and the literary scholar and not that of the traveller nor the tourist. It is here that the second intent of such traveller/theologians is apparent. This concerns those writing for a more specialized audience of other theologians in pursuit of theological inquiry. Writing both for and against their colleagues, these theological travellers might set out to write the theological equivalent of serious travel texts,[110] but return to write a form of *Baedeker* which is often taken up by their authors and contemporaries as guides and references for subsequent journeys. Modern theology is metaphorically composed of historical novels written out of a mountain of *Baedekers*: the theological traveller is writing of a journey through time where the guidebook of the present is miraculously able to describe the experience of the past. This is a past which is "the present in historical costume." In many ways this mode of journey is travel with Rousseauian intent, that Chatwinesque[111] search for the uncontaminated purity that has been lost in modern society but is believed to be still recoverable. It is, in a sense, anti-modernist, or rather Arcadian modernist, compared with much secular utopian modernist thought. Not only is "the past a foreign country where they do things differently," it was (is) a place "where they did things better." It is what I term a "back to the future"[112] theology. It is a return to correct the past to improve the present. This travel writes of the other as if it is a purer version of the traveller's homeland and a place from which the homeland should learn on the traveller's return.

The modernist traveller-theologian is in pursuit of what is believed to have been lost on the other side of the modernist divide. In looking backwards in texts (or to the exotic far country that seems to embody a pre-modern[ist] existence), their preoccupation with the perceived permanence of modernity is exposed. Such longing for a linkage outside of their context is a form of nostalgia that sits under a self-critical modernity. As such, tradition becomes critical for a reflection and self-awareness of the modern(ist) state of being, especially a tradition at counter-point to the prevailing (secular) ethos. For tradition is taken as signifying an historical authenticity that has (is read/seen as possessing) an ahistorical authority. Yet much of modern theology takes a modern perception as being in itself ahistorical. A God encountered outside/before modernity is remade/rewritten as conforming to post-Enlightenment modernity – and able to be encountered within a modernist frame of reference. All is subsumed to a pervasive *über*-modernity. The modern theologian is fighting against the imposition of a secular worldview where, if God is not dead, then God is irrelevant. The modern theologian appeals to the ahistorical notion of a normative past and tradition that, like a foreign land, is located outside of the contemporary context, and yet readily available for those prepared to make the effort (as opposed to the ease of touristic piety) to travel there. As such there are levels of encounter – the provisionality of the corporate, communal tourist and the quintessentially modern, existential lone encounter of the traveller.

But modernity itself was/is a stage and not an end in itself. That is, modernity is a project and not an accomplishment; it is a way of encountering the world and not a completed encounter. Yet the *fin de siècle* view of a normative postmodern turn raises the question of how one writes or undertakes theology in (and after) a postmodern environment when God so often seems a prisoner of the modern mindset?[113] I want to argue that far too often the modern mindset in theology is based on the self-proclamation of God as having been encountered. That is, God is, to all intents and purposes, proclaimed as static and past event-revelation. The God of the traveller-theologian is the I AM not the I WILL BE/BECOME. The I AM is able to be encountered in the texts and narratives of the past, where it is increasingly, actually, I WAS. What is written is, therefore, a form of Waring theology. The response is to develop an imaginative response, the imaginative element which attempts "to use facts as a springboard to reach more transcendent truths. Imagination is a quest for the essence of things."[114] And yet that essence is no longer there as it is represented, articulated or presented – or indeed expected. What is encountered is that which has already been written and mapped into a past existence and a past location. The challenge for the traveller-theologian – and for the reader – is one of textual expectation:

> There is a discursive or textual geography because we rarely go to a place without having read it first, without having shaped our own sense of what we want it to be. We are never innocent travelers; we arrive with ideas about the place in our minds. These ideas may be more vivid than the place can sustain when we see it; they may be more resistant to change than the place itself.[115]

Travel writers and critics have always been aware of the fictional nature of what they produce. And yet what it is they do produce is too often presented and read as if it is reportage. Part of this is a search in the modern world for a truthful encounter with the other, the exotic which it is felt has disappeared from contemporary modern, western life. The travel writer and their text provide a means to re-encounter that which is sensed, seen, or perhaps rather believed to be lost on this side of the modern divide. Yet the trip is never as presented, the encounter never as read. In fact, the expectation of what is/is not there is really a textual expectation that accompanies both traveller and reader. The traveller is seeking that which they have read was there and what they still hope to glimpse and encounter before it disappears in the encroachment of the modern world. The reader chooses to participate in the mediated experience of the other place, the other space, the other culture in the sense and expectation that it is exotic, that it *is* "other" – that "it" is THERE – if not HERE. For the great unstated truth of the theological-travel text is that I AM is actually, for the modern, always an I WAS. In short, the I AM sought is always the recovery of what is now seen as I WAS. As Bishop notes:

> Above all, travel accounts are involved in the production of imaginative knowledge. They are an important aspect of a culture's myth-making, yet this perspective is frequently overlooked.[116]

I do not want to say that travel writers and, by extension, modern theologians, are "liars." But rather, what they produce is something that reflects a specific moment of dislocation and an attempt to mediate between a sense of immanent loss and the challenge of the mass spectacle of the tourist (or the retreat into mass piety). They both exist perhaps most strongly in opposition to the mass – as one traveller in Spain found himself described. He is a traveller because he was a foreigner, but not a tourist.[117]

The privileged position of the foreigner as traveller is being someone who can and will return to where they came from. The traveller has sought, encountered, and recorded that which they believe still exists and can be encountered by the pursuit. She can fix both herself and where she came from in reference to this locatable other. There is the belief in the use of alternative experiences as the way to participate and encounter, where "the difference today lies less in the places we go to than in the way in which we go to them."[118] And yet, as always, I want to challenge this. Yes, there are always other places still there and, yes, we can encounter them in new ways. And yes, each trip by an individual traveller is a new trip – but what is it that we are visiting? Where are we actually going? How do we recall and record and report and retell it? Do we describe it in terms of what we know it is because we have read others' accounts and experiences and modelled ourselves either in their wake or in opposition to them?

For the travel text (and by extension the modern theological text) is an act of imagination and invention presented as that which is true and did occur. Howard Jacobson, in a discussion on travel writing, observes that if we have a favourite travel writer:

> you aren't reading his new book because you wonder where he's going next, you just want to be acquainted with his mind again. You want to go on a journey with him again. I'll go anywhere with him.[119]

The challenge of the postmodern world is that going with the travel writer is actually going to a place, having an encounter, experiencing that which is no longer available. It is an image (a form of simulacrum) that, rather than being not real, becomes something that "is really" in reference to that which is no longer there. The textual encounter makes, in effect, tourists of all readers and tour guides of all travel writers. All texts do become forms of *Baedekers*, telling the reader what to look for, to experience, to feel. Their readerly response is gauged against the expressed responses and encounters of the travel writer. All encounter the image of that which is no longer – yet is believed to be there. This means the I AM is located and codified. We respond then to the stability of self and I AM and, in fact, to the stability offered by our response; even if we only know of the I AM by what prior textual experiences have represented to us. But where is the I WILL BE/BECOME? For this is not the fixed, passive, controlled and controllable I AM, able to be located and written into existence. The I AM was already a past event with the advent of modernity. The I AM is past event that modern theology sought to recapture and represent as if it was still available. In a similar manner, the modern travel writer sought the unmediated, the pure, the uncontaminated, the real in the location of the other – even if that was no longer what they represented it as. In the postmodern world the challenge is that the I AM is no longer there – it never has been. The I AM was really that religion which Bonhoeffer wanted us to go past, the domestication of the sacred that made it permanent and present. The I AM made Christianity into the worshipping of religion. The postmodern world is that which needs to deal with the loss of the I AM and the challenge of the I WILL BE/BECOME. Yet perhaps the challenge can only be met if we first come to terms with the possibilities afforded and offered, perhaps even demanded, by the loss. We find ourselves, in postmodernity (and beyond), on the other side of the real. We find ourselves dislocated from what is permanent or present, separated from that which we viewed as located and able to give us location. We are exiled perhaps from where we made our home – and need to reassess where and how we are. Only then may the I WILL BE/BECOME become apparent.

So it is here that we now turn to the third trope. If the package (i.e. destination) is the experience for the tourist, and the journey itself is the experience for the traveller, then for the exile, loss is the central experience.

3 The Exile: This Location = Dislocation

In this chapter I want to further develop the inter-textual theological tropes by engaging with the trope of the Exile. More specifically, I wish to do this by connecting the trope of the exile with the trope of the postmodern theologian. To perform this task I will continue with the particular reading strategy I have followed. This method can probably be best described as a secular re-theologizing hermeneutic. Building on the centrality of the Logos–logos dialectic, allied with the continual undercurrent of lightening flashes and short-circuits, I want to wrestle with the considerable body of texts on Exile. This wrestling is designed to open these writings up to the possibility of being theological texts. The underlying assumption is that the Logos behind the logos sits within all texts enabling a theological hermeneutic to occur.

Gianni Vattimo has talked of Christianity entering an age of interpretation which he views as "the development and maturation of the Christian message."[1] What his claim signals is a future for theology that is not a case of *belief in* but rather that of *response to* and *interpretation of* "a historical message of salvation."[2] Vattimo's locating of a response which situates itself against authoritarianism[3] can be viewed as extending into such a project as is followed in this text To retreat into authoritative statements of belief as final truth that sets prescribed limits to interpretation is to make statements of belief into the locations of authoritarian oppositions. Such positioning, in turn, situates the postmodern theologian into a space of one who articulates against the reductionist limitation of prescribed statements of belief. The age of interpretation is, maybe, the age of those who see themselves as exiled from the world of strong belief and the associated statements of authoritarian belief. The postmodern theologian in exile is in exile in the secular world, in the world of the Logos made logos text. Hermeneutics, then, becomes the starting point for a theology of interpretative response.

To begin this discussion it is crucial to understand that there is a fundamental difference between the exile, on the one hand, and both the traveller and the tourist, on the other. This difference is based in experience, specifically the experience that results in their undertaking particular types of movement. This difference also signals a hermeneutical difference between the reading strategies based in each trope. It is of crucial importance to remember that the exile is (dis)located by the experiences of coercion and denial and the traveller and tourist have the alternative experience of choice. The exile is forced to leave and then cannot return until the circumstances that forced this change are themselves changed. The centrality of Vattimo's call of response against authoritarianism becomes clear. The exile is the central figure for a theological hermeneutic based in an age of interpretation precisely because of his opposition to authoritarianism in all its guises. In comparison, the tourist and the traveller, while perhaps uncomfortable with an authoritarian home location, have managed to work out an accommodation. Somewhat ironically, many of those who fall within these earlier two tropes actually choose to venture by choice into authoritarian locations for a visit (whether as tourist/popular piety or traveller/modernist theologian) because of the attractions of such locations. Or, perhaps more precisely, the traveller and tourist can *choose* to leave home, can *choose* to enter the authoritarian space and can *choose* to return to either option whenever they so desire. In doing so they venture forth, having made the necessary accommodations that the exile finds himself unwilling to participate in. The difficulties that forced those in exile to depart are those that serve to keep them in exile.

The biblical text is perhaps the natural place to begin for any discussion on Exile and theology. It is if this book was to be a traditional piece of biblical hermeneutics. But I want to sidestep such a discussion altogether. My justification for doing so is, again, based in my particular methodological reading strategy. This discussion on the exile is concerned, in a theological sense, with those who find themselves exiled from the authoritative interpretative community. While there are many transgressive possibilities within the world of biblical scholarship whereby readings from a host of marginal and or transgressive (to orthodox belief) positions can and do occur, my act of response seeks to move beyond the biblical text. This self-positioning occurs not only out of my Logos behind the logos hermeneutic. It also occurs because of two concerns with how the biblical text has often been used as a form of authoritative regime. Firstly, it is too easy for those seeking biblical warrant for a theology of Exile to proof-text their association and present dislocation onto and out of selective reference to biblical Exile. Secondly, to develop this concern further, I hesitate to relocate a Christianesque theology of Exile as analogous to that found in the Hebrew Scriptures. The *specifically* Hebraic experience of biblical Exile is one that Christians must not be over ready to appropriate. There is the danger of either a conservative or liberal form of literalism whereby contemporary Christians consider themselves Jews by default and, in effect, colonize Hebraic texts and experiences as now universally applicable – or rather universally applicable to Christians *they* represent. In doing so, the problem becomes one of forgetting that Judaism continues and did not end with the coming of Christianity. For an exclusivist reading of the

Christian tradition of the supplanting of the old covenant with the new covenant has far too often served to erase the continuation of Judaism from too many reading strategies. Of course, any attempt to be more inclusive is also, by default, bound to slip over into forms of what could be termed textual colonization. For any Christian theological re-reading and reworking of the Jewish scriptures of the Old or First Testament is in many ways reading from a disputed position. It is not the forced dislocation from covenantal land that creates the question of "How shall we sing the Lord's song in a strange land?" (Psalm 137:4). Nor is it the same question as that asked by Lesley Max in attempting to negotiate what it means to have a *Pakeha* (European) Jewish exilic identity in New Zealand:

> How do we, staring at the Waitemata[4] rather the Euphrates, 'sing the Lord's song in a strange land'? How do we, in a secular society affirm our identity without using a religious form? Yet we've devised no other lasting strategy to retain the identity, the link with the past, the hope for continuity.[5]

The exile I wish to engage with is not that of "how shall we sing the Lord's song in a strange land?" but, rather: "how can we sing this strange song of the Lord in this land?" This question is therefore a different one from that raised in a Diasporic position.

Exile, not Diaspora

In situating a re-reading located in texts of Exile, it is first necessary to note an important, if often overlooked, difference among texts commonly lumped under the generic term of "Exilic" texts. This difference is between what can be termed secular-gentile texts of Exile and Jewish texts of diaspora. It would be easy to relocate Exile *as* diaspora, and, in effect, to re-read Exile as also involving "an evolving relationship, the identity politics of one's place of politics with that of one's present home."[6] But such a reading confuses secular-political texts of Exile with what can be termed the religio-cultural-ethnic texts of diaspora. What is of crucial difference is the attitude that sits at the heart of each position: Exile is secular and diaspora is, at heart, religious. The diaspora is an attitude and a self-locating that always holds out the possibility, or rather perhaps, *the necessity*, of return. In this way, there is a degree of hope in the diaspora. By way of contrast, the exile is involved in a different sort of hope; his hope is centred on the acceptance of (and by) the place of dislocation. In that sense it is what Papastergiadas sees as a type of "exilic dialectic," where the dialectic tension between Exile and belonging is one "that informs and constitutes their meaning" in much the same way as there is a "physical border which joins and separates."[7] For the diaspora, the location of belonging is what is located in the "earlier 'elsewhere'" which becomes involved in the "active and critical relationship" of the present location, "all within the figurality of a reciprocal displacement."[8]

A thoughtful meditation on diaspora is that developed by the American Jewish painter Kitaj in his *First Diasporist Manifesto*. Kitaj, born in America, paints mainly in England, yet his work is both informed by and in conversation with the diasporic experience of Judaism. He creates what could be termed a type of diasporist ontology:

> Diasporist painting, which I just made up, is enacted under peculiar historical and personal freedoms, stresses, dislocation, rupture and momentum. The diasporist lives and paints in two or more societies at once.[9]

The diasporist is one who "knows he is one" – even through there is the future possibility of settling down and ceasing to be one.[10] The Diasporist is "both Internationalist and particularist."[11] This condition of being is echoed to some degree by what Pico Iyer describes as the "Global Soul" where someone is neither exile, expatriate, nomad or refugee.[12] Iyer's Global Soul (modelled on his own experience) is someone who is in a sense migratory,[13] a collection of selves where diversity results (hopefully) not in "dissonance but a higher symphony."[14] It should be said that the Global Soul is, for most of the world's population, a member of an über-capitalist elite: a jet-setter of business, culture, the arts, politics or academia. Here the Global Soul is a form of privilege, expressed through the possibilities of choices denied to both the exile and the diasporist. What is important is the reminder that, in the end, the physical state of dislocation in turn results in what can be termed a dislocation of the soul or the spirit. As Iyer reminds us, in the midst of global privilege, the Global Soul is always haunted by the question of dislocated postmodern identity: "who are you today?"[15]

Kitaj's response to Iyer's question would be that diasporic meanings are meant to be unfixed, unsettled and unstable. Diasporism "welcomes interesting, creative misreading."[16] Kitaj's diasporist position, and his reading of that position, is in itself inter-textual. It is also a form of secular *midrash* (that is, an "exposition, exegesis of non-literal meaning") on transience: it is "a secular *Responsa* on reactions to one's transient restlessness, un-at-homeness, groundlessness."[17] Furthermore, Iyer's question of identity is one that Kitaj sees as lying at the heart of art; that is, the central issue and question of doubt which Kitaj states means "you are never sure of the terms of what makes you distinct enough to initiate anything."[18] In short, the self-doubt of the Global Soul is perhaps the voice of conscience confronted by excess and privilege – and lacking the consoling disturbance of art. It is the centrality of doubt to the diasporist position, (the doubt central to faith) that makes it different from that of the exile. For it is the exile's certainty in herself, in her position, in her beliefs or lack of them, that forces the move into exile. In this way, the exile is also the central figure in the self-reflexive turn of modernity. The exile's certainty in the necessity for their exile arises out of modern self-knowledge and self-assessment. The exile possesses a belief in what is their true self (and perhaps "the Real") and how or how not it can or will be compromised by staying where they are. Of course doubt is central in the construction of their exilic self, but doubt for the exile is the self-reflexive turn of doubting what *was* which leads into a new certainty of what *is*. Hope cannot, therefore, be located where they came from, but that certainty in their true self may relocate them to that position or location beyond "doubt."

The Exilic position is a more permanent position, then, than that of the diaspora. This difference exists because, even if a return is sought, those who return from Exile are not the same as those who left. They have been irredeemably changed by the experience of Exile. It is really an impossibility to return. To be exiled is a permanent state.[19] John Berger argues that their experience is one that results in a dismantling of the centre of their world and "a move into a lost, disoriented world of fragments."[20] Here again is the Benjamin–Bonhoeffer dialectic: both of them being exiles in modernity. If we follow through the central deconstruction of this text being written, that is *now* the text being read, and the hermeneutic that occurs because of the gap between these two actions, then this "move into a lost, disoriented world of fragments" is what occurs in a postmodern theology of Exile. To trace this move back further, what has occurred – and continues to occur – is a form of cultural fragmentation that, in turn, results in textual and hermeneutical fragmentation. The centre of the world, that traditional certainty in the world of religion, of Christianity, of the presence of God, has been fragmented. The self-reflexive turn of modernity, focused on the claims of the religion of Christianity, compelled that centre to fragment. The tension of approaching pre-modern systems as if they apply to modernity causes great tension. The response is either to seek to perpetuate the systems (as in systematic theology) or acknowledge the shift into a world of fragments, beyond religion and religiosity, beyond the fixed "I AM" and, instead, encounter the possibilities of "I WILL BE/BECOME." This echoes a call made by Heller's discussion on the philosophy of history:

> Post-moderns inherited historical consciousness, but not the self-complacency of the grand-narratives. The confidence in an increasing transparency of the world is gone. This is not a good time to be writing systems. On the other hand, it is quite a good time to be writing fragments.[21]

The Exilic position is thus located in a fragmented state of being. What is experienced is always a position of liminal marginality that interprets "by defamiliarizing the familiar and familiarizing the unfamiliar,"[22] locating the exile "both inside and outside two cultures at the same time."[23] The Exilic challenge to systems that seek to continue the pre-modern way of being can be re-read out of Lash's critique of the systematic theological pursuit, noting that its concept of a "system":

> with its seductive, promethean overtones of panoramic organization, allows the theologian to easily lose sight of the fact that his work, like that of the philosopher, is irreducibly interrogative in character.[24]

This interrogation is what sits at the heart of the Exilic position.

Learning from the Exilic Position of Allen Curnow

Allen Curnow (1911–2001) was the major New Zealand poet of the twentieth century. Born the son of an Anglican priest in New Zealand's South Island, at one stage he undertook theological training at St John's Theological College, Auckland, in the North Island. Curnow rejected his Anglican heritage, however, by, famously, signalling his turn from Christianity and theological training in casting his Bible into the sea while on the overnight ferry between the North and South Islands. As his fellow poet C. K. Stead writes of his old friend in "Without,"[25] this liminal location signalled the turn – and continued liminality – of Curnow. Having thrown away his Bible, Stead's view is that Curnow then proceeded to "write his own," both in poems and in editing anthologies of New Zealand verse. For while Curnow might have cast aside his explicit Christianity he continued to write out of, against, and in debate with that tradition, and in what I claim could be read as the position of the exile.

For Curnow this turn from both God and Christianity was not, however, a turn from the wilderness in which God used to be located. Steeped in the language and imagery of the Old Testament, Curnow, like many modernists (*pace* T. S. Eliot) viewed wilderness, waste land and desert as sites of modernist self-reflexive revelation. What makes Curnow different is the location of his site of absence, which makes his symbolic action suddenly easily understandable. As the other great New Zealand poet, James K. Baxter, noted in 1951, for Curnow the desert (wilderness) is not primarily the interior of the South Island of New Zealand (as was commonly expressed in New Zealand literary nationalism of the mid-twentieth century). His wilderness "is the Sea, the marine desert that which [*sic*] surrounds our island desert," this wilderness being "the mirror and symbol of God."[26] This latter point is important because it has become common to see Curnow as, in the critic Mark Williams' words, "a post-religious poet."[27] But Curnow is not post-religious; he is post-Christian certainly and also secular but, if we take religious back to the Latin root *religare* "to bind together," then Curnow in this period is certainly religious. In the mid-century, both in poems and in editing a ground-breaking anthology of New Zealand verse, Curnow seeks a new secular *religare* of identity that arises out of a western Judeo-Christian cultural legacy relocated to a frontier society.

Like the Israelite prophets, Curnow looks into the wilderness to find the absent God; he sets out to find the prophetic temperament and message that will challenge the orthodoxies of the day. While God for Curnow (as a secular modern) is unnecessary, he is also wary of the claims of community and nationalist identity proffered as a communal substitute.[28] Instead, he attempts to articulate out of the dis-location of Exile. This is why his is the anti-myth, that myth of the wilderness relocated as the emptiness of modernity. This South Island Exile in the empty wilderness (conceived both as modernity and as landscape/seascape) is a deliberate rejection of the alternative to a settler satisfaction and location that T. H. Scott had noted and located as the North Island garden among the mountains.[29] In the South Island in the mid-twentieth century, the challenge of the empty wilderness was that of the necessity to find and create a new identity in the absence of meaning. The exile of the modern is one demanded by a rejection of a settler myth of providential and benign colonialism. In the South Island the empty, monumental landscape is viewed as indifferent to humanity and to European settlement. It may be sublime, but it is certainly not benign. Baxter later misread Curnow in his 1967 lecture "Aspects of Poetry in New Zealand." Here Baxter strove to link the Curnow-influenced anti-myth of isolation with the Fall, claiming:

> The myth of colonial isolation and inferiority seems to be connected broadly to the theological concept of the Fall of Man – the immigration of ancestors was, as it were, a second Fall, a departure from a garden of Eden situated somewhere in Victorian England.[30]

I want to argue that Baxter is wrong on two counts. First, like many critics, he misreads what is involved in the Fall, through a failure to take a close reading of the text involved, Genesis 2:15–3:24. Too often we read this as purely the story of temptation and disobedience, yet this reading, according to the text, is not the reason for the Exile. If we read carefully then we can see that the Fall is a fall into knowledge. The Exile into the wilderness of the world is due to the possibility this knowledge offers (Gen. 3:22–24):

Then the Lord God said, "behold, the man has become like one of us, knowing good and evil; and now, lest he put forth his hand and take also of the tree of life, and eat, and live forever" – therefore the Lord God sent him forth from the garden of Eden, to till the ground from which he was taken. He drove out the man; and at the east of the Garden of Eden he placed the cherubim, and a flaming sword which turned every way, to guard the way to the tree of life.

Secondly, Baxter locates the second Fall in the wrong place. This second Fall is not a Fall from England, but rather the Fall of the anti-myth. If we look back at the nineteenth-century boosterist myths of New Zealand,[31] the language commonly used with respect to this new land declared it to be a form of Edenic paradise, a new promised land. Curnow, as son of an Anglican priest, as "spoiled" theological student, as one born and schooled in the early twentieth century, is steeped in the Old Testament and the language of the King James Bible. This is his cultural legacy and foundation of his imagery. Yet, having already turned his back on Christianity, he is, as a modernist, postcolonial sceptic, also critical of the boosterist myth, the "godzone"[32] myth, and the Edenic myth. In this second move he situates himself in a place of double Exile. He is exiled from his upbringing and Christian heritage, but he further exiles himself from the cultural mythology of his society. Curnow, acting as secular prophet in the wilderness, pushes for a Fall – a Fall echoing the first Fall: but this time another Fall into knowledge. Curnow has eaten of the modernist tree of the knowledge of good and evil. He sees the materialist fallacy of New Zealand life. This is really the great theme of his epic anti-myth poem "Not in Narrow Seas." The wilderness stands against our materialist hopes for ease – a life that will give us the security of living for ever. The wilderness, the location of the absent God, is where time and the winds of change are located. The wilderness of the sea confirms our deserted status. Life is a "godzone" Tower of Babel that Curnow, as prophet, seeks to cause to fall. The anti-myth is the longing for Exile so we can be free of the Edenic myth and free of the God of materialism and provincialism which Curnow believed to be as limiting as the jealous Christian God.

Peter Simpson notes some of this in his 1986 essay "The Trick of Standing Upright"[33] claiming:

In Curnow's mythology the colonial is both expelled from the garden (separated from his true home) and is the spoiler of the garden he enters. To be a New Zealander, therefore, is to be trebly fallen (on personal, universal and national levels).[34]

And yet Curnow's anti-myth is actually the seeking of the act of redemption that the Fall engenders. For Curnow's exilic Fall is a Fall into a secular freedom. It is a Fall that frees the emerging, naked nation to wander in the wilderness, free from the unnecessary ornamentation of

God and "godzone." Curnow is aware of this, locating his defiantly modernist and cultural nationalist anthology of New Zealand poetry as part of "our 'spiritual' – or call it 'imaginative' – history of New Zealand."[35]

So Curnow also became a poet of Exilic religion; he is a poet of the secular questions of religion. Because of this central modernist dislocation he often focused on the issues of Exilic identity and how they might be represented. In his magisterial, epoch-making introduction for his anthology *A Book of New Zealand Verse 1923–50*, Curnow, writing of the poets D'arcy Cresswell, A. R. D. Fairburn, Ron Mason and Denis Glover, states:

> The real question was not what they were going to write *about*, but whom they were going to write *for*. A refugee in this country said this to me when we were talking about New Zealand's verse or its writing in general. About his audience there can be no certainty for the New Zealand poet, trying to keep faith with the tradition in the language while his imagination must seek forms as immediate in experience as the island soil under his feet. The best verse we have now is from this viewpoint admittedly tentative and 'transitional'.[36]

This sense of being "transitional" in a "new" context occurs in a "movement" "as the country becomes a point of departure for the imagination."[37] Here we have what I would call the poetical/theological task. The call is to attend to "a conflict of the exiled spirit"[38] arising out of the awareness of "the tension between the New Zealander and the land his body inherits but his spirit has not yet won."[39]

Mark C. Taylor, in *Erring*, his classic work of deconstructive a/theology, also refers to this tension when discussing the position of liminality, in a manner that can be re-read as analogous to Exile:

> Suspended between the loss of old certainties and the discovery of new beliefs, these marginal people constantly live on the border that both joins and separates belief and unbelief. They look but do not find, search but do not discover.[40]

Such a liminal theology of Exile will invert established meaning and subvert everything once deemed holy. It will thus be utterly transgressive."[41] The echoes are obvious here to Marx's famous description of the impact of modernity. What is interesting is how Taylor links Marx's prophecy not only into modernity but also as causing, even demanding, a nascent postmodernity to be found in the experience of liminality.

To re-read on from Taylor-*cum*-Marx, I want to claim that it is the location, or rather the dis-location, of Exile which engenders the transgression of liminality (and the liminality of transgression). The exile, in her act of *total* rejection (the spiritual/intellectual exile is finally expressed in bodily Exile), is transgressive to those she has left behind. Yet, in a further act, the exile, in her continuation of her "home" identity in the new location (her reference is to that which has forced them into exile) transgresses what is regarded as real and authentic in their new dis-location.

Such transgressions further arise from that dual perspective: viewing where they came from now from afar and yet viewing where they now reside, always partially mediated through the perspective of the pre-exilic location. This situation means the transgression is a dual one – of both past and present from the fragmented, liminal position of Exile. Both past and present are inverted and subverted through the other. Any attempt at Exilic theology will necessarily be that arising out of and expressed as "fragments" and not as "systems."

Two comments pertinent to the condition of the theological Exile are made by Kramer in his study of Exile. The first is the centrality of mediating the Exilic condition and experience through "textual traditions and meanings."[42] Reading further via Kramer, this first comment in turn becomes the basis for what could be termed "the dialogic challenge of exile," which raises questions "about tradition and convention." Such questions act to open "the ideological center to creative assaults from the periphery."[43] One result is that the exile can often articulate and discuss what others "may have known or felt *implicitly*"[44] but were unable to explicitly describe and discuss. Kennedy cites Henry Miller to similar effect:

> I'm not an American anymore, nor New Yorker, and even less a European, or a Parisian… I'm a neutral.[45]

This neutral state of Exile is, of course, not a neutral positioning of the self to any claims made or demanded. The exile is always an exile in response to, and in rejection of, claims and demands. Rather, the neutral state is one where the exiles are imaginatively, creatively "neither *here* nor *there*," where their origins are denunciated and they assume "an ambiguous position between 'outsidedness' and 'insidedness'."[46] Kramer's second insight is related. The exile's relocation to the new environment results in them coming across "new books and new theories" which establish a new dialogic challenge of a "critical analysis both of their own intellectual tradition and the one in which they live as outsiders."[47]

In a re-reading via Zizek and Bonhoeffer-Benjamin, these new books and new theories are the source of the dialectic lightening flashes and short-circuits that demand the inter-textual response. This Exilic challenge is perhaps the starting point for all secular theologies and is why they are theologies born of Exile: they are too secular for traditional Christianity and too Christian for secular society. Such theologies arise out of the transgressive liminality of attempting to articulate Christianity in modernity as self-reflexive moderns. In such attempts, the challenge to secular theologies and secular theologians is similar to that which Bauman notes is always directed against the Jewish diaspora: that is one of "non-choice" which manifests itself in always having to move out of the position of neutrality into the location of assimilation – or to move elsewhere.[48]

Following Bauman's objection, I want to re-read further to claim that the postmodern secular theologian must also resist this dual pressure to assimilate. This push to assimilate can occur in the form of a drive to put away the dislocation of Christianity, or more specifically theology – to become "just secular" – or, less commonly, it can also be expressed in the impetus to turn from the secular world back into the religion of Christianity. In response to both these counterclaims, the fight of the exilic secular theologian is the fight for the right to remain in Exile, "renovating their beliefs under the pressures of a strange land."[49] In the remainder of this chapter I want to discuss, therefore, how the experience of Exile is one that seeks to resist the demand to assimilate and continues "the renovation of beliefs under pressure."

Rethinking Exile

While Exile is used as a postmodern condition in this text, for much of contemporary theory Exile is viewed as perhaps the defining modernist condition. In this view Exile is traced back through our immediately past "refugee century" via an existentialist commentary into the formations of twentieth-century literary modernism which seems, so often, to have needed Exile to arise.[50] This is often Exile as (self-forced[51]) choice which becomes represented in that "host of Euro-American modernist tropes: exile, solitude, distance, emptiness, nostalgia and loss."[52] Kennedy observed of the modernist exiles in Paris:

> insofar as exile marks a rupture with the past, a loss of the familiar, a relocation amid alien surroundings, and a persistent sense of estrangement, it thus provides a suggestive model for the experience of modernism.[53]

These are the qualifications and qualifiers of those whom Gertrude Stein famously labelled "The Lost Generation": those writers and artists who abandoned post-World War I America for Europe and articulated a modernist consciousness. Yet, in re-reading the words as one of this coterie, Malcolm Cowley describes this generation, the experiences and laments of many postmodernists, some sixty to seventy years later, comes to mind:

> It was lost, first of all, because it was uprooted, schooled away and almost wrenched away from its attachment to any region or tradition. It was lost because its training had prepared it for another world than existed after the war (and because the war prepared it only for travel and excitement). It was lost because it tried to live in exile. It was lost because it accepted no older guides to conduct and because it had formed a false picture of society and the writer's place within it. The generation belonged to a period of transition from values already fixed to values that had to be created… They were seceding from the old and yet could adhere to nothing new; they groped

their way toward another scheme of life, as yet undefined; in the midst of their doubts and uneasy gestures of defiance they felt homesick for the certainties of childhood. It was not by accident that their early books were almost all nostalgic, full of the wish to recapture some remembered thing.[54]

Postmodern theology is often permeated by such modernist experience and sensibility; it can maintain a precarious balancing act with a foot either side of the modernist/realist and postmodernist/non-realist divide, shifting intellectual weight from one foot to the other as the winds of challenge and change blow. Even those who choose (or, are forced to make) the permanent leap across to postmodern non-realism still experience the *frisson* of dislocation and continual adjustment. It is not surprising that we need to consider how Exile has been discussed in the modern/postmodern world.

While Exile may be seen as either the condition lying beneath modernist tropes, or as that experience which represents postmodern dislocation, I have no wish to assign such a "literal periodization"[55] of Exile. Instead, Exile itself becomes part of a reading strategy. But what we do need to remember in this re-reading is the challenge of too easily privileging this metaphorical Exile, which is something, as Buruma notes, that "only people who face no real danger can afford."[56] Now, of course, this warning is not to dismiss the experience of metaphorical Exile which, while perhaps not resulting in political danger, does involve something else: choice.[57] The *choice* of Exile is profoundly different from having been *forced* into Exile. To choose to move from the homeland, and so locating yourself in opposition to what was there, is different from having been forced from the homeland and being defined by the homeland as being in opposition. In the first move, you retain your autonomy and agency; in the second you are always defined by others and so lose it. The metaphorical Exile refers to those who choose to dislocate themselves in their appropriation of the Exilic trope; the real Exile belongs to those who are forced out and who have, in effect, no choice. This difference means that the Exilic choice of dis-location in this reading is no more, really, than an extension of the modernist traveller. Conversely, for the "true" exile it is the forced change – that imposed, demanded change of dis-location, the condition of having Exile imposed, of being made an exile without a choice that separates them. The exile of choice can always go back whereas the forced exile cannot. For the latter, the Exile that has been forced upon them is the demand which is enforced, in part by who and how they are, but more so, by where they came from.

Exile and Absence

Jan Morris asks the question of location in her meditation upon Trieste, that city of exiles that itself so often seems exiled from where it should or wants to be: "Far away from where? Exile is no more than absence and it can take many forms."[58] In short-circuiting Morris, the central question of this book is "perhaps the Exile is that of an absence of and from God?" This question is also in short-circuit with Mark C. Taylor's reminder that: "Absence is merely one of the guises through which God's presence continues to haunt us."[59]

Exile has thus become an increasingly important theoretical position in the contemporary world. On the one hand it is perhaps all too easy for intellectuals who are settled, have tenure and are located to appropriate a term of the dispossessed and dislocated and, in a manner, domesticate it. And yet, in a work that is attempting to be a form of Exilic theology, there also needs to be the restatement that Exile is a theological position: Exile is a theological (dis)location, a theological identity and perhaps *the* theological position for those who locate themselves with the God who is the I WILL BE/BECOME, and not the settled, located, religious God of I AM.

Dietrich Bonhoeffer is the presence that haunts this book – and also, increasingly, my theological thinking. In many ways he is the liminal short-circuit, the trace of the lightening flash that sits behind all my questions. Of course Bonhoeffer himself is an absent presence, his posthumous texts being the replacement for the man himself. It is acknowledged that the 'possibility' of such use of Bonhoeffer is possible because he is not present and his thought remains in fragments. And yet, the fragmentary nature of what we have, in fact, allows him to speak across time and space in a non-systematic fashion. His fragments can be re-read because they are fragments; most famously, they are prophetical challenges that are re-read now in retrospect. His challenge was twofold: the call to a religionless Christianity, and the related, confrontational question: "what *is* Christianity, and indeed what *is* Christ, for us today?" In attempting to engage with these it is worth remembering the centrality of Exile to Bonhoeffer's thought and challenge:

> God is teaching us that we must live as men who can get along very well without him. The God who is with us is the God who forsakes us (Mark 15:34). The God who makes us live in this world without using him as a working hypothesis is the God before whom we are ever standing. Before God and with him we live without God. God allows himself to be edged out of the world and on to the cross.[60]

This discussion on Exile needs to be framed by the Bonhoefferian challenge: to do theology in the contemporary world is to engage in a new form of Exilic thought and identity – *which is more than just displacement*.

An important discussion on the centrality of Bonhoeffer and Exile for any attempt to think/do (and is there a difference?[61]) theology in the contemporary world is that undertaken by Eberhard Bethge in *Dietrich Bonhoeffer: Exile and Martyr*. Bethge is careful to make a distinction between Exile and displacement. Central to Exile is the experience of "being excommunicated from the hitherto existing unit of people and language."[62] The difference is that the exile "is a living reproach to his native country" while the displaced person "is a living reproach to the outside world." The exile is "overlooked and concealed" while the displaced person is to be "exhibited and spoken of as loudly as possible."[63] In what can be re-read as a challenge to popular theologians of displacement and dislocation (that is, those who bemoan how much the church must change to suit the modern world – or their expectation and experience of it), Bethge pithily states:

> The position of the exile creates or demands self-examination, self-analysis, self-knowledge; that of the displaced persons encourages self-pity.[64]

The tensions arise out the type of language used:

> The exile is tied by his native language to his mortal enemy and separated by it from his new friends. But native language separates the displaced person from his enemies and joins him to his friends.[65]

For the Exilic theologian, (harking back to Bonhoeffer) the dilemma is the challenge of continuing to think and use theological language in a manner and a world that separates him from the world where these words are still used. How do we speak of Christianity and Christ when we do not reside in a Christian world, when we are exiled from the world of Christianity – or at least from the religion of Christianity? For we speak the language of our religious enemies – and yet using theological language separates us from our secular, non-religious friends. Displaced persons give up on using theology and theological language. They seek a separation from their enemies in theology and religion and locate themselves as displaced with and within their secular friends. Yet Bonhoeffer's call and challenge is that of the exile, a call and challenge to be exiles and not to relocate to the new religious position of the displaced who seek a new I AM of "IS I." That is, God becomes an aspect of the self – something settled, domesticated, ordered and ordering. In contrast, the exile has rejected the religious I AM and is still speaking the language of I WILL BE/BECOME. The exile is opposed not only to their "religious" enemies (though they can never cut the ties of language); they are also opposed to the self-pity of the displaced and their new religion of "I AM = IS I."

The challenge of the exile is to move away from the settled-ness, the security, the capture and control of "knowing" that occurs with what could be termed the "lost in translation" of the I AM. This is the discipline of the misread/mis-heard *located* presence that churches and theology too often attempt to replicate.[66] Bethge notes, "Baalim were always more tempting than Jahweh"; and "nature and homeland always more tempting than desert and exile."[67] Here is perhaps the central challenge of Barth to Brunner[68] regarding natural revelation, and the restating of the necessity for the *"Nein,"* the necessity for the perpetual challenge to be dislocated, Exilic, to be in the desert. The perpetual challenge is to not succumb to the temptations of Baal, to not misread, not mishear, not mistranslate I WILL BE/BECOME as I AM. The Exilic position raises again the question of idolatry: has Baal now taken new shape as church, as institution, as piety, as religion?

The Exilic theologian locates himself with Bonhoeffer and with Barth as saying *"Nein"* to those who wish to shift the Christian, to shift God, Christ and church out of Exile and into settled-ness with and for Baal. Of course I make this claim recognizing there is a certain irony in using the challenge of Barth, the challenge of the ultra-transcendent God, in using the neo-orthodox affirmation of the centrality of Christ to express what could be termed a postmodern theology of Exile, a theology of glimpsed absence/presence. And yet neo-orthodoxy itself has only ever been, in the twentieth century and into the twenty-first, a theology of Exile. I read it as a theology that leads into Exile, a theology that locates itself in Exile from the world of Baal and a theology expressed as challenge to those theologies who wish to infiltrate the Baal of the I AM over and against the challenge and the tension of the I WILL BE/BECOME.

We need to remember that the 1960s death of God movement was a challenge driven by those who had been formed by Barthian neo-orthodoxy. Their challenge was against a domestication of neo-orthodoxy that, in its institutionalization and in its orthodoxy, had lost the prophetic edge. Too often the neo-orthodox Jahweh had become just another Baalim: "nature and homeland," institutional, settled, a God of weekly piety and domestication. What is often overlooked is that the death of God was, in fact, the death of Baalim. For what occurred in the death of God was the challenge that Christianity was to be rediscovered in Exile, that the identity of the Christian could only proceed, as Bethge notes, from "the loss of identity in exile." Here a necessary step occurs whereby "[i]dentity destroys itself by denying its own history and is regained in accepting it."[69] This move is heralded by the death of God theology, a move that proved too challenging, too difficult and too confrontational. To lose your identity in order to gain it is to move into and beyond Bonhoeffer's religionless Christianity. It is to attempt to work out Bonhoeffer's call in practical faith. It is to proceed to what could be termed post-Christian Christianity whereby, only by moving past the religion of Christianity, is Christianity discovered and regained. Only in moving past God who is exposed as Baalim is Jehovah encountered. Only in moving away from the I AM is the I WILL BE/BECOME glimpsed. Only in the dislocation of Exile is the true location discovered.

Again Bonhoeffer provides the prophetic challenge, by beginning his call for Protestant renewal not with *Romans* as is usual (and in so locating himself in a different position from Barth), but with The Sermon on the Mount "which negates any fixation with a homeland."[70] The Sermon on the Mount (the deliberate echoing and transcending of the Mosaic journey up Mount Sinai to receive the covenant, thus revealing the basis of the new covenant) is itself a call into Exile – with Christ. The I AM is challenged by the I WILL BE/BECOME. That which we thought we knew is now being made known in ways we do not know and do not want to understand – or follow. This textual shift is not to discount the necessity of *Romans*, but *Romans* is directed at those who are, already, in effect, in Exile. We need to remember that it is The Sermon on the Mount that resulted in the necessity and challenge of (Roman) Exile. Out of this conviction arises Bonhoeffer's central paradox of the godless world:

> When we speak of God in a non-religious way, we must not gloss over the ungodliness of the world, but expose it in a new light. Now that it has come of age, the world is more godless, and perhaps it is for that very reason nearer to God than ever before.[71]

Bonhoeffer's call is for the Christian and the *ekklesia* to relocate and recognize themselves in Exile in the secular world. He argues that we should "not [be] conceiving of ourselves religiously as specially favoured but as wholly belonging to the world."[72] Here remains the challenge of speaking "in a secular fashion of God," but in a manner that is aware of the possibility that "perhaps we are no longer capable of speaking of such things as we used to."[73] The dilemma for those in such Exile is that they are still tied to the language of the enemies (that is, the language of religion, of non-secular theology). Such language separates us from secular friends, but is not wanting to – in fact, is unable to – move into the self-pity and piety of displacement.

The Challenge of Liminal Christianity

To seek a way out, to rethink an Exilic Christianity, we should move back in Bonhoeffer's writings to his Christology and his expression of the liminal Christ, a Christ he expresses as *pro me* – that is, standing:

on the boundary of my existence, beyond my existence, but still me... Here Christ stands, in the centre, between me and myself, between the old existence and the new. So Christ is at the same time my own boundary and my rediscovered centre, the centre lying both between 'I' and 'I' and between 'I' and God.[74]

Slavoj Zizek has been one thinker who, existing on the borderlands of faith, has attempted to grapple with this liminal challenge of Christianity. In what can be seen as a further extension of Bonhoeffer's Christological liminality, Zizek, in discussing *Belief*, considers "the enigma IN God Himself...IN AND FOR HIMSELF" that results in "an unfathomable Otherness in Himself."[75] It is because of this internal Otherness, Zizek argues, that "Christ had to emerge to reveal God not only to humanity, but TO GOD HIMSELF."[76] In other words, God was exiled in and for Godself. Furthermore, it is only the self-disclosure of Christ that overcame the exile of God from humanity – and of God in and for Godself. This liminality of Christ is expressed by the Exilic God who is always I WILL BE/ BECOME not the static, total I AM. As has become apparent in this re-reading of Exile, the I AM is no liminal God, no liminal Christ, no dislocated Exilic revelation, but rather a Baal of nature and place. The challenge we can read out of Bonhoeffer and Zizek is threefold. Firstly we should acknowledge the primacy of the self-revelation of Christ (the liminal revelation of true God and true humanity to humanity – and of true God and true humanity to God). Secondly, we can recognize the centrality of this new liminal exilic, religionless Christianity that the Exilic Christ makes known. This Christ is exiled from what God was and exiled from what humanity self-desired. This way of understanding results, thirdly, in the recognition that it is only in the liminality of Exile, in the I WILL BE/ BECOME, that both God and humanity come to truly know themselves – and each other. Reading further via Zizek, we can argue, the I WILL BE/ BECOME is now known in the abandoned Christ, when the separation, the gap between Humanity and God "is transposed into God himself."[77] This Exilic separation, the basis of all Exilic separations, is that which occurs first within Godself. It is this dislocation that enables us to encounter the liminal Christ. This Christ is the one who, by being the first exiled, allows us to recognize ourselves in our Exilic status. We truly are ourselves – and truly are most close to God when, as Zizek and Bonhoeffer note, we feel most cut off from God. For, in the experience of abandonment, in the location of the other of Exile, to repeat the words of Bonhoeffer:

The God who is with us is the God who forsakes us (*Mark* 15:34). The God who makes us live in this world without using him as a working hypothesis is the God before whom we are ever standing.[78]

And as for Zizek:

> I identify myself with God only through identifying myself with the unique figure of God – the Son abandoned by God.[79]

Zizek further asserts:

> Our radical experience of separation from God is the very feature that unites us with him… – only when I experience the infinite pain of separation from God do I share an experience with God Himself (Christ on the cross).[80]

It is this experience, occurring (half a century apart) in modernity with Bonhoeffer and in fragmenting postmodernity with Zizek, which challenges us. It is only in the experience of abandonment by and of God that we are actually closest to God. It is this experience that sits under a postmodern theology of Exile.

Toward a Postmodern Theology of Exile

Being in the liminality of Exile challenges us to recognize the liminality of Christian faith. This is the liminality of Exile experienced as being "not settled" or "not being at home" in either where we came from or where we are. In short, the Christian faith is faith that dislocates. It forces us on from whenever and wherever we feel settled. It is the challenge of Christianity against Christendom; it is the challenge of Christianity against culture.

The liminality of Exilic faith is the constant reminder of the challenges that arise because we do not give up speaking our old language (of God, of Christ, of theology), even though it may separate us from our secular friends amongst whom we are exiled. It is in the self-Exilic God (found in Christ for both God and humanity) where the postmodern radical encounters God. It is in the liminality of Exile where those who seek I WILL BE/BECOME encounter the One who challenges the false security of Baal who is misread as I AM. It is only in the provisionality of liminal Exilic space that religionless Christianity, that a religionless theology, can begin to be articulated.

For the postmodern theologian it is *only* in the liminality of Christ or, rather, it is *only in his liminality* that we can reside. The postmodern theologian begins out of response to the Christ of religionless Christianity, who stands as border between me and myself, between me and God, between presence and absence and between self-knowledge and self-abandonment. By situating ourselves in response on this border of the Christ of religionless Christianity we dislocate ourselves as exiles. It is *only* here, by response, that we can make our "only reliable home…never able to settle fully on either side."[81] It is on (and in a theological sense, in) this border that, in response to the challenge of the abandoned Christ in a secular, godless world, we must, as exiles, "make our lives over from scratch."[82]

The situation of Exile is especially "permanent" for the postmodern theologian. We cannot return from postmodernity, for the modernity we react(ed) against is (in the progressive nature of modernity) "no longer there."[83] As such, the postmodern theologian is in intellectual Exile on the other side of the great realist divide. To return would involve a recanting of belief and a denial of oneself and of one's newfound Exilic self. And yet, like all exiles, there is always a certain nostalgia for an Arcadian, idealistic version of the home we had to leave. In fact, we still speak the new language with the accent and inflections of home. We can never be a citizen but only a permanent resident of this new (dis)location.

This, then, is the challenge to the postmodern theologian. Do we find ourselves in the position of the Exilic intellectual, possessing a form of "elite marginality," of being a "hybrid intellectual, who reflexively acknowledges her dependence on the centre while struggling against it[?]."[84] What occurs, then, if we re-read the centre for/as the language of traditional modernist Christianity? What occurs if we re-read the centre expressed in the language of what has too often been appropriated by religion – the I WILL BE/BECOME mistranslated and misread as I AM? It is against this centre that those who seek to express the challenge of an Exilic Christianity and theology must struggle. That it is a position of elite marginality is also something the theologian must always struggle with and against. And the privilege of this struggle is undertaken in the knowledge that there is also a responsibility towards those who do not constitute this elite but whose experience is embraced. The experience of abandonment is perhaps the wound that the Exilic theologian carries with her as a reminder of both the struggle and of the grace that is encountered.

The challenge to the Exilic theologians seeking, graspingly, woundedly, to articulate the challenge of the Exiled and Exilic God is one where they themselves may, as exiles, constitute the border. With reference back to Bethge's definition that the exile "speaks with the language of their enemies in language that separates them from their friends," the theological Exile in the secular world replicates JanMohamed's critique that "borders are neither inside nor outside the territory they define but simply designate the difference between the two."[85] Because of this, intellectuals (and we can expand the deliberate misreading to religionless theologians of Exile) come "to constitute themselves as the border"[86] – in which can be (mis)read the point of centre and boundary in Bonhoeffer's Christology. Yet that which is the border is not, in this, the intellectual or the religionless theologian mistaking himself for Christ. Rather, the border is located in his abandonment, in her acknowledgment of the Exile that religionless

Christianity forces *between* religion and the secular world. In this tension, in this wrestling, is experienced that sense of abandonment which is the border of the *imitatio Christi*. This experience is both the abandonment of religion and abandonment from/by God that is the exile of Exilic religionless Christianity. For in the dislocation and lack of settled presence of I WILL BE/BECOME is found the Christ who stands as challenge to the settlement of I AM. This is the theology of those who, following Bonhoeffer, become what has been termed "the specular border intellectual." While familiar with two or more cultures (the religion of Christianity and secular society?) she is "unable or unwilling to be 'at home'" in them, and so subjects them to "analytic scrutiny rather than combining them."[87]

So, while still owning that sense of what had been, the exile is also in a valuable position. She possesses both a critical distance from which to critique her homeland and the Exilic liminality allowing a critical eye to be applied to her present location. In many ways this postmodern liminal (theological) Exile is reminiscent of the refugee consciousness articulated by Trinh T. Minh-ha:

> Living at the borders means that one constantly threads the fine line between positioning and depositing. The fragile nature of the intervals in which one thrives requires that, as a mediator-creator, one always travels transculturally while engaging in the local 'habitus' (collective practices that link habit with inhabitance) of one's immediate concern. A further challenge faced is that of assuming: assuming the presence of a no-presence and vice-versa.[88]

This situation resonates for the postmodern Exilic (post)theologian because:

> The named 'other' is never to be found merely over there and outside oneself, for it is always over here, between Us, within our discourse that the 'other' becomes a nameable reality.[89]

If we re-read these statements in an inter-textual mode and posit "god" as both "presence" and "other,"[90] then postmodern theology is most definitely a theology of both Exile and of a "refugee consciousness." As the French Canadian author Hubert Aquin states: "exile is first and foremost a linguistic phenomenon, a matter of coming to terms with alienation within language."[91] But, following on from this first step, as all postmodern (Exilic) theologians know: "Ultimately, exile is a political rather than an artistic concept. Exile is when you can't go back."[92]

At face value such a statement is too absolute. Exiles have always seemingly returned. The Chilean Exile Fernando Alegria reminds us that

> only an exile who intends to return has a true exile's consciousness. There is no exile without the intention to go back.[93]

Of course, Exile is not just a physical state. It is not just the re-location of the body. For Exile can become permanent in a variety of ways. Firstly, it should be remembered that for the exile to return to that un-changed location/context which originally forced her into exile would be to deny the validity of her original identity which necessitated such a move. To recant and return in such a manner would be to deny not only *who she was*, but also *who she is now*. This is the second way in which Exile is a permanent state for, in a paradoxical occurrence, to return from Exile is in many ways to re-Exile. This situation occurs because the location to which she returns has not stood still. It has changed and altered while, at the same time, she is not the person who left, having been influenced and culturally "infected" by the location of Exile. So, for the exile, "this" location is fated to always be dislocation.

Edward Said duly commented:

> Exile for the intellectual in this metaphysical sense is restlessness, movement, constantly being unsettled and unsettling others. You cannot go back to some earlier and perhaps more stable condition of being at home; and, alas, you can never fully arrive, be at one with your new home and situation.[94]

The Exilic state, once undertaken, is always then a permanent state. It is so even if the location of Exile changes. The exile has entered a new state of being that signals a new orientation to the world experienced in liminality. It is a state marked by the constant tension of dislocation. The option offered by Said is to pursue and respond to the

> provisional and risky rather than the habitual, to innovation and experiment rather than to the authoritatively given *status quo*. The *exilic* intellectual does not respond to the logic of the conventional but to the audacity of daring, and to representing change, to moving on, not to standing still.[95]

With all exiles there is a lingering, perhaps defining, sense of loss that tinges any new freedom. For exiles live with the knowledge that both the new location and those left behind will always be aware of them as exiles, always viewing them and their work with a conflicting hermeneutic of suspicion. The liminal being is never fully trusted by those who feel no such conflict because liminality is a direct challenge to their dualistic sensibilities of "one either *is* or *is not*." For example, in both theology and theory the challenge arises that "postmodern theology is neither" – that is neither postmodern (from secular postmodernists)[96] nor theology (from modernist/orthodox theologians).[97] And so the postmodern theologian is in a double exile, a liminal Exile, a theological "border town refugee" distrusted by their new hosts and unwanted by their "land of origin."

The exile must therefore begin again. Indeed, the philosopher George Santayana saw this imperative in religious terms:

The exile, to be happy, must be born again: he must change his moral climate and the inner landscape of his mind.[98]

Such a change is not a repudiation of all that drove them into Exile. It is more a stage of accommodation within their new dis-positioning. Such a challenge means that the problem for the postmodern theologian is how to hold together the internal tension that reflects their wider dislocation.

Tertullian, in equating philosophy with heresy, once asked, "What indeed has Athens to do with Jerusalem?"[99] A similar question could be asked of postmodern theology: "What has Paris[100] to do with Jerusalem"? The task of the Exilic postmodern theologian is to propose an answer to this question. The situation is reminiscent of the task faced by Andrew Gurr in contrasting the state of Exile with the focus of the English poet John Donne who sought to find a home in God:

In the twentieth century the idea of God as our home has tailed off into a pallid cliche, an unconvincing assertion of wish fulfillment, the idea of getting away from it all taken as far as it will go.[101]

The postmodern theologian is neither resident in Jerusalem nor Paris but somewhere in between. In fact, the home is often in the more marginal locations in that this tension reflects a further "tension in the world." For every postmodern theologian located securely in a major university or theology programme, thousands more find an Exilic home in minor universities, seminaries and provincial locations. This physical Exilic status is often the response to their prior theological status. God (Jerusalem) can no longer be their home, yet they are not yet a resident in "Paris" (secular postmodernism). As such they are homeless migrants in perpetual Exile attempting to reformulate "Paris" through their memories of home – and conversely attempting to reconceive their past in light of "Paris." The Cuban-American exile Gabriella Ibieta refers to a state of Exilic simulacrum, of projecting a nostalgic past onto an Exilic present and so inhabiting "this mythical country of nostalgia and kitsch"[102] which is, in many ways, a most apt description of postmodernity.[103] Yet this Exilic reworking of home is not sentimental, but rather a rigorous reassessment of home through the contextual lens of the location of Exile. Gurr concludes: "The freedom of exile works paradoxically as a constraint, a commitment to create a fresh sense of identity through the record of home."[104]

Exilic Thoughts on "Home"

What the Exilic theologian often discovers is not only a new freedom to pursue the theological task but also, because of the challenges of the Exilic context, a new way of thinking about home.

> Our home is the place from which we originate, and toward which we turn to look from an ever-increasing distance. Our home is a point in time which we have lost, but can always rediscover, along with details which we would not have noticed *then, on the spot*.[105] [emphasis original]

So, how can the exile rethink, recapture, re-imagine home? Is it the choice Nikos Papastergiadis identified between deferring "homecoming for an idealized time in the future, to find a substitute home in the here and now, or madness"?[106] Or alternatively, is Exile, like Kennedy claims, continually a "futile longing for *nostos* (home), for a ground of being"?[107] Maybe this is what occurs if home is taken as the stable I AM, that which is challenged by John Berger's claim that "home is no longer a dwelling, but the untold story of a life being lived."[108]

McKenzie Wark discusses what I term the validations of home:

> It seems impossible to make a new home without another's granting of that right. Impossible to return to what was once home which will now be marked by betrayal of its right to validate existence.[109]

Wark's second sentence sits at the crux of Exile: where and how is existence validated? Exile is the search for provisional validation over what is perceived as inauthentic. That is, the home that *was* can no longer be home. The inauthentic nature of what *is* forces a move out of that location and into another whereby the past *is* becomes a present *was*. And yet, what is the *is* of the location the exile finds themselves in? That which has been left behind is marked by a mutual betrayal. It is characterized by an inability to validate the exile's existence and also by the exile's inability to accept what it offers (demands?) as validation. For the home left behind, the exile is now inauthentic. For the exile the past home is itself newly inauthentic. For the exile their new location is also not authentic, however. It happens to be just less inauthentic than that they have left behind. For the exile is someone who is aware that all locations and experiences are now deemed inauthentic through the Exilic gaze. They are inauthentic insofar as they are now revealed as perpetually provisional, open to constant change and challenge. And yet perhaps the desire for the singular, situated, orthodox authentic place and experience is what is initially and ultimately challenged by the God who is I WILL BE/ BECOME. The true authenticity is to be found, paradoxically, in what those seeking the permanence of the I AM view as inauthentic. The dislocation and the recognition of the inauthenticity of any claims to human permanence sit at the heart of the Exilic condition. The Exilic gaze emerging in this perspective belongs to those who ask that central (and now modified) question: "How do we sing that strange song of the strange Lord in this strange land – *because* we can do no other." Likewise, for the new location, the exile is not one who has properly made their home here. This is because the hosts are always aware of the challenge of "that strange song being sung." Rather, exiles always retain their Exilic identity of liminality – an exile *from* one location and an exile *in* another. This provisionality is expressed by Trinh T. Minh-ha:

> Home for the exile and the migrant can hardly be more than a transitional or circumstantial place, since the "original" home cannot be recaptured, nor can its presence/absence be entirely banished in the "remade" home.[110]

This claim is important for our reconsideration and re-reading if, as argued, God was (is?) our home. That which was original God, that is the I AM, cannot be entirely banished in the Exilic home haunted by the presence/absence of God who is claimed to be I AM. There is also the constant reminder that there are many in the new Exilic location who prefer to keep the legacy rejected by the exile as a permanent view of that which must "be," so as to be rejected. It can be a type of hyper-reality of repudiated nostalgia. This situation means that the liminality of the God who is I WILL BE/BECOME is always referenced against that which was/is taken as the expression and religion of the I AM. The pursuit of a religionless Christianity does not seek to recapture the original I AM of religion, but neither can it be totally overcome. So, having initially rejected the diasporic view for an Exilic gaze, perhaps now we need to venture into a liminal diasporic position, situated between Exile and diaspora? In the end, perhaps for postmodern theology, its biblical antecedents of diaspora force a liminal relocation, whereby the gaze is a constant shifting between a repudiated past, a dislocated present – and a future hope. Perhaps this is why Papastergiadis can claim that: "The homeland is, for a diasporic sensibility, both present and absent."[111]

The Diasporic Sensibility

We can perhaps respond to Papastergiadis with the statement that if our home is in the I AM of religion then in the modern/postmodern world we are in a perpetual diasporic sensibility. This is a world where maybe we are all displaced in "the inhuman landscape of postmodernism" because we are denied "the grounding which would allow us to locate and define our lives."[112] If we think of ourselves in diaspora, rather than in the permanence of Exile, then there *is* a home; there *is* a possible homeland that we can one day (hopefully) return to – even if, in the diaspora, we have never been there.

The New Zealand writer Peter Calder was born into what can be seen as a diasporic sensibility. Raised in 1950s New Zealand, he grew up with dreams of what was real being located in the diasporic homeland of England:

> I was entranced with the idea of leaving these mediocre and provincial shores and making my way in my spiritual homeland.[113]

And yet, not only was Calder New Zealand born, so was his mother who "grew up regarding herself less as a New Zealander than as an Englishwoman marooned in an alien land."[114] When his mother, now in her eighties, comes into an inheritance, Calder decides to accompany her on her "trip of a lifetime" to England to "take her home to a place she's never been."[115] Calder had travelled to this other home as part of assuaging his diasporic sensibility that "the world always seemed like something other than where I was"[116]; as part of overcoming the feeling of "being stranded on the edge of the world as far as may be possible from my natural home."[117] For him, the experience of the other had awakened a realization of New Zealand as "home." So, for him, the real England he travelled to with his mother was not the "imaginary" England that his mother travelled to and experienced on the same journey. His mother revels in the possibility of return (to the "home" she has never been to) – and yet with it comes the expression of a certain type of diasporic resentment:

> "I love it here" she says. "I wish, in many ways, that I had been born in England. I wish I had been born English. Because it's in my blood and yet it's not. I'm of the soil, my blood is English, but I'm just an ordinary common-or-garden New Zealander and I resent that in a certain fashion… Hamilton is so ordinary to me. I'm English to the core and I wish I had been born in England.[118]

The resentment of the diasporic experience occurs out of an original belief that one's true home is somewhere else, coupled with the disappointment on arrival in the realization that the sought-for home is *not home*. This personal epiphany forces yet another change in self-identity, a challenge to long-held beliefs, and a change in what is deemed self-authentification. Calder's mother returns to New Zealand and reassesses her situation, acknowledging that diaspora is now actually home – but a modified one:

> But I don't feel in exile here. I'm a New Zealander, but I'm an *English* New Zealander.[119]

Peter Calder's travels with his mother are a reminder that diaspora takes many forms – as do the attempts to re-accommodate the diasporic experience. Yet, as his mother came to realize, the diaspora is not Exile because the diasporic condition is, in truth, one of two homes, of being "an *English* New Zealander." By way of contrast, for the exile there is no possibility of such an accommodation. The diasporic location is not one of liminality as is experienced by the exile who remakes a *liminal* diasporic position. The crucial, if subtle, difference of the diasporic location is one of being able to relocate in one or the other and thus spanning or accommodating the dislocation. It must be said that the critique of the diasporic position is here directed not at those who experience the authentic Jewish diaspora. Rather, it is a reading from within the position of postmodern Christian theology, against such expressions of Christianity which too easily and uncritically appropriate such a diasporic trope. The Christian diasporic sensibility is perhaps that most open to the critique of Bonhoeffer's religionless Christianity. They are able to accommodate the competing claims of religion in a secular world and have two homes, two identities, of religion and secularity. For the diasporic sensibility in Christian piety and theology seeks an accommodation; it seeks a commonality which seeks to overcome otherness. The diasporic sensibility belongs to those who, when in one location which is "other," have always *another* home, *another* location elsewhere that they can turn to.

The Desert(ification) of God

The exile is the one who has no location. The exile is the one who exists in the liminality of dislocation. And is always confronted by Cioran's aphorism that "god is the burial ground of transcendental vagrants."[120] For God, so Cioran claims, is that without which "everything is nothingness" and yet paradoxically, "god is the supreme nothingness."[121] De Certeau attributes this dialectic to "the discourse that makes people believe is the one that takes away what it urges them to believe in, or never delivers what it promises." Here is opened up the "room for a void"[122] that allows the space for liminality.

What too often occurs, both historically and more recently in theory, is the turn to the desert in order to express that void. What we have here is a consequence of a turn to the nomadic sensibility all too readily appropriated by urban, settled, western intellectuals – as was archly noted of Bruce Chatwin, for whom "talk about nomads was like a medieval theologian discussing the Trinity."[123] In such moves there is a conflation of "God" and "desert" where the liminal nothingness of God becomes physically experienced and theoretically expressed as "desert." There is a further problem in this desertification of God inasmuch as talk of God too easily becomes yet another form of Rousseauian romanticism: God is the preserve of the "noble savage" – or their imitators.

Out of this sate of affairs arises the claim that God is, in the words of John the Baptist in the film *The Last Temptation of Christ*,[124] "a God of the desert." In Scorsese's film we know that the Last Temptation sequence is false and not from the God of Israel. Jesus descends from the cross not into the Judean desert but rather a lush, green wooded valley. This sequence follows in the tradition of Judeo-Christian tradition where physical absence signals divine presence. The God of no-place is to be found in the non-place. The place we may want to be, the comfortable, settled, lush valley of everyday domestic life, is actually the location opposed (and of those opposed) to God. In response there exists that romanticist re-reading where the "God of the desert" is read as literally *a god of the desert*. In this legacy follow all those desert travellers who seek that which is pure and uncontaminated by modern, western, urban experience. And so the Rousseauian traveller and theologian seek a purity in the absence of the desert – and amongst those non-western, non-urban people who live there. This results in claims such as:

> The experience of the desert is an experience of the overturning of human finitude, the opening of human being to the mystical basis of its identity. This is the place where the divine as "god" empties itself into finite human being and where finite human being discovers its own deep participation in transcendence.[125]

Theologians have always been partial to such desert romanticism, in a lineage that can be traced from the desert fathers into the present-day syncretic New Age desert practitioners. In his meditation on *The Sacred Desert* David Jaspers describes the experience of travelling to the Texas desert and "sacred Indian lands" in South Dakota. It was like encountering:

> a place which is neither exterior or interior, and remote…a place which has been familiar all along but hitherto largely unfrequented by me. It is a place all know individually, but rarely, if ever visit.[126]

This liminality has, of course, echoes of the Exilic position, but occurs where Exile is merely a repetition of the place of original encounter. This desert liminality becomes actually a form of theological essentialism and romanticism. Such desert theologies imply that to be truly authentic necessitates a journey to the liminal desert (*any* desert it appears) to encounter the sacred termed God. Such journeys take the authentic liminality of Exile out of the exile's predominant location – the modern, urban, western world. What occurs is a rejection of Bauman's noted turn of experiencing modernity as the urban desert. For Bauman's dislocation is, first and foremost, a philosophical and metaphorical claim. The romanticized turn of the desert theologian is actually a form of theological literalism. Here the turn is against the non-presence of God where humanity exists and to the presence of God where there is no humanity. The theological implications are too easily overlooked. For the God to be found and experienced where humanity is not is a God who is a rejection of the incarnational, Trinitarian "God with us" – and who may yet be experienced as absence. The problem is the literalism of Jasper who claims that the dissolution of Christendom will enable the beginning of "the radical theology which has always been the theology of the desert."[127] His theology of the desert is primarily that of the physical desert and not the socio-theological desert of modernity.

Do we then have to follow in the wake of Richard Kearney and ask:

> Can we draw a line in the sand between deconstruction as desertification[128] of God and desertion of God?[129]

Jacques Derrida, the one to whom this question is directed, perhaps understandably replies "There is no line… [because] that is the end of faith. You can be sure that God has left."[130] In other words, the desert is only ever a metaphor and should not be sought as a substitute for, nor as authentic encounter place of, God. The turn to the desert is to seek to replace faith with place which is, in effect, to give God a being of desert, a deserted being. It is to attempt to read the presence of God into the physical absence of desert; yet this is a desert which while void, is still physical, is still presence, is still as "desert" a *very real* place. Rather, we can return to the challenge of Mark C. Taylor who states:

> In the desert that has become our world, there is only exile – chronic exile – without beginning and without ending… [which means] our questions are as infinite as the displacement that feeds them.[131]

The fragmented Exilic location understands that the dislocation and questions of Exile is also where the promise of the encounter of the absence/presence and presence/absence of God occurs. It understands that located in Exilic texts are those infinite questions where the encounter and the promise may yet be re-read.

If God is the expression of religion, then the expression of religion never delivers God. It might deliver an experience, or rather a reference back to the solidity of the I AM which enables the diasporic sensibility for those feeling "at home but not at home" in religious and non-religious locations. But the God who is I WILL BE/BECOME, the God encountered in Bonhoeffer's liminal Christ, is the God who exists *on the other side* of the belief of religion and the religion of belief. This encounter occurs in the void of Exile. What occurs is the recognition that the exile's home is in God, in the God of I WILL BE/BECOME, in the encounter of the liminal Christ. Here then is the recognition that the attempt to express what may be a religionless Christianity is one born of the experiences of dislocation and no permanence. The issue of what home may mean in today's world becomes a central question. Karamis notes:

> the search for home is a constant state of arrivals and departures, exits and entries to and from various locations. Home no longer exists as a fixed site of belonging but is transformed into a space which is simultaneously curved and parallel, sometimes crossed by roads and sometimes more intangible, shooting off a high speed down the highway.[132]

Home in this cultural meaning has become *some* thing, *some* place that we move through. Home is *some* "that" which may be glimpsed and which may be glancingly noted, as we are on the move. The theological implications of such a short-circuit reading positions our home in God as a paradoxical experience of dislocation. The modern city, that is the desert of modernity, is actually the non-place where our home in God is experienced. So home, in both the theological and socio-cultural senses, may be relocated within the experience of dislocation in the modern world as, paradoxically, located *in* the act of dislocation as we attempt to find our way through and within it. Pico Iyer observes: "The modern city is a place where everyone's a stranger, so it seems, on his way to somewhere else."[133]

It is to this dislocated location, to the modern city, the "place where everyone's a stranger" that we must turn, if we wish perhaps to posit a way out of Exile and into what I offer as the new theological trope, that of the theological *flaneur*.

4 No City of God...

The modern city may be where Bauman locates the new desert of modernity. To understand fully the theological implications of his claim we should rethink the modern city as a theological text in itself. What primarily activates the tourist, the traveller and exile in the contemporary western world is the experience of living in the modern city. This is because the dislocation that is experienced in the modern city appears to be a primary reason for undertaking re-location in pursuit of what is deemed lost or not present at home. Is such a re-location, however, actually due to our inability to recognize what "home" means in modernity? Does our pursuit of a located home now become a form of nostalgic, romanticized longing? Furthermore, if for Christians home is in God, then to seek a new home of locatedness elsewhere is to confuse God and place. In other words, is the rejection caused by the dislocation of modernity in favour of physical locatedness really part of a turn away from the challenge of Christianity back to a Baal of Christendom and locatedness?

In order to discuss these issues, this chapter will occur in two distinct, yet connected, parts. The first is concerned with the rise of the modern(ist) city. The city in modernity is variously that home which is not a home, that place of presence that is an absence, that location which is dislocation, that place of relocated and internalized exile. While I am aware that there might be claims that we have moved out of modernity and into postmodernity (and indeed as I will posit, into a new era which I term "soft modernism") all this occurs in cities that are the embodiment of modernity. The past is always present, even if only as barely discerned trace, but has often now become romanticized as heritage. In fact, much of the urban modern past has predominantly been reduced to a Potemkinesque façade, that hyper-reality of gentrification whereby the external remains but the internal is new. Such moves that occur physically in architecture also occur conceptually and theoretically, often in dialectic. In both architecture and theory, the moves into postmodernity are attempts to repudiate the dominance of modernism, often in an attempt to express a more vernacular environment. Such moves often result in postmodernism becoming just another series of variations against a perceived internationalism, however.

In considering the clash of modernism and postmodernism in architecture, most people, I would argue, exist in these cities without being overly aware of just what their environment is meant to represent. Yet, as the modernists were wont to proclaim, modernism in architecture was a "spiritual expression" of the times. That "spiritual expression" was/ is "the death of God." We live in cities that express the death of God and yet also express a form of alternate spirit of the age – that of the secular world. The distinction is intentional for the death of God is not necessarily the same as existing without reference to an absent transcendent God. The secular world is perhaps where theology *after* the death of God by necessity occurs. Gabriel Vahanian reminds us that the secular is the starting point for all our theological reflection, for secular derives from *saeculum* – that is, the world of shared experiences.[1] We too easily forget by an all too easy retreat into transcendent spiritualizing that it is actually *in* this material world where grace is experienced. This encounter occurs because the *saeculum* is actually first and foremost the world of shared experiences of God and humanity, most centrally in the incarnation. Yet the challenge of an urban, secular theology is one often seen as inauthentic precisely because it is a challenge to our traditional conceptions of where and how God is encountered and reveals Godself. In this chapter I wish to begin to engage with where and how a re-thought urban secular theology may be expressed.

That the tourist and the traveller often seek a non-urban authenticity can be read as a dislocation. They want to live in the secular city but also want to be able to visit the romanticized authentic, believed now to primarily exist as transcendent or non-urban experience or, conversely, as the spectacle of the hyper-real resort. By comparison the exile often seeks to relocate from one city to another – seeking in his dislocated liminality to live authentically in his exilic authenti*city*. Therefore the charting of the ontology of the buildings *in* the modern city (and *of* the city of modernity) is necessary in order to undertake the second part of this chapter. This section is the discussion of the theological option I posit exists over and beyond the reduction to tourist, traveller and exile. Here is the possibility and challenge of the theological *flaneur*. In order to understand the *flaneur*, however, we need to understand first that which she *flaneurs* through. I will thus first consider the modernist city before turning to the possibilities that a re-reading of the *flaneur* offers for those of us who live in the city after God.

Loos-ing and Mies-ing God: Building "Boxes of Absence"[2]

> Architecture is either the prophecy of an unfinished society or the tomb of a finished one.[3]

In 1908 an Austrian architect and cultural philosopher presented the first reading of a paper that was to have a profound effect upon the way the twentieth century was lived, thought and, most crucially, built. It was firstly in Vienna that Nietzsche's claim of the death of God was secularized, commodified and repositioned into the aesthetic heart of twentieth-century life. The result was the rise of what was termed the international style in architecture, the rebuilding of our city centres into canyons of glass towers and, finally, desecularization in the rise of postmodernism. It was the postmodern turn, initially as an architectural movement, that can be viewed as heralding Berger's famous recanting of his secularization thesis due to the return and rise of New Age, Pentecostal and fundamentalist forms of religions as we moved into the twenty-first century. To make such a claim for a little article written in Vienna may seem somewhat audacious, yet Adolf Loos, the forgotten author of this piece, was a seminal figure in early twentieth-century cultural theory and a thinker whose influence should not be overlooked.

Loos' lecture was entitled "Ornament and Crime." His central thesis was succinct, simple, brilliant and wonderfully persuasive in a Europe variously in the grips of *fin de siècle* remnants, *beaux arts*[4] ostentation, a wondrous fear of immanent technology and the sense that modern progress was a *tabula rasa* on which could be written great achievement.[5]

Loos begins his challenge by drawing on the legacies of anthropology and social profiling. Using what is now distinctly exclusive language (yet that was precisely his intention), who, asked Loos, in this day and age wilfully decorates themselves and their environments with unnecessary decoration and ornamentation in the manner of the undeveloped child or the uncivilized Papuan? His answer was that in modern society there were only two groups who did so: those with criminal tendencies and the degenerate aristocrat. Loos' claim was that to be modern, to be progressive, to be cultured, to be civilized was (and is) to live your life with control, order and discipline. To be modern, in Loos' assessment, is to live your life without the support and excess and distraction of unnecessary ornamentation; and that ornamentation, post-Nietzsche, included God. In other words, God was part of the unnecessary ornamentation that the modern project strove to overcome.

While Loos' article was repeated and printed in various forms throughout Europe, it did not find its true audience until following the horror and destruction of the First World War. This securing of an audience occurred in France where those attempting to articulate a utopian hope of a new technological and pure future translated and published Loos' paper in the second volume of *L'Espirit Nouveau* (November 15, 1920). Here it was retitled "as a purist manifesto that demanded the total suppression of ornament ('Ornament IS Crime')."[6] This mistranslation (that coincidentally horrified Loos[7]) became one of the aphorisms that underwrote the onto-theological secularization of architecture and modern life. The other aphorism was Mies van der Rohe's oft-cited statement "less is more" (which he himself seems to have borrowed from Peter Behrens).[8] Together these two architectural aphorisms drove a modernist aesthetic that took Nietzsche's death of God, secularized and then respiritualized it within the architect's brief. In the process, the architect became the prophet and priest of a new modernist aesthetic,[9] the high priest of modernist technology who would strip the world of unnecessary ornament and attempt to re-cover it in boxes of absence.

In a similar vein, at the end of the twentieth century, Mark C. Taylor stated "with the death of God, the high priest of salvation becomes the architect of New Jerusalem which will finally be built."[10] Taylor's claim is one that not only looks back over the history of theology in the twentieth century, but also forward into a God-less postmodern future. I would argue that the importance of Taylor's statement occurs not so much in his future vision (which is contestable depending on how "the death of God" is viewed) but rather in his historical assessment. It symbolizes what was to become the driving force of modernist architecture: the attempt to build temples of humanism that signified the absence of God.

To understand just what this might mean we need to return to another of Loos' claims. In 1910 Loos had begun working out the implications of his call to banish ornament in a lecture entitled architecture. In this he claimed that:

> Only a very small part of architecture belongs to art: the tomb and the monument. Everything else that fulfils a function is to be excluded from the domain of art.[11]

This reference to the tomb and the monument is part of Loos' classicism which itself became an important underpinning of the modernist movement. In Loos' vision, to be progressive and modern was being able to acknowledge the strength and truth of a past tradition that could be remade here in the present:

> You are permitted to change the accepted method of construction only if the innovation represents progress; if the opposite is true, preserve the tradition. Because the truth, be it secular, is closer to our lives than the lies that march at our sides.[12]

(In here perhaps lie the hints of the Bonhoefferean "religionless Christianity" and its turn to truth now encountered in the secular world that will be activated in the theological *flaneur*.)

This concern with the necessity both to recognize and create a new truth for the modern world occurs because of the societal shift demanded by the death of God. The pursuit of a secular truth in architecture is in effect the pursuit of constructing truth. Such a vision arises out of the perception of truth as a technology – a *techne* – that is, something which is created. Such a linkage is no mere speculation, but rather originates in Nietzsche as has been noted by Kostka in his discussion of Nietzsche's use of the word architecture:

> the word *architecture* relates to the search for a strong form in the shadow of the crumbling of all forms after the death of the Great Architect himself, God.[13]

Furthermore, Neumeyer states that the Nietzschean motto "Everything decisive happens despite" was also "the maxim of Loos."[14]

It is important to note this link, this continuity, for what modern architecture attempted to do was work out the implications of the Nietzschean noting of the death of God. The task of modern architecture became the attempt to overcome the "indifference" that Nietzsche claimed lay at the root of God's death. In response, modernist architects attempted to provide a body of architecture, attempted to build an environment that would challenge and would overcome this indifference. My use of the term body is intentional for modernist architecture, for all its focus on absence was also focused on a societal embodiment. The theological implications are deliberate. The body of architecture created was to signal a new way of being in the world. The embodiment of a new epoch of secular identity, this new architecture was to make present that which was to be revealed as the new spirit of the age. Such buildings were to be a modern, secular revelation of how humanity was now to be: unornamented, functional and universal.

The modernists attempted to construct an architecture of meaning that challenged indifference, not through a turn back to religion but rather, as Loos decreed, through innovation that represented progress, be it secular. This progress in the modern world was not to be distracted from the pursuit of truth, order and discipline by any ornamentation that hid what was built behind a façade (or perhaps, reading Bonhoeffer through a modernist, Loosian, architectural lens, the hiding of "Christianity" behind "religion"). In a sense it was the articulation of a belief in an aesthetic essentialism that could be recaptured, yet remade, in modern times. As Loos went on to state as the purpose of architecture:

> But he who knows that the purpose of art is to take the man further and further, higher and higher, to make him more like God, understands that to give art a material function is a profanation of the highest order.[15]

The echoes of Babel here are prescient. Later, in America under Mies and his disciples, the profane Babel of the glass tower would attempt to restore a common language where there had been disorder. The international style that held sway over mid-century western architecture was a style deliberately attempting to implement a new onto-technological rhetoric as built environment. Such a move was the construction of truth as a modern, progressive, unifying secular embodiment of the tomb of the absent God – and also as a monument to his departure.

For modernism is an act of secularism. It is an attempt to order that which God was seen to disorder. It is an act of humanism over and against religion. As such, modernism is both utopian and progressive – and necessarily secular. The challenge for theology is that paradoxically modernism is *both* the secular apocalypse *and* the attempt of living in an immanent kingdom of the absent God. Often this was not recognized until well into the mid-century of twentieth-century modernism. For while Bonhoeffer signalled the implications of this move, it was not until the 1960s in America that such a paradox reached a wider western public. While Gabriel Vahanian had published *The Death of God* in 1961 and Paul van Buren, Thomas Altizer and William Hamilton were all writing and teaching in American universities and seminaries they had failed to make a popular impact. What caused the brief outpouring in the popular mind was J. A. T. Robinson's popularization of secular theology in his *Honest to God* (1963). Robinson in this book, however, was always primarily a reporter of other people's ideas. Rather, it was in the United States that, for a period in the 1960s, modernity and the death of God came together in theology. The way in which the American debate came to be played out was increasingly configured into a battle between the seminary and the church. For, while Robinson was, it seemed, happy to locate revelation in secular society, the American experience was the secular society mediated *through* the seminary and university.[16] It is indeed the intellectual, academic nature of the American experience that allowed for revelation's dismissal, marginalization and later excision.[17] What is important about this movement is its focus upon the contemporary, secular, urban world as the location from which western theology must be done. Writing in the preface to their anthology *Radical Theology and the Death of God*,[18] Thomas Altizer and William Hamilton noted radical theology's links to the death of God in the nineteenth century, the collapse of Christendom and the rise of secular atheism. They note its debt to Barth and neo-orthodoxy, to Tillich and Bultmann and also its location in an American context. There is also the specific secular challenge that modernity laid down for theology:

> It reflects the situation of a Christian Life in a seemingly neutral but almost totally secular culture and society. Hopefully it also reflects the choice of those Christians who have chosen to live in Christ in a world come of age.[19]

This challenge is stated even more explicitly when, in 1966, in his deliberatively controversially titled *The Gospel of Christian Atheism*, Altizer would claim:

If there is one clear portal to the twentieth century, it is a passage through the death of God, the collapse of any meaning or reality lying beyond the newly discovered radical immanence of modern man, an immanence dissolving even the memory of the shadow of transcendence.[20]

Behind all of this of course, as behind the project of modernity itself, lingers the shadow of Nietzsche.

While Nietzsche often seems to get both the credit and blame for almost anything and everything that has occurred within the twentieth century, it is the gnomic brilliance of his aphorisms that lays him open to such use and abuse. Invoking Nietzsche can as a consequence be a fraught undertaking with associated tensions and mis-readings. That said, his quest to move past a redundant Christianity that had tied itself to culture offered the possibility for many to rework their efforts to create society anew after the seemingly apocalyptic experience of the First World War. What Nietzsche saw was just how tied the western world was to the Judeo-Christian ontology, yet for many this God had already died. It was now evident that an increasing number of people lived without any necessary reference to God – and yet western thinking and life often continued as if that God was still alive. What the death of God signalled, in part, was the death of the God of a specific western Christian culture: the God of a redundant Christendom.

The recognition of the death of God unleashed a cultural turn that is still being felt today. For modernity *is* the age of the death of God. Often, in an implicit way that only became explicit under Nietzsche's searing critique, all that seemed solid does *indeed* crumble when the God posited as the original author, maker, builder, creator or architect dies and is dismissed. The tomb to enclose and commemorate the body of the one made *imago dei* now becomes simply a receptacle of disembodied flesh. The monument to celebrate *imago dei* attempting an imitation of divine activity becomes now the ultimate humanist statement. For Nietzsche's secularization reduces buildings to receptacles of human self-contemplation and self-discovery.[21] Nietzsche even forces a reassessment of our attempts to build churches and cathedrals in modernity. To build such a *particular* building in modernity becomes, in effect, an explicitly anti-modern statement.

The rupture of modernity and its central secular turn exposes the limitations of attempting to continue a Christendom model in a death of God world. To do otherwise is to reduce us to a theology and culture of nostalgia. No longer can we build "for the glory of God" except to celebrate his absence by attempting to locate him with a particular type of building – here the church is like a cage or prison. Such an attempt is, post-Nietzsche, the attempt to re-institute Christendom by default – even if done so unwittingly. The God that ornamented our buildings and our lives is no longer there.

The secular world of modernity means that we now build through *our* will, not God's grace; we build to celebrate *our* strength and possibility, not as symbols of human frailty hiding meaning behind decoration. We now no longer contemplate or glorify God, but contemplate and glorify our selves. In modernity, the architect becomes the one who will directly challenge this Christian past of associating Christianity with cultural expression and representation, for what the architect will do is directly challenge Christian teleology. In turn, modernity with its dislocation of Christianity from the culture of Christendom is, in fact, returning Christianity to its origin as proto-modernity.

In an admittedly controversial re-reading, the Marxist-Lacanian philosopher, Salvoj Zizek, in articulating the need for a re-expressed Christianity *against* cultural essentialisms, claims Christianity was the first expression of modernity, stating:

> One possible definition of modernity is: the social order in which religion is no longer fully integrated into and identified with a particular cultural life-form, but acquires autonomy so that it can survive as the same religion in different cultures.[22]

The rupture of Christianity thus occurred, as the first modern religion. But, when Christianity became institutionalized and essentialized as Christendom, it stopped being modern. It became Baal instead. The problem for Christianity occurs, then, when Christianity becomes a culture rather than being *intra* and *counter* culture. The death of God really is then the death of the Baal of Christendom, the death of the God of Christian "culture"; the death of I AM. Today, the rupture occurs anew as the religious expression of modernity – as the secular Christianity that rejects location. As the Russian theologian and philosopher Nicholas Berdyaev pointed out in *The Bourgeois Mind* in 1934:

> A Christian has no city – he is in quest of the City of God, which can never be the city of "this world"; whenever an earthly city is mistaken for the New Jerusalem, Christians cease to be pilgrims and the bourgeois spirit reigns supreme.[23]

The modern architect seeks, then, to create in reference to human not divine truth. In 1922, the influential Dutch architect J. J. P. Oud claimed:

> Spirit overcomes nature, mechanics supercede [*sic*] mere animalistic power, philosophy replaces religion.[24]

The spirit that is evoked in various forms becomes far more a variation of Nietzschean will than Christian salvific grace. As the great Dutch architect Theo van Doesburg observed, also in 1922:

the coming style should spell out 'religious energy' but not 'belief and religious authority'.[25]

This recognition of the spirituality of modernist architecture needs to be remembered: it lies at the heart of this spirituality's ability not only to create disciples but also explains why it seeks to act as a global evangelistic ethos.

In modern(ist) thought, the death of God did not lead to the death of the spirit. Rather the spirit, which was trapped behind and within superfluous ornament, was set free as the guiding force of human creative endeavour. Part of being modern and progressive was to acknowledge the need to express a new spirit of the age (*L'Espirit Nouveau*) that took Loos' Nietzschean-derived aesthetic as a new way forward.

Le Corbusier, the great Swiss-French modernist architect, writing in, *L'Espirit Nouveau* in 1925, claimed:

> But in the twentieth century our powers of judgement have developed greatly and we have raised our level of consciousness. Our spiritual needs are different, and higher worlds than those of decoration offer us commensurate experience. It seems justified to affirm: *the more cultivated a people becomes, the more decoration disappears* (Surely it was Loos who put it so neatly).[26]

If Loos and Nietzsche laid the foundations, the triumph of the box of absence was built by one of the masters of twentieth-century architecture, Mies van der Rohe. It was Mies who came to be seen as the vanguard of a new movement that, under his disciple Philip Johnson, invaded America in 1934 and, post World War II, spread the secular aesthetic as part of a globalizing modernism that sought to locate the New Jerusalem in the earthly plane – but now this New Jerusalem was composed of towers of pre-Babel universality. To understand this new movement we have to first locate its origins in the utopian hope of the collective of artists, designers and architects known as the *Bauhaus*.

The Spirit of the New

Arising out of the reassessment of post-First World War Germany, Walter Gropius and his *Bauhaus* laid the foundations for what became the dominant ethos and secular spirituality of western architecture in the mid-twentieth century. The *Bauhaus* sought a new gnostic hope out of the ruins of a destroyed world:

> The object of the *Bauhaus* was not to propagate any 'style', system, dogma, formula or vogue, but simply to exert a revitalizing influence on design. We did not base our teaching on any preconceived ideas of forms, but sought the vital spark of life behind life's everchanging forms.[27]

Gropius was influenced by Loos' ethos and linked it with the early Modern belief in the redemptive powers of an incipient machine age. Gropius believed the machine age would act in tandem with the human spirit to create a new, inevitable utopian experience:

> A breach has been made with the past, which allows us to envisage a new aspect of architecture corresponding to the technical civilization of the age we live in… [This new architecture is] simply the inevitable, logical product of the intellectual, social and technical conditions of our age.[28]

Gropius proceeded to outline what he perceived to be the new liberating freedom for humanity offered by a technological age of standardization. This freedom set "hand and brain free"[29] in the service of humanistic aims:

> The standardization of the practical machinery of life implies no roboticization of the individual, but, on the contrary, the unburdening of his existence from much necessary deadweight so as to leave him freer to develop on a higher plane.[30]

This higher plane of development was to find its purist expression in the *Bauhaus* style of architecture later reformatted and redefined as the International Style. The new architecture was to be based on four elements that lie at the heart of the Modern aesthetic: rationalization because of "its purifying agency," liberation "from a welter of ornamentation," "emphasis on structural forms" and "concentration on concise and economical solutions."[31] Not to be forgotten was the case that

> The other, the aesthetic satisfaction of the human soul, is just as important as the material. Both find their counterpoint in that unity which is life itself.[32]

Such a cultural turn also required a new ontology. This way of being became expressed as the machine age which, *pace* Loos, looked to the dynamic industrialization of America as its model. Loos had indeed remarked in his essay "Culture" (1908):

> …the American worker has conquered the world. The man in overalls.[33]

This new future of the technological modernism, the age of man as *techne*-creator, sits at the heart of *Bauhaus* spirituality. Here was the spiritual expression of humanity who lived in modern, urban, technological, secular societies. Gropius, referring to "the predominantly materialistic mentality of our age," concluded:

> Believing the machine to be our modern medium of design we sought to come to terms with it.[34]

This coming to terms was the attempt to speak into the world as it was. The *Bauhaus* is, in effect, another signpost along the way to Bonhoeffer's desire to speak of "religionless Christianity." His "World come of age" was also a world of technological achievement which happens to create without necessary reference to God. Joseph Hudnut discerned within the revelatory powers of *Bauhaus* buildings:

> An aspect of our own civilization made express and visible, they reaffirm, in the language of our own era, *that which the cathedral and temple have taught us.*[15] [emphasis added]

This secularization of the religious building into the building of the machine age is an attempt to overcome the indifference of the Nietzschean death of God. It is an attempt to overcome that sense of absence that many now felt precisely because of the death of the cultural God. The secularization of the machine age is, as such, designed to re-present presence in the midst of indifference. Here were buildings of meaning attempting to express the progressive ethos. These were buildings expressing the spirit of the age and which sought to challenge indifference. They were a claim to reassert meaning and intention – a secular ontology – into and onto the city. Their challenge is that transcendence can still be glimpsed, can still be made present as it once was in the cathedral and the temple before indifference made these iconic forms of building meaningless. But the transcendence now expressed is a secular transcendence. It is transcendence that is a human creation: it is a *techne* – a technology. And here we have the transcendence of secular modernity.

Such a secular transcendence can be linked into a secular expression of I WILL BE/BECOME. To persevere with the cathedral and the temple as the sign of transcendence and presence, as that which is believed to still express the spirit of the age is to perpetuate the I AM. It is this uncritical belief in *what was* which situates the tropes of Tourist and Traveller as anti-modern expressions. The Tourist and Traveller relocate themselves in order to view the cathedral and the temple as the sight and site of what *was*, but now *is lost*. Their travel to the cathedral is now to a museum of faith; their travel to the temple is to an authenticity lost on the other side of modernity. Cathedral and temple are now both viewed as part of the romanticization of faith as culture. The urban Exile in the modern city, by way of comparison, is set down among attempts to express and make visible what the past has taught us – but what now cannot be expressed in that language. That architectural language of faith as culture is what, Zizek reminds us, stops religion from being modern. The Tourist and Traveller seek a lost I AM, not seeing, not recognizing that I WILL BE/BECOME is present in that world they seek to turn their backs upon. Ironically, it is the Tourist and Traveller who express the indifference that results in the death of God. Their indifference is primarily due to a nostalgic longing for what has passed away. Their indifference is an indifference to the new revelation of secular transcendence that is encountered *where they are.* The modernist city did, after all, offer an alternative to nostalgic longing, but one that demanded an overcoming of indifference.

Le Corbusier is, of course, famous for describing a house as "a machine for living in." His influence can never be dismissed or diminished. But it was, as Padovan notes, the brilliance of Mies to take the machine ethic of Gropius and Le Corbusier and respiritualize it through the modernist, yet medievalist, ethos of *Baukunst*:

> Mies' buildings, before they are functional shelters or even objects of "aesthetic contemplation," are sources of "spiritual sustenance" – that is, of food for the mind… For Mies, as for Le Corbusier, the house was a machine a *mediter*. But where for Le Corbusier it was merely a machine to meditate *in*, for Mies it was a machine to meditate *with*.[36]

Mies van der Rohe is the architect who more than anyone took Loos' dictum on ornamentation and remade it into the secular city of the pre-Babel skyscraper. Like Loos, he was the son of a stonemason. Educated in a Catholic school in Aachen, Mies took his conception of Modernity as a return to discipline and order over and against the ornamentation of the prior *beaux arts* movement. In a tangible signal of his "Modernity," Mies himself remade and reordered his life. In 1921 (one year after Charles-Edouard Jeaneret assumed the name Le Corbusier) Ludwig Mies separated from his wife and children, remade his Berlin apartment into a bachelor pad, destroyed the records of his previous years and signalled a new Modern, clean move in his architecture by changing his name to Mies van der Rohe.[37]

His personal remaking as a modern being was further evidenced when three new major elements entered his work. The first was the plan in 1922 for a skyscraper made of steel and glass. A design quintessentially modern in being open, clear and unornamented, it was a universal tower of clear intention. This new expression of modernity was to find post-war and re-located fruition in the Lakeshore Drive apartments in Chicago (1948–1951) and his magnificent Seagram building in New York (1954–1958). The latter became a temple[38] to modernity complete with the forecourt as sacred space.[39] In both buildings, what became the trademark Miesian glass curtain (that is the walls of glass and steel) opened up the interior to the gaze of humanity. What made them of crucial importance is that these temples to modernity no longer lived under the eye of God as had their cathedral predecessors; now they were open to the eye of man. Though their walls of glass reflected other buildings, they reflected not the glory of God but rather the secular glory of humanity.

The second element that signalled Mies' modernism was the use of the flat roof of the horizontal plane. This design was a rebellion over and against the pitched roof of the past. The flat roof is a statement of immanence; the gaze is kept this-worldly, flat and secular. The spire of the cathedral, by way of contrast, pointed upwards to God, lifting the eye and the soul away from the earthly realm towards heavenly rule, truth and inspiration. The pitched roof could be seen to imitate the cathedral; its effect is to make the house the cathedral in secular miniature. The modernity of the flat roof of either the Miesian tower or the Miesian house is that it radically secularized the spiritual plane. In a very visible expression, the spirit that Mies believed lay as inspiration behind the modern age was no longer located on a transcendent plane. The spirit of modernity was secular and immanent.

The third element taken up by Mies was an increased use of whiteness (though not as much as Le Corbusier) and an associated opening up of space within his buildings. This opening of space is best shown in his magnificent pavilion for the 1929 Barcelona International Exhibition. An epoch-defining expression of modernity, it has echoes of classicism in both the use of marble and an outside sculpture. Here is a return of the temple in its horizontal roof and open spaces. For Mies' Barcelona pavilion is a temple of and for modernism – and the building that really made his name. What it signalled was a new internationalism that expressed itself beyond any contemporary cultural particularities. It was a re-conceptualized Modern version of a classical temple now expressed and secularized as a house, designed by a German and exhibited in Spain. International modernism was born.

Whiteness was, and is, an important part of these boxes of absence. At the heart of the modernist aesthetic stood the white cube unadorned and unornamented. Simple, logical, an enclosure of the nothingness of space, it echoed the puritan simplicity of the pursuit of the aesthetic of white as the unadorned clarity of a new spirituality.[40] Theo van Doesburg went as far as to locate white as the highest phase of the development of humanity as exemplified by the De Stijl school:

> WHITE: This is the spiritual colour of our times, the clearness which directs all our actions. It is neither grey nor ivory white, but pure white.

> WHITE: This is the colour of modern times, the colour which dissipates a whole era; our era is the one of perfection, purity and certitude.

> WHITE: It includes everything.

> We have superseded both the "brown" of decadence and classicism and the "blue" of divisionism, the cult of the blue sky, the gods with green beards and the spectrum. White pure white.[41]

White represented an ontological *tabula rasa* on which the new Modern, utopian future of humanity was to be written. The clarity of vision was built into being. Unmarked by a past of ornamentation, white buildings were to be a New Jerusalem of the immanent secular kingdom. In *I Lived in Modern Times,* her novel of the attempt to build a Modernist utopian state in Israel, Linda Grant's narrator, Evelyn Serf, sums up perfectly this utopian dream in her description of the *Bauhaus*-inspired white city, Tel Aviv:

> I was in the newest place in the world, a town created for the new century by its political and artistic ideologues: the socialists and the Zionists, the atheists and the feminists who believed with a passion that it was the *bon ton* to be in the forefront of social progress and in a place where everything was new and everything is possible, including a kind of rebirth of the human spirit.[42]

Le Corbusier's aesthetic saw whiteness as a move of purist spirituality against a decorative religion in a way that has prescient echoes to Bonhoffer's call for a religionless Christianity. Writing in 1925 Le Corbusier claimed: "The religion of beautiful materials is now no more than the final spasm of an agony."[43] To move past the religion of beautiful materials was, in a sense, to move past all that humanity created to obscure the truth. The aim was the truthful form of the white cube that enclosed a space that exhibited the ontological truth of the Modern age: there was nothing until it had been built, but the building of the enclosure brought the truth into view.[44] Le Corbusier proclaimed:

> Listen: *a new period has begun, animated by a new spirit.* The hour is favourable. Clean away. On this void let us build something new, animated by a new spirit. Today, we see clearly![45]

This truth could no longer be disguised by beautiful materials or by decoration that reflected human conceit. What was left was the pure white of immanent truth.

And yet, as Wigley concedes, whiteness is itself a form of decoration:

> What has to be concealed is the fact that white is a layer…modern architecture is not naked. From the beginning it is painted white. And this white layer that proclaims that the architecture it covers is naked has a very ambiguous role.[46]

In one reading, this point of view could be seen as an attempted return to Edenic existence. Nakedness is the natural state of being, white buildings are naked and, therefore, find themselves in the continual presence of God in a pre-lapsarian world. The difficulty with this point of view is that in being the expression of modernity, whiteness occurs post death of God. By extension there is no Edenic state to which we might return. This whiteness, this nakedness is rather a conscious fake and conceit; it saying that we can start again post-God. The radical claim of secular modernity is that No God means the Fall no longer matters. We can negate our Fall and return to an original state by our own literal design. So, following Le Corbusier, Wigley claims:

> The whitewash facilitates the development of new forms, understood as new ways of looking at the world... The whitewash is able to effect this transformation by being inserted into the gap between structure and decoration in a way that constructs a space for architecture that is neither simply bodily or abstract.[47]

This architecture of universal liminal presence is what lies at the heart of modernist architecture. The box of absence, the cube of white walls with open space, the glass and steel tower able to be seen through – all have their ontology in the barrier of the wall, and in the paradoxical open expression of enclosure. The enclosure of no-thing is the enclosure of nothing-ness. It is the open space that is enclosed which gives function and form to the enclosure. Form does indeed follow function. Furthermore, there is no longer any need for decoration: the presence of the building is decoration itself. No longer is there need to reference either transcendence or total immanence. The modernist aesthetic is one of liminal presence. What is seen as within is discerned on the surface. The modernist aesthetic becomes a universal yet particular expression that becomes the new post-Babel tower to the self.

Mies was an architect who sought to return the immanent universality of a new *Zeitgeist*. His Barcelona Pavilion acknowledged classical architecture and sought to remake it in the age of technology. At the heart of his vision was what he termed *Baukunst*. This approach has been translated variously as the "art of building, the art of construction or building art."[48] Mies himself in 1923 described his underlying theory of *Baukunst* as:

> the will of an epoch translated into space; living, changing, new. Not yesterday, not tomorrow, only today can be given form. Only this kind of building is creative. Create form out of the nature of the tasks with the methods of our times. This is our task.[49]

The spirituality of Mies' task was to be heavily influenced by Aquinas. In an interview he gave in 1964 he recalled:

> I was interested in the philosophy of values and problems of the spirit... I allowed myself the question "what is the truth? What is the truth?" until I stopped at Thomas Aquinas, you know. I found the answer for that.[50]

For Mies the answer was in his translation of Aquinas' definition of truth: *Adequatio intellectus et rei*. The Latin meaning is "truth is the correspondence of thing and intellect." For Mies it became "truth is the significance of fact."[51] Mies' reduction replicates the reductionism of his building. The discipline and order he read into Aquinas was read against the prevailing cultural pessimism as expressed in Oswald Spengler's hugely influential elegiac lament *The Decline of the West* (1918–1922). In Mies' approach, modern architecture was an expression of hope for a future that positioned itself against the decline of western civilization. The new world of modernity was a necessity against a spirit of decline. It offered hope in the present age against romanticized, ornamented nostalgia. To build in the spirit of the age was to build against the decline of the past century, against the *beaux arts* mentality, against the lack of art in the face of deliberate artifice. Cultural pessimism and unnecessary decoration in art, life and thought all pointed to a spiritual crisis that thinkers such as Mies saw as in need of the discipline and order that modern architecture could exhibit and inspire.

The key to understanding what modernist architecture attempted is to be found in the term the International Style. While "internationalism" was first used in architecture by Gropius in 1925,[52] the phrase as we have come to know it today was coined for an exhibition at the Museum of Modern Art (MoMA) in New York in 1932, curated by Philip Johnson and Henry Russell Hitchcock. The cultural critic Tom Wolfe, in his disparaging attack on modernist architecture, still manages to exemplify the impact of this exhibition, citing Hitchcock and Johnson:

> Little did they know that they were but the messenger Elijahs, the Mahaviras, the Baptist heralds for an event more miraculous than any they would have prayed for: the coming.[53]

In particular, the coming was the coming of Mies, and Johnson became his most ardent disciple: promoting, supporting, copying, developing the Miesian ethos – and ultimately radically challenging it with his return to ornamentation heralding postmodernity with his "Chippendale"[54]-affixed AT&T[55] building.

For some forty-odd years[56] the Miesian influence reigned supreme. America was the new world order and the displaced European ethos of Mies became the new American dream of a modernity that could be translated and implemented anywhere, any place, any time. Here was an inclusive modernity that built on the post-war notion of the need for a *tabula rasa*. Of course, society never was a *tabula rasa*: at the very least the trace of what went before was always present. The aim of the modernists was to signal a new start that expressed an inclusive utopian hope that sought to overcome difference. For the modernist creed was a universal belief that built local expressions of the universal idea of a modern, technological, secular, progressive humanity. The grid, the cube, the white house, the glass and steel tower, the horizontal roof over the pitched – all this was the imposition of a new universal order that looked to the human spirit and not the divine as the location of truth. Rem Koolhass described the new Miesian orthodoxy thus:

> Mies does not design individual buildings, but a formless condition that can manifest itself as a building anywhere and be (re)combined in an infinite number of configurations.[57]

I want now to consider what occurs if we undertake what can be seen as a deliberate theological (mis)reading. This reading strategy is the continuation of re-reading non-theological texts and ideas *as if* they are theological. In considering Miesian modernity through such a strategy, the links of modernity to particular claims of Christian universalism can be discerned. Out of such a re-reading, I wish to claim the understandably contestable view that Miesian modernity is the building of the negative presence (through absence) of God. What this claim intends is a particular liminality as a form of presence/absence (absence/presence? Which comes first is an ongoing debate) that can be relocated anywhere – similar in a manner to Barthian neo-orthodox high Christology. For in both claims, the particular becomes subservient to the belief of the universal revelation. Miesian modernism can be read as a form of secular revelation that stands over and against any vernacular religion. It claims to provide the embodiment of the secular *tabula rasa* which seeks to start again over and against the vernacular religion of the past. Just as importantly, its progressive hope is over and against the indifference that just results in nihilism. This secular vision of Mies was often expressed in his lectures: "This world and no other is offered to us. Here we must take our stand."[58] But taking this stand meant building what seems the paradoxical undertaking of constructing transparent presence. Mies sought to construct buildings that "enclosed space while transfiguring it" with the aim "to make space a mystical entity, the immaterial manifestation of the higher truth."[59] Such an undertaking occurred in part to answer the question Mies posed:

> Is the world as it presents itself bearable for man?... Can it be shaped so as to be bearable to live in?[60]

Within twentieth-century modernism, Mies became the expression of the new grand architect, the man who through *Baukunst* was reordering the world out of the chaos of the absence of God. Robert Hughes reckoned:

> Mies seemed to be the epitome of reason – straight lines, rational thought, and extreme refinement of proportion and detailing. If an architect copied him, he would not be copying a style but emulating revealed Truth.[61]

Mies himself saw his task as ontological, claiming in 1924:

> the entire striving of our epoch is directed toward the secular. The efforts of the mystics will remain episodes. Although our understanding of life has become more profound, we will not build cathedrals... We do not value the great gesture but rationality and reality.[62]

It is the Miesian promotion of order that stands at the heart of the modernist ontology. Order, the grid, straight lines, white walls, glass and steel, horizontal planes, all act to impose a universal order and direction upon life. This order operates in two ways. On the one hand, it promotes a human ethic and ontology; human rationality now orders, disciplines and controls life. Central to this view is the claim that God is absent. His absence is built into being in temples to human order. Yet behind this, in the banishing of ornament, something else is happening. Ornament was not merely representative of the transcendence of the secular. For the modernists, ornamentation was a type of deceit. Ornamentation was a sign of the absence that had to be brought into the clear white light of secular life. This was necessary because ornamentation was used, they contended, to cover the reality of the absence. The modernists believed that the act of covering absence with decoration and ornamentation was an intentional attempt to persuade people that the absence was not real and did not exist. Modernism saw itself, as such, as the revelation of truth long obscured. The French philosopher Jean Baudrillard had identified something similar in his discussion of the perception of the iconoclasts. He contends that the iconoclast seeks to destroy the icon in their recognition that the icon (the simulacra) is, in fact, the *only* thing that exists – "indeed that God himself has only ever been his own simulacrum."[63]

Preceding the modernist turn, the architect Louis Sullivan had already intimated such moves in America at the turn of the twentieth century. Sullivan covered his essentially proto-modernist buildings with Rococoesque ornamentation, expressively playing one off against the other, as if marking a transition point.[64] The young Adolf Loos was strongly influenced by Sullivan and often cited him as an influence. What Loos did was note the iconoclastic nature of Sullivan's ornamentation. To place the presence of ornamentation on top of the absence of the grid is to draw attention, not so much to the decoration, as to that which has been so decorated.[65] Sullivan, by separating ornamentation from the building beneath, opens up what I term a secular space, a gap that became developed into the liminal universality of whiteness, or conversely, of steel and glass. The centrality of the secular gap is that it forces a separation between decoration and the decorated. It then sows a doubt as to the necessity of decoration. For once no longer intrinsic, decoration can be discarded as unnecessary.

The other element revealed by Sullivan's ostentatiously decorated modernism was the limitations imposed by decoration. What became apparent in his proto-modern move was that, while the underlying structure seemed to represent some universality, the applied ornamentation not only seemed to locate the building in a particular place and time, but also to date it. I wish to link this by a theological mis-reading to being similar to the critiques applied to a Christology from below, or conversely, as similar to Bonhoeffer's pursuit of a religionless Christianity. The rejection of "vernacular Christologies" and the associated claim for a religionless Christianity are both quintessential modernist pursuits.[66]

The American theologian and philosopher John Caputo clearly lays out the underlying modernist aesthetic that sits under this critique:

> The moderns have a rigorous sense of boundaries, limits, and proper domains, and they make everything turn on drawing these boundaries neatly and cleanly.[67]

Mies saw his task as replicating in the cultural realm that order of disciplines, limits and proper domains exhibited in the technical and economic realms. In his opinion:

> Things by themselves create no order. Order as the definition of the meaning and measure of being is missing today; it must be worked toward anew.[68]

This statement lay at the heart of the modernist ontology: God, the giver of order, was no more. The task of ordering the world was now a human task. If God, the Great Architect, could no longer order and plan, then the human architect had to take his place. The first task of the newly ascendant human architect was the restoration of the truth of order over and against the ornament that sought to obscure the new truth.

This order had three essential elements: space as opposed to mass and solidity, regularity as opposed to symmetry and obvious balance, and elegant materials, technical perfection and fine proportions as opposed to ornament.[69] This oppositional modernist trinity took the form of a new universal secular revelation. It signalled the break with a now dismissed past and the turn to a new society. The clarity and apparent simplicity of the International Style was seen as symbolizing a new aesthetic that reflected a new secular hope of Loosian-derived modernity.

It was this sense of building a new secular age into being that lay at the heart of modernist architecture. That is why I headed this chapter with Lewis Mumford's aphorism, which we need to remember: "Architecture is either the prophecy of an unfinished society or the tomb of a finished one."[70] The modernists, of course, saw themselves as fulfilling the first option. Often socialist in politics, futurist in expectation, secular and humanist, the modernist architects saw their creation of an ordered form and space as offering technical, materialist and spiritual order to a society seeking a new way forward. Not surprisingly, the architect Carl Kocjh saw "Mies as the simplicity out of chaos,"[71] while Eero Saarinen saw Mies as composer of a new state of being:

> Then one man, Mies, really came along and codified all these attempts into one beautiful line and it became the gospel. It became one straight line and it was a beautiful clear thing. It was open for everybody to copy if they wished... That was the state of things in 1950.[72]

Perhaps it was Mumford's second alternative that really describes modernist architecture, however. What it attempted, a modernist utopia, was never achieved.

By the 1960s western society had begun to attempt to live out the prophecy of the erasure of unnecessary ornament. The rise of secular man, the secular city, the cry (some eighty years after the Nietzschean fact) that "God is Dead" occurred against an urban background that had already built these sentiments into being. For architecture the question became, what next?

The postmodern architect and critic Charles Jencks has located and dated the death of Modern architecture to the blowing up of the Pruitt-Igoe housing scheme in "St. Louis, Missouri on July 15, 1972 at 3.32 p.m. (or thereabouts)."[73] However, I believe that this was more a symbolic purist expression similar in its destructiveness to the misquoting of *L'Esprit Nouveau*. What this event-spectacular symbolized was, in reality, the re-assertion of the modernist aesthetic against what was seen as unnecessary ornamentation of a failed vernacular modernism. Rather, to encounter properly the beginning of the end of modernist architecture we need to go back to the late 1960s when Robert Venturi was attacking Miesian grid and order, famously claiming "More is not less" and "Less is bore."[74] Tom Wolfe has defined this shift as bringing "modernism into its scholastic age."[75] Venturi's critique is central because such a proclamation was itself an act of iconoclasm. He recognized that what had been at first new and transgressive had itself become a new form of uncritical decoration and ornamentation. The Mieisan expression had been institutionalized and enforced by architects who constructed in the style of Mies, without an attendant understanding or belief in his creed. Modernism had itself become religion – not a revelation. The move out of order, or rather beyond or after order – a post-order – is what lies at the heart of postmodernity. And crucially it found its most potent symbol in another tower.

Loos' aesthetic was strongly influenced by his time in America in the late 1890s. We need to remember that he prophesized in his lecture "Architecture" that "the American worker has conquered the world. The man in overalls."[76] As discussed above, the American worker that had conquered Loos was Louis Sullivan who strongly influenced him, and was often cited by him. What is crucial to Loos' reading of Sullivan is the recognition that ornamentation stopped the structure from being modern "just now," becoming instead, contextually, "back then."[77]

The Loosian-derived modernist aesthetic sought to construct "decoratively absent" towers whereby their presence alone was necessary ornamentation. Less *is* More for Mies because "less" signals "more" immanent presence: you see the immanent truth; you are not opiated by ornamentation. The contrast is with postmodernism. Being after-modernism in a dialectical progression sought "More as More." The failure of modernism occurred because people no longer could read the absence as presence. In a literalist reading they read absence as absence and so sought direct presence. In a further theological mis-reading, such a demand for direct presence against the absence of modernity is seen in the turn to the direct presence of Pentecostal Christianity and fundamentalism. In both cases, architecture and Christianity, the fact that ornamentation *had* been deemed unnecessary made it what *was now* necessary.

In the world of architecture, what brought postmodernism to public awareness in both physical form and through the pages of *TIME*[78] (itself the apotheosis of modernist information) was Philip Johnson's AT&T building. Here again the similarities to the world of theology are informative and striking. For just as it was ex-Barthians (who had stressed the complete transcendence of God) such as Altizer and Hamilton[79] who tended, in the face of secular society, to become "death of God-ers," so it was the über-Miesian disciple, Philip Johnson, who signalled his departure from the flat-top grid of Miesian orthodoxy with his "Chippendale"-top ornamentation of the AT&T building in New York in 1978 (finished 1984). This new, ornamented tower heralded a new state of play. Here in a very physical, material fashion was ornamentation and decoration as postmodern eclecticism. It was the return of the building that "pointed up to heaven." And yet it was expressed in a manner that suggested we could now remake the past and its traditions, in a personal, ironic, eclectic manner. What was constructed signalled a new possibility. It was no longer the flat-top Miesian slab, but neither was it the finger pointing to heaven. Rather it combined and corrupted both prior forms. In this building the slanted pediment echoes pinching fingers, a hand pulling the transcendent down, a hand grasping for what may just be out of reach. What is expressed is a tension-filled claim: there is more than just the horizontal plane, yet what exactly there is to be grasped is perhaps still out of reach...

Here, expressed in this particular building, was the return of ornamentation almost twenty years before Peter Berger recanted his secularization thesis.[80] If Loos had deemed God an unnecessary decoration back in 1908, it took over half a century for this to become sociological orthodoxy. Architecturally there had been almost forty years of building absence into being. Loos had meant less which signalled the loss of God, religion and transcendence. The modern mind was, it seemed, rational, logical, in sway to secular reason and scientific proofs and principles. Order and discipline, as Foucault (*Discipline and Punish*, 1975) attempted to show, lay at the heart of the modernist aesthetic and sense of progress. Berger's promotion of a secularization thesis promoted a new secular orthodoxy subscribed to not only within sociological circles but also, interestingly, increasingly within liberal Judeo-Christian circles. The secular apocalypse was expected to occur not as some cataclysmic event but rather as a gentle withering away expressed as disenchantment. It was expected to be a slow withdrawal, the Arnoldian permanent low tide of

Dover Beach.[81] God and religion would be the preserve of the unenlightened and the deviant, the intellectually weak and the fundamentalist. To be modern would be to live without transcendence.

Yet, increasingly, secular ideas attempted to exist in a postmodern environment. The tension occurred as Less attempted to express itself in a world of "More is More." Here something interesting occurred both architecturally and in the wider realm of human spirituality – but at cross-purposes. What occurred was the triumph of the internal world. In postmodern design and architecture, while the outside may have been eclectic, the inside was often inclined to promote an austere, commodified minimalism. You entered the postmodern (literally through the door) and found yourself in the world of not less but of *no* ornament. Inside the eclectic, ornamented buildings was an environment that sought to constrain and often banish ornament. The minimalist interior was a muted world of refuge from the exterior decorative chaos. Purist sensibilities had triumphed at last. In the world of the individual, however, the reverse was happening. The purist sensibility of the radically secular individual was under challenge from the rise of spirituality. There arose an eclectic, commodified, mix-and-match postmodern ethos where spiritually you could mix epochs, cultures, religious traditions – and invent new ones! You too could be the spiritual equivalent of the AT&T building or that postmodern favourite, the Bonaventure hotel.[82]

Just as modernist architecture acted as a useful herald for the secular turn, and postmodernist architecture in turn signalled the postmodern society, architecture is again heralding a new cultural move. While the globalized world seems to be uncritically embracing postmodernism, as we see the return of "unnecessary ornamentation" in piercing and tattoos, in the rise of spirituality and fundamentalism, architecture has conversely thrown off the ornamentation of postmodernism. In the last few years we have seen the beginnings of a move to what is termed soft modernism.[83] This shift is seen as a humanized update of the modernist box. On the one hand, it is perhaps a referencing to the order of the past and the enclosure of space. But, on the other, this box is now a space for living in. What occurs is the return to order, control and discipline, but expressed in a manner that is humanized and not sterile.[84] Here we have a casual modernism.[85]

Something more (or rather less) is also happening. Modernity hinged on a broad axis: reduction (less/loss/order/control) and progress. Postmodernism acted as the polar opposite: excess (eclecticism/ornament/chaos/diversity) and relativism. If modernism strove for an International Style, postmodernism promoted the vernacular.[86] If modernism sought an end yet to come, postmodernism stated the end has come and so let's celebrate its demise in carnival (hence Bauman's noting of the tourist as the carnivalistic representative of the postmodern society).

To attempt to understand the rise of soft modernism, we should firstly think in terms of Hegelian dialectic. Modernity is the thesis, postmodernism the antithesis and soft modernism[87] its synthesis – perhaps. The provisionality is necessary because too simplistic an application of Hegelian dialectic obscures a crucial point. What is happening is a modernism without theory and without context. Too often this is modernism that exists as style alone. In a very postmodern fashion, the reduction of the minimalist interior often occurs in the homes of those with eclectic forms of transcendent spiritualities. Modernist reduction is linked with New Age beliefs in Feng Shui, Western Buddhism and Kabbalah. The lack of ornamentation occurs in the homes of those who are themselves unnecessarily ornamented. The reference point for this soft modernism is not some future utopia, nor some computer age futurism but rather a retreat from modernist progress in the fetishization of a retro modernism. The past becomes a design to be copied and lived within. This is a modernism that stands against the Loosian demands. Such soft modernism seeks to replicate the past that is perceived as only representation and image. It is neither an innovation that represents progress, nor the preservation of tradition. Rather, authenticity becomes a commodity of the simulacra. For we have finally reached the Benjaminesque apotheosis: the pre-postmodern work of art has finally lost its aura after the postmodern age of mechanical reproduction.

The life that is referenced in soft modernism is lived looking backwards, not forwards. This is not modernism but, rather, kitsch. Here the stylist, the second-rate draftsman, the architect who copies, has ended up presenting the holographic museum. The reduction is now from the eclectic present. It is the retreat from the vernacular to an unthought-out imposed retro modernism that is dislocated in time and space. Less is now the loss of presence in the present. Like the narrative of Martin Amis' *Time's Arrow* (1991) life is (almost) lived in reverse.

The stylist of minimalist, retro modernist interiors and the draughtsman/ architect of humanized modernism now live out the second part of Mumford's aphorism. They live their lives in perpetual recurrence of an authenticity believed to lie on the other side of postmodernity. The clinical nature of their interiors, the attempt to resurrect the past as the new progressive, the promotion of lifestyle and the style of life as worth living and emulating, all only result in a dislocation in both time and space. It is not modern, it is not postmodern, it is merely inauthentic.

It is also important to note what I term organic technological monumentalism as the other, very public expression of the inauthentic in the wake of postmodernity. This is the communal expression of the inauthentic as public building. For retro modernism is primarily a domestic expression (that is, "the house" and/or "living space") of the pursuit of a technologized existence. As such, retro modernism is

> the ultimate statement of separation from normal humanity [where] the very rich and the very self-aware can live a life that is in itself a form of performance art, merely by dressing a certain way and inhabiting a certain space.[88]

What is often not recognized is the close association retro modernism has with such newly iconic works as Frank Gehry's Guggenheim museum in Bilbao. These are new, titanium clad, computer enabled/designed/ generated (the jury is still out as to the degree the software *really* is "a tool not a partner,"[89] not "a generative device but...an instrument of translation"[90]) public/corporate buildings. In themselves such buildings exist as a form of performance art that unintentionally mimic Louis Sullivan's proto-modernist façades. For with such buildings the focus is on the ornamented exterior as decoration to cloak the real intent of that which it decorates. (Again, in theological mode, they are similar to the postmodern fundamentalist/arch-conservative/Pentecostal churches that may present themselves in high-tech surroundings and contemporary worship expressions – and yet have at their core a biblical literalism and anti-modern sectarianism.)

The inauthenticity of such buildings occurs in the extent to which the public interest and debate is far more concerned with the exterior of the building than with what it actually exhibits *within* its walls. In this sense the Bilbao museum is actually the exhibition of itself (or indeed of Gehry plus computer) being ultimately a presence with no interior meaning. It is apposite that situated outside is the postmodern artist Jeff Koons' kitsch classic topiary Dog, as both the building and the Dog represent the inauthentic excess of kitsch and the collapse of depth. For if retro modernist domestic space mimics an imagined past dislocated to some cyborg future, and so stops it being *modern*, computer aided design (CAD) dislocates the present from both history and the vernacular. As soon as it is built, such retro futurism is already dated and categorized into what Charles Jencks terms "Bilbaoism."[91]

Jencks' emphasis in this term is architecture that appears to be inherently self-referential. Yet such CAD emphases actually shift the reference from the prototypical building such as Bilbao into the possibilities of software and new materials that reference the exterior event as pure ornamentation. This exterior presence occurs in a form that in its organic rhetoric actually creates a type of replicant cyborg architecture that is as minimalist (and inauthentic) as the return of the modified square white box.

While Jencks might have allocated the term ecstatic architecture to such forms of architecture that appear so excessive as to induce "a trancelike state in the onlooker,"[92] the ecstasy is here linked to a typical postmodern New Age/neo-romanticist focus on nature as the location of the authentic. So Jencks refers to such "non-linear/complexity architecture" as "closer to nature in its infinite variety"[93] with its computer-generated basis of fractals as "self-similar, not modernism's same-similar."[94]

What organic architecture really represents is the dislocation of nature into a hyper-real transcendence of pure technology as un-natural presence. Nature now becomes contemporary (and so immediately dated and located). This promotion of contemporary Nature signals a de-humanization of the built environment far more than the Miesian skyscraper or the square white box ever did – or does. The modernist representations were attempts to locate the secular, humanist plane as the basis of authority and identity. The banishing of unnecessary ornament was articulated as a sign of hope, freedom and authenticity. Bilbaoism pursues the artificial representation of the organic as something that is identifiable and desirable. Bilbaoism's promotion of the organic as pure surface representation is the architectural equivalent to genetic modification. Nature gets remade by technology into the representation of the essentialist forms of nature – yet within an unreferenced oxymoronic purist manifesto. As Hans Ibelings notes with regards to what he terms Supermodernism:

> Today's minimalism, incidentally, is purer than ever before, thanks to improvements in technology and materials.[95]

If the Miesian modernists located the expression of the contemporary within human experience (i.e. the "death of God" and secular existence), what Bilbaoism does is dislocate the contemporary to replicant versions of techno-organics, where humanity itself becomes unnecessary ornamentation. The presence of such techno-organic shells is the flip side of the loss of presence of retro modernism. CAD Bilbaoism completely collapses function into form or, rather, into the representation of technology as necessary ornament.

The postmodern theologian Mark C. Taylor sees such moves as the evidence of an "emerging network culture"[96] where, especially in Bilbao, "form becomes complex"[97] and the modernist grid becomes "dynamic" and "organic."[98] I want to argue that there is an essentialist mis-reading occurring here that takes network technology as the location of the real. In effect, it replaces pre-modern religious transcendence with postmodern technological transcendence. Just as cathedrals pointed to a normative reality believed to exist external to secular experience, so too does CAD Bilbaoism. Only now technology replaces (the pre-modern) God as that which exists independently of humanity.

The challenge of Mumford is to seek what comes after the tomb. The minimalist retro tomb is empty, while in Bilbao the "tomb" may as well be empty... Do we worship the empty tomb?

The Response of the *flaneur*

Architects are among the shrewdest readers of our globe, I often think, not only because it is their job to gauge the future but also it is their task to make their most abstract ideas concrete.[99]

In this next section I want to posit a new theological figure, that of the *flaneur*. In order to understand the re-reading I want to offer of the theological *flaneur*,[100] we needed to have an overview of that which the *flaneur* wanders through. While the *flaneur* was conceived as a modernist figure, in postmodern theory claims were made that the *flaneur* could be dislocated from modernity and reappropriated by postmodernity. With the rise of soft modernism, the *flaneur* becomes, in my articulation, a figure who wanders *against* the context. The *flaneur* is one who not only transcends the dislocation of Exile but also actively seeks that dislocation as the location of anticipatory presence in the absence of modernity. The *flaneur*, in effect, undertakes a form of willingly sought Exile *within* their location, so that it is seen anew from the perspective of dislocation.

The turn to the *flaneur* in contemporary theory can be traced back to the work of Walter Benjamin, in particular his textual city of *The Arcades Project*. For Benjamin the *flaneur* embodies a particular response to the liminal challenge of modern urban existence:

the gaze of the *flaneur*, whose way of life still conceals behind a mitigating nimbus the coming desolation of the big-city dweller. The *flaneur* still stands on the threshold – of the metropolis as of the middle-class. Neither has him in its power yet. In neither is he at home. He seeks refuge in the crowd.[101]

Half a century later, Jonathan Raban presented his own version of the *flaneur*'s environment, writing of the liminal context of what he terms *The Soft City*:

Cities, unlike villages and small towns, are plastic by nature. We mould them in our images: they, in turn, shape us by the resistance they offer when we try to impose our own personal form on them... The city as we imagine it, the soft city of illusion, myth, aspiration, nightmare, is as real, maybe more real, than the hard city one can locate on maps in statistics, in monographs on urban sociology and demography and architecture.[102]

Raban's discussion of the soft city is what sat as unacknowledged presence behind the first part of this chapter. The prior survey was not so much a monograph on architecture but rather a discussion as to how the modern(ist) city was itself "the city as we imagine it" attempted to be made real. It was undertaken as the necessary reminder that the hard city is really the attempt to make the soft city solid, presentable, present. Yet each participant in the hard city is actually responding to the attempt to make the soft city present. Raban notes:

> The city as a form is uniquely prone to erode the boundary between the province of the imagination and the province of fact.[103]

This soft city experience that erodes the boundary is where the *flaneur* becomes dialectical. For the *flaneur* is variously the one who "wanders the streets, ambling through its passages, and revealing its undisclosed secrets"; he is also the one who when, "distracted among a crowd," makes "unconscious and unwitting connections" and, so in the process, "reveals the mythological secrets of society."[104] The dialectic occurs, Benjamin argues, within the *flaneur*, where the city "opens up to him as a landscape, even as it closes around him as a room."[105] This interiority–exteriority dialectic is, I want to argue, also the condition of those who could be termed secular theologians in the profane world. For such secular theologians combine in themselves and their position what Benjamin presented as the "dialectic of *Flanerie*":

> on the one side, the man who feels himself viewed by all and sundry as a true suspect and, on the other side, the man who is utterly undiscoverable, the hidden man.[106]

I want to argue that the secular theologian is the one who combines both sides of the dialectic of *flanerie*; she is the hidden suspect. That is, secular theologians are those under suspicion by both the members of the religion of Christianity and by those who seek the purely secular. Yet the secular theologian is, in a sense, hidden in – and yet in opposition to – both. The theological *flaneur* wanders through both cities: the city of religion/city of God and the secular city.[107] In this wandering the theological *flaneur* is distracted in both cities, often by the secular when seeking religion and by religion when seeking the secular. Furthermore, in his pursuit of what could be termed religionless Christianity, he actually both hides and exposes himself by his exposure of the mythological secrets of society.

The theological *flaneur* undertakes her *flanerie* in two ways. The first is the physical *flanerie* of wandering through both the city of God and the secular city. That is, more broadly, wandering through the institutional church and wandering in the secular, physical world. But, secondly, and perhaps more crucially, the theological *flaneur* wanders textually. Walter Benjamin, in his discussion of *flanerie*, notes:

> We know that, in the course of *flanerie*, far-off times and places interpenetrate the landscape and the present moment.[108]

This interpenetration occurs in the architecture of the city the *flaneur* moves through. Both the city of God and the secular city have architectural "far-off times and places" within them; and, furthermore, the people of these cities are never monocultural. But textually – or, more so, in texts and ideas – the theological *flaneur* is one who in wandering through a city of texts and ideas has, in their observation and encounter, the dialectical moments that create a new angle of vision. These are those moments of interpenetration that a theologian could call grace.

In this way, this book is really an account of being a theological *flaneur* – of wandering through a variety of cities – physically and more so in texts and ideas – that result in moments of interpenetration and reassessment. It is, in an act of theological deconstruction, an account of being struck by grace. This act of being struck is sought in a sense of wandering around the city and seeing things differently. Benjamin observes that there needs to be the acknowledgment that doubt "seems to be the proper state" for the *flaneur* – which is part of their "peculiar irresolution."[109] The sense of doubt that sits at the heart of the *flaneur* is not only a reflection of his liminality, but also a response to the liminality of what he perceives and exists amongst. The *flaneur* is the one who moves in response to the continual challenge of the liminal I WILL BE/BECOME. She does not consider it viable staying put with the solidity and security of the I AM.

Graham Ward in his *Cities of God* argues for the centrality of the trope of the city for the practice of contemporary theology. For him the city provides a context in which the question that theology "does not handle," the question of "what God is in relation to the world," *does* become addressed. It becomes addressed in the question of "that relation and that world…[which] is a question about history and salvation…the question becomes very specific; it becomes the question concerning 'what time is it?'"[110] That it is a question implies, I want to claim, a series of central necessities for contemporary theology. These are the necessity of doubt to faith, of doubt to the encounter with grace, of doubt to the whole project of theology. Furthermore, this central necessity of doubt is to be experienced in our contemporary urban world through a form of secular theology as experienced by the theological *flaneur*. The *flaneur* is one who exists inside, yet outside of time, whose answer to the question "what time is it?" is always time to move, to wander, to observe – not time to settle, not time to locate. As Ward states:

> Time is the unfolding of God's grace, of God's gift of God's self in and through creation and being created.[111]

In my re-reading, time, God, creation and being are all part of the expression of I WILL BE/BECOME, not the permanence of I AM. Here the theological *flaneur* is truly *imago dei*: the *flaneur* is the wanderer who wanders as God wanders, the one who questions and challenges as God questions and challenges humanity, the one who is continually on the move, challenged and challenging. In what is an admittedly bold statement, I wish to claim that the *flaneur* is, in our contemporary world, the most suitable theological response to the cities in which we live. For, as Ward reminds us, "the Bible is ambivalent towards cities... If Abraham represents the righteous Jew, the ideal is a wanderer, a nomad, not a city dweller – city dwelling, like the need for a king, was later sanctioned by God, but ambivalently so."[112]

I want to argue that the *flaneur* is not only the authentic response to the city, but also the authentic theological response to this ambivalent environment in which most of us live. Harvey Cox noted four decades ago that we should not attempt to "desecularize and deurbanize modern man, [sic]...[that] to rid him of his pragmatism and his profanity is seriously mistaken."[113] The ambivalence of God toward the city is reflected in the ambivalence of the city toward God. In a sense the modernist city/the city of modernity, in building its boxes of absence, is the epitome of this ambivalence and indifference. And yet, as Cox reminds us, to reject the state of secularization and urbanization is to wrongly presuppose "that a man [sic] must first become 'religious' before he can hear the Gospel."[114] In noting that I have located 'religious' back with the settled misreading of I AM, if I continue with Cox then I can re-read his call for secular humanity in the secular city as that for us to take up the project of the *flaneur* so as to encounter the gospel of the I WILL BE/BECOME:

> Pragmatism and profanity, like *anonymity* and *mobility*, are not obstacles but avenues of access to modern man. His very pragmatism and profanity enable urban man to discern certain elements of the Gospel which were hidden from his more religious forebears.[115] [emphasis added]

In the *Secular City*, Cox argues for the mobility of Christ. Such mobility is not only concerned with the incarnated Christ but also with regards to the despatialization of the ascension. Here we have a refusal for Christ "to be localized or spatially restricted."[116] That is the theological reason, I would argue, why the modern city is where the pursuit of God and the challenge of grace is be encountered. The modern city is constructed of boxes of absence that refuse to locate solid presence. As Cox further states:

> The ascension in its simplest terms means Jesus is mobile. He is not a Baal but the Lord of all history.[117]

The modern city, the place of the representation and construction of indifference, is also the place where Christendom broke down. The modern city is the rejection of "a sacral civilization," the rejection of the attempt to "transmute the Christian Gospel into a Baal cultus...a fatal respatialization of Christianity."[118] The trouble with both the theological tourist and traveller is that they attempt to encounter the respatialization of Christendom elsewhere. They reject the challenge of the presence of absence, the challenge of the liminality of contemporary secular, urban despatialization and seek its relocation elsewhere. The theological Exile too is one who, in a sense, is always referenced back to the spatialization of Christendom – even though he now exists in the despatialization. In the contemporary world, it is the theological *flaneur* who represents the return to the despatialization of the Gospel, who responds to the presence/absence of the liminal Christ, who is the follower of the God who is I WILL BE/BECOME not I AM. Cox again acts as a prophet of the theological *flaneur*:

> But by and large the mobile man is less tempted than the immobile man to demote Yahweh into a Baal... Perhaps the mobile man can ever hear with less static a Message about a Man who was born during a journey, spent his first years in exile, was expelled from his home town, and declared that he had no place to lay his head. High mobility is no assurance to salvation, but neither is it an obstacle to faith.[119]

How might the theological *flaneur* proceed, then? Anke Gleber defines the *flaneur* as a reader of modernity, who responds to it "by incessantly reflecting on and recording his impressions," and as one who is located "as an individual and solitary outsider amidst the crowd."[120] The *flaneur* is situated within a liminal modernity. A different version of this liminality occurs in Michel de Certeau's ontology of walking that has distinct echoes of the Christian life: "To walk is to lack a place. It is the indefinite process of being absent and in search of a proper [sic]."[121] Yet there is a purpose to this *flanerie* of "walking through a city slowly and attentively, one's appreciation bolstered by learning,"[122] for it is an activity which acknowledges that "[t]he city itself is a writing within which all other writings are circumscribed."[123] The *flaneur* is thus one who undertakes a series of intertextual readings of that which they wander through, of those they encounter and observe and of themselves in motion, of themselves as liminal beings in a liminal encounter in a liminal environment. Underneath there is a sense of redemption which occurs always from the position of outsider and mobility:

> *Flanerie* moves according to this impulse to write, register, and redeem what has been seen.[124]

The reason that *flanerie* occurs in the city is because it "is the arena of the modern, its stage, its location."[125] So any attempt to represent a modern, secular theology has to be a theology of the city. It is the response of the theological *flaneur* who moves through the texts of modernity, both written and built (words and buildings), seeking to observe, to glimpse, to re-read anew:

> the observation of the fleeting and the transitory...the activity of the sovereign spectator going about the city in order to find the things which will occupy his gaze and thus complete his otherwise incomplete identity; satisfy his otherwise dissatisfied existence; replace the sense of bereavement with a sense of life.[126]

Zygmunt Bauman posits that the *flaneur* is but the mirror image of the modern world. That world is "the original *flaneur*" because "neither the world nor the solitary wanderer knows to where they move or what is to be found around the corner."[127] This is why we need to be aware not only of the boxes of absence of the modern world, but also aware of postmodernism's failed attempt to build presence and further aware of the (re)turn back to the absence of soft modernism. The modern world *is* the Modern city, in all its expressions and attempts to represent modernity. Furthermore, Bauman challenges us to become aware of how for both the modern world and *flaneur*, "[t]he aimless stroll is the aim; there could not be, there should not be other aims."[128]

This aimless strolling is the world of religionless Christianity, the world of the secular theologian, the world where the wanderer glimpses the I WILL BE/BECOME but refuses to settle with the Baal of I AM. The aim of the wandering that the *flaneur* wanders in search of[129] is the liminal presence/absence of I WILL BE/BECOME. Here is the liminal Christ of Bonhoeffer, and the closeness to God revealed in the absence. This is the Christ who *flaneurs*, the Christ who is not spatialized but present and absent everywhere. This is the Christ who as Word of God is textualized in and yet not in the world. This is the Christ to be glimpsed in re-readings, not imprisoned in religion, in Christendom or in institutions. For the *flaneur* wanders in the liminal space of the street: that metropolitan "site of encounter and confrontation."[130]

In the street, the theological *flaneur* wanders with imagination and observation: re-reading, re-observing, on the move, seeking the encounter that is liminal yet offers the ongoing glimpse of grace. She reads and re-reads that which the settled, the comfortable, the institutional do not. She continually re-reads and deliberately mis-reads. *She* wanders with and against the crowd, as an individual, as one of those reading the city that is the challenge to the Baal of Christendom. For the theological *flaneur* is not content to be told that "this" (that is, the religion of Christianity) is where grace occurs, that "here" is where grace is to be found, that grace is to be mediated and defined. He recognizes such claims to grace as the siren call of Baal, who seeks to halt the *flaneur*, to impose Christendom over and against the liminal absence/presence of secularity. The *flaneur* recognizes the world as a text that is in continual need of re-reading. The *flaneur* recognizes that texts need to be re-read to find that which may be glimpsed within them. The *flaneur* is the inter-textual theologian who reads Bibles, Baedekers, buildings, whatever – because the grace of God is not settled, the Christ has not found a home to lay his head, the I WILL BE/BECOME is not that which is claimed to be I AM.

5 Rethinking Location and Christology

The challenge of the *flaneur* forces a radical reassessment of the theological task in the modern world. The *flaneur* situates himself as dissident voice to the prevailing orthodoxies and institutional claims. Traversing the liminal boundaries between theology and the secular world, the *flaneur* acts as internal dissident to both cultures. This liminality is further emphasized in the various responses to his claims. To the secular he is a secular *theologian*, while to the world of theology he is a *secular* theologian. The differing emphases of response are both attempts to question his legitimacy. Both theology and the secular view him with a certain and understandable degree of distrust because he refuses to be constrained by boundaries or expectations. To the theologians the *flaneur* is too immersed in the secular world, its views and theories. To the secular world the *flaneur* is viewed as one who unnecessary traverses within the claims, worlds and language of theology and religion. To both he seems a dabbler; that is, he is someone who refuses a full immersion and focus within either world: he is too theological for the secular and not theological enough for the theologians. And yet I wish to state that the trope of the *flaneur* is perhaps the best expression of what is involved in undertaking cross-cultural theology in the modern world. The *flaneur* is cross-cultural both to the culture of theology and the culture of a secular world.

The interruption and disruption of the trope of the *flaneur* has also occurred within this text itself. Originally, this text was to be a discussion on re-reading theology through the tropes of tourism, travel and exile. But as the actual writing of the text occurred, I realized the limits of what I had attempted. More so, I realized the need to move beyond the exile into articulating a new position. I realized the limitations of the trope of exilic dis-location as the location to undertake theological thought in the contemporary world. To move past the excluded position of the exile forced the articulation of the *flaneur* as the position of self-chosen liminality and dissent. In this sense, the *flaneur*, whose position arises from her basis of self-reflexivity, emerges as the quintessential modernist figure. However, most work on *flanerie* is, understandably, secular in nature. The *flaneur* is the secular modern individual undertaking liminal assessment against the mainstream of society. The *flaneur*, however, also forces a reassessment of the theological task – in particular, the engagement of theology with the modern, secular world the *flaneur* arose within. To rediscover the *flaneur* means also, for theology, the re-encounter with European theology of the early and mid-twentieth century.

Often such theology, linked as it is into neo-orthodoxy, is viewed with suspicion in today's world. This understanding is especially true in theologies and cultures attempting to express a contemporary theology of particular cultures. The hegemony of neo-orthodoxy is an accepted orthodoxy itself in many theological minds. And this state of affairs is often held with good reason insofar as neo-orthodoxy has itself often been expressed as a particular expression of power. Such an expression is itself, I would argue, however, a perversion of the neo-orthodox basis in the critique of cultures as revelatory in and by themselves. The problem exists because contemporary expressions of neo-orthodoxy often seem to be the result and the articulation of what Rowan Williams terms "meaningful action." In his perceptive introduction to *Theology and the Political: The New Debate*, Williams is careful to position "meaningful action" against "acting intelligibly." Meaningful action, when successful, does not invite response, critique or revision. An expression of "meaning is power," it is a "specific disposition of will. It does not require understanding."[1]

I want to argue that both the attempt to impose contemporary neo-orthodoxy as hegemony and the outright rejection of the neo-orthodox challenge to culture are attempts towards "meaningful action." Both positions will treat the theological *flaneur* with suspicion and distrust because he moves within and yet against both views. The alternative, positioned by Williams as arising out of Augustine, Hegel and Marx, is to "act intelligibly." In doing this:

> …we expose ourselves to the process of language. This is to say, we have offered a *representation* of something prior and shaping reality into a continuing narrative of uncovering through response and question.[2] [emphasis original]

The position of uncovering through response and question is that of the theological *flaneur*. As such the *flaneur*, in this self-reflexive uncovering within modernity, is also, at the same time, a figure engaged with the legacy of the Enlightenment. In fact the *flaneur* engages with the two legacies that combine to create modernity: Christianity and the Enlightenment. This means that both legacies as the past (the "something prior") can be part of an ongoing response versus "meaningful action" and especially against *Volkgeist*[3] in all its forms.

The issue for contemporary society is thus not to repeat Lyotard's claim that the postmodern is the return to pre-modern ways of thinking.[4] Central to this argument is the role of theology, precisely as the articulation of universal reason *within* the secular *against* un-reflexive and un-critical belief. As the Frankfurt School came to argue, in the words of Eduardo Mendieta, "theology is reason in search of itself by way of the demystification of social reality."[5] This quest occurs, so Max Horkheimer argues, because theology, in attempting to "reconcile the demand of the Gospels and of power" was assigned an "indispensable task" of reconciling Christianity and power, "to give a satisfactory self-awareness to both high and low with which they could do their work in a corrupt world."[6] In reading Horkheimer, we can see that out of this tension, inherent in the task of the response of theology, arises one basis of modernist self-reflexivity.

On the road to modernity, this self-reflexivity became posited against theology itself. In effect this was the secularization of belief away from Christianity to non-Christian power. Now, with the rise of various theological and cultural hegemonies, theology again regains its position as necessary tension – but a *tension of secular theological response* to both gospels and power. As such it is the liminal counter-cultural movement of the *flaneur* expressed as the critical response of "acting intelligibly." This centrality of theology for secular western society occurs, as Helmut Peukert explains, because:

> ...theology, as a methodologically controlled reflective form of religion, has been concerned with the basic problems of advanced civilizations that developed simultaneously with it.[7]

Therefore, in positioning themselves against the return of *Volkgeist* belief in contemporary society – whether as theological claims or as cultural necessities – "[b]oth projects, theology as well as enlightenment, need to enter into public conversation with each other to continue."[8]

John Milbank notes that Marxist atheists such as Badiou[9] and Zizek[10] are re-engaging with Christianity in an attempt to challenge the return of *Volkgeist* because

> Christianity was the very first enlightenment, the first irruption of an absolutely universal claim.[11]

The response of political theology against the return of belief is the attempt to continue the Enlightenment project that is, in itself, secularized Christianity. This occurs because, in this new type of modernity,[12] there is yet again the need to reassert the Enlightenment by a response to and with Christian theology – even against Christianity (as implicit Christendom) itself.

The centrality of Christianity in articulating the turn versus the *Volkgeist* of post-secular[13] belief occurs because Christianity enacts, as Milbank states, "a universal *event*, which has the consequence of relativizing in practice cultural particularity and allowing a universal human association."[14] The centrality of Christianity means we respond to the legacy of two universal events: the Incarnation (for Christianity) and the Enlightenment (which is a secular incarnation in that it enacts a new universal event). The necessity of Christianity for this response occurs because, as Milbank, Badiou and Zizek would all note,

> Christianity is universal because it invented the logic of universality; it constituted this logic as event.[15]

The issue of response, as "acting intelligibly" against "meaningful action" means, like the Marxists, secular western society can respond to the claim and legacy of Christian universality as that which sets the logic and base of universality. The importance of response is that it follows the encounter of the *flaneur* – the one who responds to that which they move within and against. In the manner of the *flaneur*, the Christian legacy of inclusive universality that transcends cultural logic and belief is that which we respond to which *negates* claims that seem to privilege either cultural logic or theological hegemony. The logic of the event of universality is that which we can refer to as a legacy *from response* versus any new claims of cultural or theological particularity.

The theological *flaneur*, therefore, finds her origin in the liminal position expressed by the early Karl Barth. The role of neo-orthodoxy was originally to act as caution to both secular and religious society. Tim Gorringe notes the importance in Augustine, Luther and Karl Barth of the "same sense of the ambivalence of culture... all three see the barbarism attached to culture."[16] Gorringe, in a similar turn to Badiou and Zizek in their articulations of the necessity of a secular political theology, links the discussion into Walter Benjamin, specifically his "sixth thesis on the philosophy of history":

> ...there is no document of civilization which is not at the same time a document of barbarism.[17]

The role of theological *flaneur* arising out of its modernist neo-orthodox roots is also one of *response as critique* to a belief in civilization free from barbarism – either as *Volkgeist* or perfected Enlightenment. Theology is the constant reminder to religious civilization that as civilization or culture it too contains within it the barbarism that in turn demands the response of ambivalence to culture.

To explore more closely the situation of the theological *flaneur* as response and critique, we should to turn to Karl Barth's 1926 essay "Church and Culture." Here Barth makes clear the distinction between belief as confession and belief as action, statement or as credit.[18] For Barth, belief is something personal that in itself contains by necessity, unbelief because of the very nature of humanity. The necessity of the acknowledgment of unbelief within belief *as confession* is the distinction of response. For belief as action, as statement or as credit, let alone as culture, all exclude the possibility of unbelief and so become imposition and non-contestable *Volkgeist* and theological hegemony. In short they become what Williams critiques as "meaningful action."

For Barth, culture is what reminds humanity of sin and separation from God. Culture does this because culture is the confrontation of humanity with the problem of our existence. Culture is where theological response occurs – both as a summons to cultural activity (because culture means humanity[19]) and yet also as the response to culture of "ultimate, sharp scepticism."[20] Here is the situating of theology as internal response versus belief in culture. To read further, in modern society, theology is the critical voice against both the return of "religious culture" and of "culture as religion." Following Barth, the role of the theological *flaneur* is built on the critique of religious culture by and from theology whereby the response is the combined critique of "ultimate, sharp scepticism."

Barth is careful to claim that, "throughout its whole course, the Church swims along in the stream of culture."[21] Yet swimming in culture does not mean the acceptance of it as the norm. Here we have the recognition that culture is the location from which critique *must* be made – even as those making the critique cannot locate themselves, as humanity, outside culture. In this manner, theology is itself inherent to modernity's self-reflexivity. For the *flaneur* the legacy for theology is a theology that speaks a critique "with society, without society, against society; in season and out of season."[22] This liminal position of the theological *flaneur* as *within and yet against* both cultures of religion and secular society means I find myself returning again and again to the challenges laid down by Dietrich Bonhoeffer. The reason for this is because central to the liminal position of the *flaneur* are two questions: how should I align what I am attempting with his continual challenge to express a "religionless Christianity" yet engage also with the often unspoken challenge of "where does Christology sit in this?"?

In attempting to express a secular theology, the move from theology to Christology is not as simple as perhaps many would believe. On the one hand, the Trinitarian challenge of Christianity always locates Christology as central to any attempt to speak theologically. Yet, on the other hand, we need to also remember that to speak of secular theology is perhaps easier than to attempt to speak of secular Christology. The specific claim of Christology cannot be easily subsumed into a general secular theology which can often be far more unitarian than trinitarian. But any attempt to wrestle with the implications of a secular theology in a Christian framework has to deal with both the core question of the Christ: "Who do men [*sic*] say that I am?" and the answer of Peter: "You are the Christ" (Mark 8: 27–30).

Often the easiest response in secular theology is not to talk of the Christological challenge at all. Too often secular theology becomes unitarian by default, if not by design, and merely states "God" and lets that suffice. The implication is that readers can respond to such a proclamation as they please. For being strongly linked into liberal readings of Christianity, secular theology often becomes the preserve of those seeking a human Jesus who is, at the very most, a "god-filled" man. In such views Jesus is the Christ as fully human and not divine. The more I progressed in this work the more I felt the challenge to deal with the Christological issue which sits at the heart of Bonhoeffer's challenge. Why this is so is because the basis of a secular theology arises in the encounter of neo-orthodoxy with modernity. It is the encounter of the twin oppositions to the challenge of religion as *Volkgeist* in modernity. The challenge of religion as *Volkgeist* presents itself as that which seeks to negate the universalism of both Christianity and Enlightenment-derived modernity.

I am fully aware that I am not a systematic theologian, nor have I specialized in Christology. And yet the challenge of the Christ is what I found lurking behind all that I set out to do in this book. The challenge of the Christ both to and within secular theology meant that I had to venture on from the exile to introduce the trope of the theological *flaneur*. Such a move was undertaken because I am working toward a position where the secular Christian, as theological *flaneur*, is where the *imitatio Christi* occurs in "religionless Christianity." Furthermore, it is the opening of the *flaneur* to the world that allows the encounter with the Christ in the religionless world.

Sacred Space?

One way in which I could articulate the question of Christ in the world is by re-reading God as sacred space. This is what I term a populist unitarian approach whereby "God" becomes a textual and cultural signifier that is singular, not trinitarian. An example of this can be shown by re-reading Peter Bishop's definition of sacred space as (primarily) referring to God:

> Sacred space has been defined in terms of its separation from the profane world, by the limited access accorded to it, by a sense of dread or fascination, by intimations of order and power combined with ambiguity and paradox. Sacred places also seem to be located as the periphery of the social world.[23]

Such a re-reading whereby God and sacred space conflate into each other could, I imagine, easily result in affirmation by many in a post-Christian world. This practice is especially evident in a culture dominated by New Age syncretism. But such a literalist re-reading does not serve our purpose. Rather I wish to follow my deconstructionist re-reading strategy and situate such a strategy within the challenge of secular theology. Under such a challenge, this claim of re-reading God as sacred space only makes Christological sense if we continue the re-reading and think of Christ as the *axis mundi*:

> At the center of the sacred place is the *axis mundi*, the world axis, the link between heaven, earth and the underworld.[24]

To think of Christ as a form of *axis mundi*, as that which is the centre of God, yet a God located on the periphery of the profane world, is a challenge to Christian thought – and to those such as myself grappling on the edges of faith and non-belief. It is a challenge because such an approach locates God and the Christ who is the *axis mundi*, in effect, as elsewhere, as that which is not "here." Such a re-reading works for those adopting the trope of tourist, traveller or exile, for their expectation and experience is located in opposition to what is seen as profane. In their readings and experiences, the profane is to be left behind in either physical movement or memory so that a form of journey to the authentic sacred location can occur. Such movement, however, whether textual, theological or physical, is opposed to the task and challenge of secular theology. For those like myself seeking some engagement with the trope of *flaneur*, to locate that which is responded to on the periphery of profane space is to make inauthentic the location where the challenge of the Christ occurs. In other words, it is to seek the Christ as located on the periphery of the profane and so to limit him to where we feel he *should* be. The challenge of the *flaneur* is to be open to the possibility of the Christ in the profane world – that is, to be open to where he *may* be. The challenge from the position of the *flaneur* is that the attempt to look elsewhere for authenticity is yet another retreat into religion and a sectarian response that posits Christianity as religion which is to be sought and found over there.

Coupled with this is the challenge thrown out to theologians in modern times by Charles Taylor, reminding them that:

> [while] they may still think in theological terms…this is theology in quite a different register. They have to speak as theorists in a profane world.[25]

This profane world may actually be, as Gabriel Vahanian insists, the *only* place in which we can ever do theology. This profane world is the *only* place in which God in Christ is encountered – or, from a *flaneur's* point of view, fleetingly glimpsed. Vahanian's point is "that secular does not mean the opposite of sacred. Rather, the term secular refers to a *saeculum*, or a shared world of human experience."[26] It is in this *saeculum* that humanity and the divine encounter each other. This is why I have made use of what are termed secular texts to undertake what could be termed secular theology. These texts have been re-read because the theological *flaneur* responds to the God in Christ who is encountered (perhaps only fleetingly) in the *saeculum*. The challenge from the *flaneur* is against any attempts to reduce the texts we use both to encounter and express our response to self-delineated (self-consciously?) "religious" texts. For to limit God to the realm of the sacred or the religious, whether in texts or places, is to have already prescribed, limited and defined the boundaries of this encounter – and our response to it. From the position of secular theology and from the situation of the theological *flaneur* this is to make religious texts and places religious. That is, to make them the texts and places of I AM. The challenge from secular theology and from the position of the theological *flaneur* is to be open to the God who is I WILL BE/BECOME. It is to be open to the God who may act and seek response outside of religion and religious texts. It is to be open to the God who does not limit encounter with humanity to how and in what texts or places humanity may desire.

Therefore, in following Charles Taylor's challenge, to speak as a "theorist in a profane world" is to use the theory and the texts that have been defined as profane as now *possibly* the site and sight of the encounter with God. The challenge of theology in a different register is to register that theology is not religion, that theology is a response – and not a demand or an encoding. Rather, to undertake such theology in a different register is to *be challenged*. It is to wrestle like Jacob, risking injury in our encounter. Like Jacob it involves acknowledging that blessing and encounter do not come without some permanent dis-locating away from what we were – and what we thought God was and is. And most importantly, this wrestling occurs in the *saeculum* – because our current state is neither beyond God nor incarnation. Because it does occur in a secular world that is both post-Christian and post-Christendom, it does require a new form of theology. This new theology may of course be termed heresy, but it is a necessary heresy so that God's potential action and freedom is not limited.

It is in response to this understanding that I wish to stress the importance of the *flaneur* who wanders through the *saeculum*, over and against the pietist who withdraws. The problem of the pietist is that to withdraw to the world of religion is actually to withdraw from that place of encounter; it is to withdraw from where humanity and the divine meet. The pietist withdraws into an anti-world where humanity creates the directional and controlled space and limits for that encounter. So the problem of the withdrawal from the secular of the pietist is that he encounters I AM, not I WILL BE/BECOME.

Vahanian sees the secular as "what outgrows religions":

[I]t looms on the incomprehensible horizon of memory as what's left when religion is loosened from the fossilizing effects of memory and fades into hope… The secular is not merely secular. Nothing is secular that is not at the same time symmetrical with something religious.[27]

The challenge of the theological *flaneur* is one of turning to the secular without retreating to the safety of the religious. Because of the quintessentially modern nature of the *flaneur* the challenge of religionless Christianity is precisely born out of this tension that Vahanian notes: there is the world of shared human experience where Christianity states the mutual encounter of humanity and the divine occur. And yet the anti-modern *religion* of Christianity seeks to distort, to limit and to prescribe this encounter. It does so not as the expression of hope and grace but rather from the limitations and prescriptions of memory.

The Italian philosopher Gianni Vattimo reminds us that the question of religious faith in western culture is "the recovery of an experience," that "none of us…begins from zero…"[28] That is, the question of faith, the challenge of Christianity, the possibility of grace, the revelation of God-in-Christ (and I acknowledge I am here expanding Vattimo beyond his statement) is that which is our starting point. This is the "different register" which we who are "theorists in a profane world" must engage with – and against. We must engage *with* it acknowledging we did not begin with, from or in a *tabula rasa*. We must also engage *against* it when those claims have become religion – that is human expressions of the I AM, not the dis-located challenge of the religionless I WILL BE/BECOME. The challenge, therefore, is to work against the religion of geopiety – and the geopiety of religion.

Against Geopiety

Geopiety is "that curious mix of romantic imagination, historical rectitude and attachment to a particular place."[29] Geopiety is the inverse of Christ as *axis mundi*, whereby religion and its expressions lie at the centre of any expression of sacred space. In geopiety, the Christ of place becomes the object of piety. Christ becomes the located, spatialized Christ who is containable and domesticated – and at the service of religion.

The theological *flaneur* undertakes an attack upon geopiety. She responds to the call of I WILL BE/BECOME to move on from location through dis-location to a liminal wandering that exists on the far side of exile. The theological *flaneur* understands religionless Christianity as seeking to follow the Christ who wanders the streets of the secular city, the Christ who is not the *axis mundi* of geopiety, but a Christ who goes unnoticed by most.

This is the Christ who does not assume the *persona* of what is expected. This is the Christ who continues the disturbance to piety, to fixed notions, to fixed beliefs, to fixed expectations. This is the Christ who is opposed to the fixity of religion. This is the Christ who refuses to limit himself or the offer of grace to those within the institutions of religion. This is the Christ who lays down the challenge of the discomfort and dis-location of religionless Christianity. To follow such a Christ is to follow more an absence than a presence. To search for such a Christ is predominantly to see where he is not. To follow such a Christ is to locate yourself in and with that and those that religion sees (rightly) as opposed to what it demands.

In opposition to the theological *flaneur*, the siren call of geopiety is what calls the tourist and the traveller. It is the location of geopiety which is able to be located, visited, and commodified. As such it exists and is encountered as domesticated, controlled, mediated, disciplined and constructed space specifically for the religious encounter. The problem for Christianity of such an encounter occurs because the Christ of geopiety is that which is there because we are told he is. For the religious expectation and demand of the Christ of geopiety is that he is located and able to be encountered over there, over here, in this place, in this experience. What is often not understood is that the Christ of geopiety is a Christ who is located and locatable precisely because his presence is controlled, delineated and ordered – that is, constructed. This means that the Christ of geopiety occurs as an event to be visited, as an event to be recorded and souvenired. The Christ of geopiety thus becomes a Christ who fits *our* expectations and demands. Such a religious Christ of geopiety is available to those who are prepared to pay the price – and so becomes a repeat business experience. In short, he becomes a spectacle. He is a Christ who is not to be found and encountered in the mundane and everyday. He is rather a Christ who is exotic and different, who is authentic because he is so different to where we are. He is a Christ whose encounter marks off those who encounter him as special, as seekers, as searchers, for the geopiety is never where most of us live. So, just as the Christ of the tourist is a repeat-event spectacle easily encountered in the institutions and locations of defined religion, the Christ of the traveller is an exotic event located *not* in your home location and *away* from where the tourist Christ is. Both follow a Christ of geopiety, however: a Christ of place, a Christ of special place, a Christ to be found over there, away from everyday life. Likewise, the Christ of the exile is a Christ who is to be found in dis-location, where the geopiety is one that is more remembered than experienced. Where once the exile encountered Christ now they are aware of his absence. Christ was encountered in what has been left behind. For the exile Christ becomes reduced to what is encountered in what is now only a memory, a dis-location.

In opposition to such reductions of Christ by forms of religion, I want to argue that it is the Christ of the *flaneur* – and indeed the *flaneur* Christ – who is the Christ of religionless Christianity. The *flaneur* wanders through the location which the tourist, the traveller and the exile all view as inauthentic. For the tourist and the traveller, it is that location that must be left behind in pursuit of what is deemed authentic and real. For the exile, it is that location which serves to daily remind them of what they have been forced to leave behind. Only for the *flaneur* is this location the authentic location; only for the *flaneur* is this location the site of encounter. For *the flaneur* is the return of the position of openness to encounter *within this secular world* on divine and not human terms and conditions. While there may be a journey at the centre of the encounter with the Christ, for the *flaneur* the journey is one that occurs *here, where we are* – not over there where we are not.

Christ and the *flaneur*

Roberto Calasso, in discussing the photographs of the traveller Bruce Chatwin, offers the challenge of rethinking grace:

> What was the first journey, or at least the model for us of every journey? Certainly not the Odysseus, which was a homecoming. A homecoming can never have the essentially freewheeling quality of real travel, *which is a total surrender to the unknown.*[30] [emphasis added]

The challenge occurs because Calasso prefaces this statement by stating what he sees as holding together the books, photographs and character of Chatwin: "that element lying at the heart of all theological writings: Grace."[31] At this point it would be easy to extend such a line of reasoning and state that travel is the encounter with grace in a secular world and so tourism is nothing more than cheap grace and exile is thus the experience of the death of God. But to do so would be merely to continue along the religion of geopiety. The alternative is to follow what, reading from McKenzie Wark, I could term "*flanerie* knowledge":

> To refuse to develop knowledge within a category. Knowledge should be botched not batched. *The discipline of indiscipline*, making tracks, not monitoring borders.[32] [emphasis original]

The development of such knowledge, I propose, has to occur alongside what the post-colonial scholar Stephen Turner terms "frontier knowledge":

> For the frontier is the first and last place to know: the first to confront the new, the not-yet-known, and the last to understand what it means, how it is understood in the most general sense, theorised, and returned to the margin.[33]

These two readings of indiscipline and the frontier, which incidentally arise from Antipodean perspectives,[34] I want to argue express where the encounter with the Christ occurs for the *flaneur*. While I do not want to totally dismiss Calasso's insight of that *"total surrender to the unknown,"* I also do not want to locate that experience in a site of geopiety. Rather I want to return all three challenges of surrender, indiscipline and the frontier to the *flaneur*. For the *flaneur*, who is to be found in the undisciplined crowds of the city, wanders the streets of the known, open to the unknown. The challenge of the frontier is that which is within each *flaneur*, because the frontier is that which is found in our encounter with the Christ.

For the theological *flaneur*, the challenge is that laid down by Bonhoeffer's liminal Christ, a Christ he expresses as *pro me* – that is, standing:

> on the boundary of my existence, beyond my existence, but still me… Here Christ stands, in the centre, between me and myself, between the old existence and the new. So Christ is at the same time my own boundary and my rediscovered centre, the centre lying both between "I" and "I" and between "I" and God.[35]

The benefit and challenge of such frontier knowledge lies in the experience of being encountered by and acknowledging the liminal Christ. The position of the *flaneur* is that while we know, we do not yet fully understand. The frontier for the *flaneur* lies between the old me and the new me. It is the frontier that is between Christ and me, between God and me. And yet, for the *flaneur*, Christ is also the centre where what is new is fully understood. From this understanding of Christ the centre arises the *flaneur's* new understanding of that encounter of and at the frontier. For the frontier encounter I might perceive as primarily between myself and the world (wherein I am primary and the world is secondary) occurs firstly between Christ and me, between God and me. The frontier encounter with Christ reminds me that I am secondary in all encounters with the world because, in Christ, God has *already* encountered the world. Furthermore, this encounter is not merely an historical event but is rather an ongoing encounter which challenges all our attempts to reduce it to the historical. This encounter occurs through the discipline of indiscipline, through making tracks and not marking borders. This encounter continues through not marking borders between me and Christ, between me and God, between Christ and the world. It occurs, as such, with the transgression of the *flaneur* who is not constrained by expectation and claims to order. For the *flaneur* wanders open to encounter within the modern environment deemed by many as now empty of any such encounter. The transgression of *flanerie* encounter occurs in the wilful botching of borders of knowledge. For the theological *flaneur* this occurs in both the knowledge of transgression and the transgression of knowledge.

In this paradoxical encounter we deconstruct and reconstruct our readings of ourselves and Christ in encounter with each other in the world.

Underlying the encounter of the *flaneur* is Barth's reminder of where we meet God – which is not in a place but in a person:

> We can meet God only in the bounds of the human which he has determined. But just within these bounds we may meet him. He does not spurn what is human. Quite the contrary. That is what we have to hold on to.[36]

The human encounter with God is what takes place in the Christ, the Christ who is to be found in this world, the world of humanity, not separate from it as sacred place. The importance of Barth's reminder is that the Christ is to be encountered within our *contemporary* world, the world of *our* here and now. For it is the *flaneur* moving among the crowds *of where we are* who is the one fully open to the God who meets us in the human. The *flaneur* does not seek the exotic other or place as the sight and site of revelation and encounter, nor does she believe that the authentic encounter is only to be found in the past, in another time and place and people. The theological *flaneur* acknowledges that the encounter with God who has made himself available in "the bounds of the human" is to be encountered *in* the "bounds of the humans" where we are – and, as we are:

> The presence is a concealed presence. But it is not as though God were concealed in the man [god is God in the man Jesus]; rather this God-man as a whole is concealed in this world in the likeness of a man.[37]

The theological *flaneur* is one who is open to this concealment in the world, in the cities and the streets where they wander. Furthermore, transposed to the textual world, the *flaneur* is open to this concealment in the texts in which they wander. The *flaneur*, in being open to the possibility of concealment, is observing all and not limiting his gaze. This is because the concealed Christ is the Christ who is concealed in the crowds of the secular world and in the world of the secular city. The concealed Christ is not an exotic presence open to observation elsewhere as a spectacle, as an event. The concealed Christ is not one who is to be sought over there in a manner that makes there authentic and here inauthentic. The concealed Christ is where the exile *is* as well as where the exile was. For the concealed Christ is encountered as presence in the present and not just as a memory.

The theological *flaneur* is thus open to the concealment of Christ, but is not, as Bonhoeffer warns, one who "interprets either the full manhood or the full Godhead of Jesus at the cost of qualifying either one or the other."[38] The theological *flaneur* is one who wanders open to the challenge of the incarnation in the *saeculum*, an incarnation in which full humanity and full Godhead are both present. This wandering is a wandering in the midst of bodies, as Graham Ward reminds us, indeed as a body within the midst of bodies that are all "situated and given significance" within the "permeable, transcorporeal, transpositional"[39] body of Christ, body of God. By wandering in our body we are wandering within the body of Christ; by wandering amongst other bodies we are wandering amongst the body of Christ; by wandering through other bodies we are wandering through the body of Christ. The challenge encountered by the *flaneur* is that it is *here, in* our bodies, *amongst* other bodies, where our bodies *are,* that we encounter the incarnation. It is indeed in this modern, secular world of the present that we are challenged by the incarnation, that we are challenged by "permeable, transcorporeal, transpositional" grace that is the grace of I WILL BE/BECOME and not the fixed, permanent, religious location of I AM. As Bonhoeffer declares in his *Christology*: "Christ is Christ not as Christ in himself, but in his relation to me."[40]

This relational encounter is where religionless Christianity offers the challenge both of and to the *flaneur* (for any challenge does privilege the *flaneur* in himself). The challenge occurs because religionless Christianity is also relational Christianity: it is a Christianity where the Christ, where God, where grace is not found in place but in relationship. For God in Christ and the gift of grace are found in challenge and in encounter in the present and not in the past. They are experienced as an offer in the here and now of each individual and not separated off to be sought in the "over there." They are experienced as an offer in the relations in this location, not as primarily in the relations of that location left behind. For the challenge of the incarnation is that of the challenge of God who is to be *continually* misread, misunderstood, disputed, ignored, challenged and dismissed – even by those who claim to follow and know "him." As such a reading strategy of mis-reading may paradoxically open the *flaneur* to the possibilities of encounter. The *flaneur* is, therefore, a response out of the possibilities offered by the three-fold challenge of the incarnation. This possibility exists because the challenge of the incarnation is that God in Christ confounds and confutes our expectation as to his location and action. This possibility exists because God in Christ confounds and confutes our expectation as to his association and relations. This possibility exists because God in Christ is one who stands against the religion we proclaim in his name more than he supports it.

The *flaneur* and the Bible

To understand the challenge of the *flaneur* we need to remember that *flanerie* is a response that arises out of a particular reading strategy of both the texts and cities of our Modern world. Too often, I fear, we have made the Bible a Baedeker to God. That is, we uncritically make the Bible a book of the "site and sights of God." In this manner we use it as a guidebook to Christ as Christ was once viewed. We undertake a form of literal reading whereby Christ and text are always primarily located as a form of report and encounter within the biblical world. In such a reading our contemporary world becomes the biblical world by default. On the other hand, we read the Bible in a manner whereby the biblical world becomes our contemporary world by default. These ways of reading could be broadly expressed as the populist readings undertaken by theological conservatives (the first) and theological liberals (the second). In the first the problem becomes the contemporary world and in the second the problem becomes the biblical world. Both seek a form of permanence that situates either past or present as truly authentic. One result is that both liberals and conservatives find themselves in opposition to the radical theology expressed by the *flaneur*. For both forms of reading, I would argue, are limitations of the authentic Christ. Both conservatives and liberals too often seek to limit and avert our gaze and our experience with theologies that either idolize the biblical past or the cultural present. Such theological reading strategies as undertaken by both sides are too often a rejection of the radical dis-location of the gospel. Both conservatives and liberals, in their rejection of the radical position, seek to limit the *flaneur*.

The tourist, the traveller and the exile are not *flaneurs*. They exist with a purpose that is already delineated and constrained by their experience, expectation and memory. The *flaneur* wanders the city *against* the flow of tourist and traveller, perhaps moving amongst the exiles but not possessing their sense of longing for what is deemed irretrievably lost. What makes the *flaneur* radical is, in fact, their continual openness to the disruptive possibilities of grace. For the *flaneur*, grace is more often than not encountered, fleetingly, as that which disrupts and challenges the position of the *flaneur*. For grace is what keeps us dis-located and yet, paradoxically, provides a location of relationship. And yet such a relationship is always in reference to that relationship that occurs first within Godself, in the relationality of the Trinity and is then extended, via Christ to humanity. Trinitarian grace is thus the disruptive corrective that is encountered *in* the *saeculum* that provides a new location of identity *within* the *saeculum*. Grace and Christianity for the radical *flaneur* is, by necessity, secular and religionless.

The *flaneur* of religionless Christianity must, of course, heed the Bible as the record of the encounter with God. But the *flaneur* is also aware that the Bible continually reminds us that God encounters humanity more often outside of religion, religious institutions and religious expectations than within them. In response, the theological *flaneur* wanders through the text as well as the world. But, crucially, the *flaneur* wanders in openness to those Zizekian "short-circuit readings" that occur both in the biblical text and in the *saeculum* of the world in which we wander. This openness is what makes the *flaneur* radical in opposition to either the conservative or the liberal. For to respond only to the incarnation in the biblical text is to turn the Bible into the *Baedeker* of a world lost, a guidebook to an ancient world of which we see only the ruins of today. Conversely, to respond only to what is claimed to be the expression of the incarnation in the world today is to turn the world into only a map of the now; it is a world without a past – nor a future. It is a presentism that takes "me" as the endpoint of history and as the focus of grace and revelation.

The challenge is to remember that it is religionless *Christianity* that challenges the theological *flaneur*, not just religionless theology, or even religionless religion. Of course, in the tradition of *flanerie*, the *flaneur* is open to these possibilities. He will even *flaneur* in and amongst them (even if somewhat wilfully against their general flow), observing, noting and analysing. Yet for religionless Christianity, the challenge always comes back to the incarnation that makes Christianity "*Christ*ianity." The religionless challenge of the incarnation is firstly that it occurred and occurs within humanity and not institutions; secondly, that it occurs in humanity and not religion; and, thirdly, and perhaps the most challenging part of the incarnation is that it occurs within humanity that misunderstands and dismisses what has occurred. For humanity looks still for religion, God and the sacred to be what they (humanity) want it to be, and what they want it to be *seen* to be. This occurs because of their variety of *Baedekers* that prescribe their views, expectations and encounters so as to guarantee satisfaction.

That said, both religionless theology and religionless religion do occur in response to religionless Christianity. Religionless theology is the God-talk that derives from the experience of religionless Christianity. The distinction of religionless theology is that it *is* theology, a God-talk that talks of a God encountered *not* as religion would wish. A religionless theology is a theology of absence if viewed from the perspective of religion. It talks of the God in Christ who is encountered in absence from religion, in absence from our expectations, in absence from where we seek presence. The distinction of religionless religion is the *religare* that occurs outside of the institutions and the institutional study of religion. Religionless religion occurs in those ties, those bindings together that are dismissed as variously non-religious, as secular, as profane by all those wishing, demanding or needing to control religion as Religion. Furthermore, we need to remember that the religionless approach is not only a textual production that occurs in the midst of existing discourses.[41] For the religionless approach also challenges the religion of text and discourse which too often can reduce Christology to an affirmative mirror of the contemporary, located and locational now.

Response, Not "Belief"

The mode of response *versus* belief is laid down by Gianni Vattimo's notion of *The Age of Interpretation*. A religionless theology of response occurs in and out of a Christianity that has reached a maturity whereby hermeneutics (via Nietzsche and Heidegger) is "the development and maturation of the Christian message."[42] Following Vattimo, this means that Christianity in a secular society is not a case of belief but rather a situation of response/interpretation. Interpretation positions itself against the institutionalization of religion that demands belief as a mark of acceptance and control. Belief for religion and institutions sets boundaries that are to be enforced. They serve to limit and exclude the *flaneur*, for the *flaneur* is someone who undertakes constant interpretation.

There is the recognition in Vattimo's position that, without the legacy of Christianity, we cannot understand our contemporary western society. Because of the Christian revelation we cannot make sense of either our historical existence or our culture in its broadest sense "if we were to remove Christianity from it."[43] But this legacy, expressed and engaged within a secular context, separates us off, by necessity from those who prefer still to perceive the world through a religious and institutional lens. Vattimo's *Age of Interpretation* is indeed part of a religionless theology of response conceived in terms of interpretation that challenges belief in a religion. Vattimo views such a position as continuing the democratic legacy of the Enlightenment and, I would add, is very similar, in intention at least, to Rowan Williams' claim to the necessity of acting intelligibly. This religionless theology of response and interpretation situates itself against authoritarianism. Vattimo advises against the prospect of viewing religions as belief, declaring that: "In general, a democratic regime needs a non-objective-metaphysical conception of truth; otherwise it immediately becomes an authoritarian regime."[44]

What is important for the secular, modern West is its often forgotten history of theology as the location of opposition to authoritarian and *Volkgeist* claims of truth. Or, to put this point another way, Christianity as *flanerie* (as opposed to Christendom) is "a historical message of salvation"[45] that is *responded to*, not *believed in*. The Christian *flaneur* (and by necessity the religionless theologian) is one who responds and interprets, not one who 'believes in'. The reasoning behind such a posture is because to 'believe in' is a reductionist position. It results in claims of objective religion and truth that need to be either proved or disproved. Secular society in its elimination of public belief builds on Christianity versus Christendom – and indeed all public religions. A secular religionless theology is that which, in and for the West, recognizes the centrality of Christianity within western culture, but a Christianity that cannot and should not be confused with authoritarianism or Christendom.

We can now start to outline a four-fold proposition of what appears to be involved in raising the possibility of a religionless Christology. The provisional nature of what follows is intentional given that it is based in Vattimo's notion of the *Age of Interpretation*. As an interpretative response it situates itself against the structure and authoritative clarity of belief.

A religionless Christology is a Christology that is in response to the incarnation but is not one that "believes" in such a set of doctrinal claims. A religionless Christology is a Christology that is in response to the gift of grace, but is not one that believes in such. A religionless Christology is a Christology that is in response to the resurrection but is not one that believes in this confession. A religionless Christology is a Christology that is in response to the offer of salvation but is not one that believes in this core claim. A religionless Christology is, therefore, the attempt to respond without belief. As a type of *flanerie*, it involves wandering without aim but in expectation, open to both challenge and disappointment.

Perhaps the model for religionless Christianity as a type of *flanerie* is actually provided by the *Baedeker*. In encountering the *Baedeker* we make a response. We use it as a guide: as that which alerts us to what is of note, as that which, as a compendium of prior knowledge and experience enables a fuller participation, a fuller *flanerie* with the place under observation. But we do not believe in the *Baedeker*; we do not hold the *Baedeker* up as normative truth and see *only* what it prescribes – nor *only* in the way in which it demands we see. We know that any guide is indeed that of a past time. It is the expression of another's seeing and noting. This is not to dismiss its authority or claim upon our participation; it is to recognize that what it presents is always encountered through a process of interpretation. In using the *Baedeker* we also acknowledge that things change over time, even in the time that exists between the production of the guide and our undertaking to use that guide to inform our experience. In that sense we do not believe in it but, rather, we respond to what it offers. Of course, some of what it offers will still be valid. Some of what it offers will enable the participation with place that is essentially timeless. However, the use of the guide is that of response in expectation. To believe in the guide is to privilege what *was* over what *is*. To believe in the guide is to have our impressions already formed in advance, to formulate and delineate participation and experience prior to the encounter. What the guide offers is, instead, often a challenge to what we may have seen, a challenge to what we think we see and experience, a challenge to what we thought was important and of note. To properly use the guide is to undertake the hermeneutic between guide and place that reads each out of and through the other.

A religionless Christianity is, then, cast in a form that is a response *to* the challenge of Christianity, the challenge of the incarnation, the challenge of Christ, the challenge of the gift of grace. To believe in Christianity, to believe in the incarnation, to believe in the Christ, to believe in grace is to seek to variously mediate, control, delineate and contain them within a series of prior expectations and experiences. Religionless Christianity is the Christianity undertaken by the *flaneur*. That the *flaneur* goes in and against the crowds, that the *flaneur* wanders, in effect, without aim open to constant challenge and new ways of seeing and participation means that the *flaneur* does not believe but instead experiences. Of course, the *flaneur* does not venture forth as a *tabula rasa*. Vattimo noted that such interpretation is part of making sense of what it means to live in western secular society built on a Christian event-legacy. Furthermore, the *flaneur* is only able to venture, to participate, because they have become aware of the need to do so, of the demand to do so.

To *flaneur* is to respond to the challenge of the world in which we live. It is undertaken as response to the challenge to what we expect to be, of what we expect to see, of what we expect to find. The *flaneur*, in that form, ventures forth in expectation and in response, but without belief. She ventures forth open to the world, open to humanity and open to the *saeculum* in which, theologically speaking, we are challenged by the incarnation. The openness of the *flaneur* is the constant reminder that being in this *saeculum* is the only place we can respond without the reduction into religion and into belief. The *flaneur* wanders in opposition to the retreat of the containment of the literal reading of the guidebook and the mediated, contained security of the tour party. Such positions which make the experience a function of the expectations of the tour party: you see and experience what has already been determined as worthy, important and of note. A religionless Christianity is thus a Christianity that stands in opposition to the expectations and security of belief and belonging.

It is also important to remember that religionless Christianity is not only a response to the incarnation; it is also a response to the resurrection. Too often it can appear as if attempts to express religionless Christianity only respond to the incarnation. Often the focus in religionless Christianity is concerned with a kenotic incarnation. Yet in the kenotic model, that model of God emptying Godself out into the world, there is a tendency to downplay or even dismiss the resurrection. Kenosis serves to locate Christ with us while the resurrection can be seen as that which works against this location in humanity of the incarnation. In one possible reading, the resurrection becomes seen as a return to the transcendent Godhead and the subsequent separation again of humanity and God. The resurrection is, in fact, crucial for religionless Christianity because it is a reminder that the kenosis is not the end of the Christ. The resurrection is the reminder of the centrality of the cross for any *cross*-cultural theology. It is a reminder that the death of Christ is not just the death of both humanity and God – in that in Christ we are confronted with he who is fully human and fully divine. The resurrection is the challenge that the crossing of the separation of humanity from God, by an act of divine self-giving, does not end with the death. The resurrection is the challenge of grace and Christ in his entirety – fully human and fully divine – and who is resurrected, who does begin anew. And, more so, this resurrection is not out of this world, but into this world. We have a tendency in the modern world to downplay the narrative of the resurrection and especially that of the post-resurrection encounter of Christ and humanity. In a half-thought, reductionist modernity, we are happier with the kenotic model where either the death of Christ is the death of God, or that the self-emptying is now into humanity. But such a reductionist modernity is actually the polar opposite to the challenge in response to grace of religionless Christianity. It is merely the perpetuation of religion over and against the challenge of Christianity. The religious self-divination of humanity merely seeks to make "I" the new "I AM." This is the creation of a new religion: the religion of self, the worship of humanity as the sight and site of the divine–human encounter.

The challenge of the "I WILL BE/BECOME" is a challenge to both the kenotic "I AM" or the further reduction into the "I WAS." The God who is "I WILL BE/BECOME" is the God who, in Christ, is resurrected. This is the resurrection that resurrects the closing of the gap between humanity and God. Yet this resurrection locates it still only within the Christ and not as either a reduction into death or as kenosis into humanity. The resurrected "I WILL BE/BECOME" Christ is a Christ who is the expression of the promise of "I WILL BE/BECOME." The resurrected "I WILL BE/BECOME" Christ is a Christ who is resurrected *back into* that world from which he was Exiled by death.

If we turn to the post-resurrection narratives, we are reminded that the resurrected Christ did not seek to flee from this world; neither did he permanently locate himself here. The *saeculum* becomes the place of glimpsed and fragmentary encounter with a Christ who *flaneurs*. In the post-resurrection narratives we are reminded that the resurrected Christ is on the move – and commands his followers to move. The resurrected Christ appears where and when he is least expected – and is still not fully understood. The same is true of the challenge of the Spirit who continues the "I WILL BE/BECOME" encounter with humanity. Just as with the

Christ, the encounter is *in* this world that is the *saeculum*. Both Christ and Spirit initiate encounters of challenge and critique.

In rethinking what a secular or religionless Christianity reveals, we become aware that the challenge of "I WILL BE/BECOME" is that God is perhaps the original *flaneur*. God continuously moves in and against the crowds and generic expectations and expressions of humanity. God, as the original *flaneur*, is observing, interacting, critiquing and experiencing. This is God who is opposed to and who moves counter to human aims and expectations. For just as the *flaneur* is dismissed as aimless by those who seek security and order, so too does God as *flaneur* move against human aims of security and order. Our retreat into religion and authoritative institutions is the attempt to halt the *flanerie* of God. They are our attempts to locate, control and prescribe the movements of God. In opposition to such attempts to limit God, religionless Christianity is a response of *flanerie*. Responding to God who is the original *flaneur*, the religionless Christian *flaneur* moves against the crowds of expectation and religion. She is a *flaneur* who moves through texts just as the *Logos* moves as words. For religionless Christianity responds to an incarnation that continues as challenge amongst the texts of the *saeculum*.

The Incarnational Text of God, the Original *flaneur*

The question of textual incarnation first occurred in response to the Logos-text of the Bible. In re-raising this question in this particular discussion, I recognize that I am yet again stepping outside the boundaries of institutional belief. Yet being a theological *flaneur* means that I am often wandering in opposition to the order and control of the majority. The challenge of theological *flaneur* involves raising the question of response regarding textual incarnation. If we claim that we encounter the Logos in the Bible-text, then why are we afraid of responding to it as incarnational presence? Were there no incarnation there would be no possibility of encountering the Logos in the words. Because this revelation of Logos occurs in the Logos-text of the Bible, it also occurs in the *saeculum*. For the Bible is a text in and of the *saeculum*. The Christological incarnation was the overcoming of separation by God in Christ to encounter humanity in the *saeculum*. Here and now, in the Logos-text, we have the overcoming of separation by God in Logos to encounter humanity in the *saeculum*. Yet this presence and encounter occurs in a universal availability through the act of mechanical reproduction. It was the invention of the printing press and the resulting widespread vernacular Bibles that enabled the mass production and mass consumption of the Logos-text. It meant that the text of salvation became a commodity able to be bought and sold.

To be able to purchase the text of salvation, however – to be able to purchase the Logos/logos revelation of God, raises questions of authenticity and originality. Firstly, amidst the plethora of Bibles available, what text, what words, whose words, whose texts, whose reading has the original and authentic Logos-event? To what degree can variation represent or express the original and authentic Logos-event? Even within a particular language, such as English, the variety of translations and subsequent texts means there is not a singular English-language Bible. What we are confronted with instead is a variety of translations and texts that are the creation of competing scholars and theological positions. Churches and individuals choose a translation and edition of the Logos-text that confirms their own particular theological and cultural position. The Logos-text is in some cases liberal and in other cases conservative. It is inclusive in its language or exclusive. It exists in the poetic language of past ages and in the plain speaking of the barely literate. Some texts highlight certain passages as theologically important, while others do not. Some texts provide detailed commentary in footnotes while others do not. A Roman Catholic text will contain more books within it than a Protestant Bible. In short, the Bible itself, as singular Logos-text is, in reality, a form of hyper-reality.

If we consider the universal offer of grace that sits at the centre of Christianity, then this plurality does not become a problem. We recognize that the universal offer is offered via the universal text, which exists as texts. Rather, the problem occurs when the universal text itself becomes, within communities, a singular text of religion. Here the text in its particular expression becomes itself the expression of that particular community, rather than the corrective challenge to that community. For the Logos-text is not the expression of humanity. It is rather that which is addressed to humanity in the *saeculum* as corrective and challenge. But, because it is not a text that refers merely to past events, but a text that makes the Logos present to us in our here and now, it requires interpretation. In short, the *saeculum* in itself is the demand of the *Age of Interpretation*, a demand that originates from God. A religionless Christianity is a secular Christianity that, in response to God, undertakes a reading of response by interpretation. For the Logos-text is, for Christians, addressed to all people in all times. Without interpretation it becomes the imposition of biblical textual time as normative and prescriptive. God becomes literally captured by the text. The interpretative reading is a response that frees God from our particular literal expectations of how God should be. The interpretive response frees God to be once again *flaneur* between text and humanity. God as original *flaneur* forces an encounter between text and humanity within the *saeculum* and is not separated off in sectarian piety and institutional religion. For the interpretative response frees the *flaneur* God to continue as I WILL BE/BECOME and ends the reductive, religious capture of God as I AM.

The freedom of the text of the *flaneur* God within the *saeculum* now raises new possibilities of response. What happens when the text of the incarnated God (text as both location and record of textual Logos revelation) can be purchased and read not as truth but as text? This is the response that Vattimo refers to as being initiated by the *Age of Interpretation*. That occurs when the reader secularizes this text by the act of a particular reading strategy: it is then read as a cultural and literary document and not as religious text. As we have seen, to read the Bible as a cultural and literary document, as a text addressed to and within the *saeculum*, is a reading strategy that frees it from the limitations of being a religious text. This is because to read the text from the position of the *flaneur* is to situate oneself firstly in response to the God who is the original *flaneur*.

Underlying these issues is the Benjaminesque question: To what, if any degree, does the act of mechanical reproduction limit the authenticity of the textual incarnation?

Walter Benjamin, German Jewish critic and philosopher of culture, asked the question of authenticity in a world of mass commodification in his seminal 1936 essay "The Work of Art in the Age of Mechanical Reproduction." Benjamin's concern was with originality. He claimed that what gives the work of art its authenticity is the aura of its singularity. That is, it cannot be reproduced except as a fake: "The presence of the original is the prerequisite to the concept of authenticity."[46] For Benjamin, the aura is that which stimulates a sense of wonder and reverence. The aura is the meaning that the original contains by virtue of its singularity, its one-offedness. Benjamin's identification of the singularity of the aura means that the copy is always a copy: it is a conscious fake and *is not* what was or is.

Benjamin's concern was with the role of technology upon the work of art. Specifically, his interest was with the impact of the photograph that enables a reproduction that separates the reproduced object from its location, tradition and authenticity. The central issue arises with the ability to make multiple replications of the original photograph. This is because the subsequent replicant photo is not a fake or a copy, but rather an image that is – but is not that which it represents. What we print off is not the original image and yet it is. With the photograph, uniqueness disappears. The possibilities of mechanical reproduction are those of mass replication. What you have is a multiplicity of images that exist without the aura. The nub of Benjamin's argument is as follows:

One might generalize by saying: the technique of reproduction detaches the reproduced object from the domain of tradition. By making many reproductions it substitutes a plurality of copies for a unique existence. And in permitting the reproduction to meet the beholder or listener in his own particular situation, it reactivates the object reproduced.[47]

As Benjamin states, "what is really jeopardized when the historical testimony is affected is the authority of the subject."[48]

There are implications here for our response to the textual encounter of the incarnation on two levels. The first is to remind us of the necessity of interpretation. Under Benjamin's guidance we can perceive the situation whereby we have the Word of God (*Logos*) contained within the Word of God (Bible) reproduced as words. We are made to reconsider what is meant by our Christian claims for authentic singularity. In our biblical texts we claim that we can encounter that *which is but is not*: the Logos in our own particular situation.

The challenge of the Word (*Logos*) as words in Word of God (Bible) returns us to the issue of the *Baedeker*. That is, do we use the Bible as a *Baedeker* to Christ? Are we too often like those tourists who limit their experience of what they seek by having their encounter prescribed and limited, directed and defined by the *Baedeker*? Such tourists respond to only that which the *Baedeker* defines as the located and expected site of response. The challenge to the tourist is to use the *Baedeker* as the guide to that which is responded to, not as that which is to be responded to. The challenge to the tourist is to use the *Baedeker* as a guide *to that* which is revealed, not *as that* which is revealed through the *Baedeker*. That is, we need to remember that the *Baedeker* is what points to what we think we see. The challenge of the *Baedeker* is to remember that it is, in the end, only a framing of our vision through the framing of another. Our response to what is seen is, therefore, a type of reading through the frame of *Baedeker*. If we act as biblical *Baedeker* tourists then we need to be reminded that we are reading through three frames: the frame of biblical text, a frame of Christian tradition – and the frame of the *saeculum*. The biblical *Baedeker* tourist should remember the necessity of Vattimo's *Age of Interpretation*. The multiplicity of reading frames means that the tourist's frame of encounter is not just a singularity, even though they may believe it is. Rather, the multiplicity of frames results in a type of liminal response. It is to return to the liminality experienced by Turner's expression of frontier knowledge. Such a liminal frame occurs as that inexpressible liminality which is experienced and responded to as variously the border between, the boundary through, the neither here nor there, the negative presence, the presence of no-thingness. As such it is similar to the frame of a painting, as Taylor states:

> The frame as such does not exist; nor is it non-existent. Its site, which is really a non-site, is the neither-nor of the between...the frame works by allowing appearances to appear, representations to be represented, and images to be imagined... [It is] the condition of the possibility of presentation.[49]

The frame is the liminal boundary. The frame is what has no meaning except in the act of perception. For perception is an act of response that simultaneously includes the perception of the frame and the perception of what is created by the act of framing. It is therefore a challenge and response originating in Bonhoeffer's Christology where Christ is the one who is between I and I, who is the liminal centre of our being. And yet Christ, being liminal, sits on the boundary of our expectation. This is Christ who Bonhoeffer expresses as *pro me* – that is, standing:

> on the boundary of my existence, beyond my existence, but still me... Here Christ stands, in the centre, between me and myself, between the old existence and the new. So Christ is at the same time my own boundary and my rediscovered centre, the centre lying both between "I" and "I" and between "I" and God.[50]

The framing of response is thus both one of Christ and by Christ. We do not believe in the frame, but respond to that which is framed and to the act of framing.

Conclusion

If we return to the trope of the *flaneur*, it becomes apparent they are the ones who move in opposition to those who seek to use the *Baedeker/Bible* as limitation and full expression of the site (and sight) of encounter. The *flaneur*, in comparison, seeks to create their own texts and framings out of a continual series of reframings in response to the challenge of existence. The *flaneur* seeks to create her texts and framings in both response and in opposition to what is expected, presented and encountered by most as expected, offered and regulated. The frame of vision, the frame of encounter, is, for the *flaneur*, one of a response to the anticipation of the challenge of grace. The *flaneur* wanders textually and physically in anticipation of the unusual and the unexpected, the anticipation that originates in the rejection of the domestication of grace. The *flaneur* responds against the prescribed, expected and controlled revelation and encounter of religion and belief.

What is framed in religionless Christianity is both the *flaneur* and his response to God in Christ encountered in – but against – humanity. God in Christ is the original *flaneur* in the *saeculum*: in the human world – yet not of it. The *flaneur* Christ who is continually on the move, the Logos

Christ as words that are re-authored and re-read in every encounter. For the *flaneur*, the Logos Christ is not believed in, but responded to. The Logos Christ is not found in the crowd, but against it. The Logos Christ is liminal and glimpsed in the act of framing, yet also is an act of framing that conversely reframes those using the frame. In other words, our response to the framing of Christ is that which in turn frames us for God.

The secular, religionless Christology that is responded to is thus a Christology that demands a response, but rejects belief. Such a Christology involves dislocation, not location. It is a Christology that is to be responded to within – but against – the expectations and experiences of the crowds of the secular world. A secular, religionless Christology is only glimpsed; it is not a Christology that is defined and prescribed.

Religionless Christianity is the response of those who *flaneur* through both built and written texts of the *saeculum*, framing and being framed by the Logos Christ. Such *flaneurs* are open to the possibility and challenge of the I WILL BE/BECOME and not seeking the sectarian withdrawal into the I AM of the tourist, the traveller or the exile. The *flaneur* as religionless Christian is the one who does not believe but the one who responds, who does not worship but who encounters, who does not seek grace but is challenged by it. The *flaneur* as religionless Christian is continually wandering without aim, yet is open to that world through which and against which they wander – the *saeculum* where the liminal Christ is and is not.

The tourist, the traveller, the exile all seek to believe in what is not where they are. Their problem is that they retreat from, they search for, they mourn the loss of what is actually here where they are all the time – and yet is not. What blinds their vision, what constricts their sight, what limits their encounter is that *Baedeker*/Bible of religion – the religion of the Baal of the I AM.

The *flaneur* in response to the continual challenge of the I WILL BE/ BECOME responds to that which is/is not here where we are now. The *flaneur* ventures forth with indiscipline into the frontier of the now, into the frontier of the *saeculum*. He ventures with indiscipline into that frontier which the domestication of religion serves to act as refuge against. It is on that secular Emmaus road that the *flaneur* encounters him who we do not recognize…and who disappears when we do.[51]

Conclusion

This text is a radically different one to that which I first set out to write, itself an example of what is involved in the disruption and dis-location of undertaking *flanerie* knowledge. The text is also different from the one envisaged when I actually began writing. All texts, of course, take on their own internal dialectic and hermeneutic, and my work has sharply raised the question for me as to what degree this process is constrained by what the author desires to express.

Originally, this text was going to follow a well-worn formula. It was to be an engagement with the biblical material that configures with the ideas under consideration (in this case texts referring to tourism, travel, exile), followed by a history of tourism, travel and exile in Christianity, focusing amongst other things on the desert abbas and ammas, and on pilgrimage. I intended to follow this with a re-reading of tourism, travel, and exile from a postmodern perspective As I said, this was the original intention and yet obviously this has not been what you have read, as my studies forced me into new directions, pushing into areas I had initially attempted to keep peripheral. In fact, initially peripheral thought became central.

One key shift in focus related to the claims of Dietrich Bonhoeffer. This was not only a response to his well-known calls for a religionless Christianity in his *Letters and Papers from Prison*, but also, perhaps even more centrally, a response to his dialectic Christology. This is to be found in his *Christology* that was posthumously derived, edited and reworked from lecture notes kept by his students. A second challenge emerged from an alternative reading of the name of God: reading it as I WILL BE/ BECOME instead of the traditional I AM. For me, the possibilities and challenges raised by Bonhoeffer and the radical rethinking demanded by the re-naming of God were increasingly engaged in a dialectic that demanded a refocusing of this text. It became apparent that to write the original text would in fact be to conform to and confirm that which Bonhoeffer had challenged! It would be to conform to and confirm that which the alternative reading of the name of God confronted; that is, it would merely serve as a continuation of the religion of Christianity. In turn, this not only forced a re-evaluation of the three original tropes I had proposed, it also made clear the demand to move on from what I now saw as the still religious stance of the exile. Then I became aware of the possibilities offered by what became the continual undercurrent (and indeed counter-current) of the trope of the *flaneur*, who refused to be limited by the constraints of the original tropes of tourist, traveller and exile.

In particular, the *flaneur* seemed to open up the possibility of moving on from the backward-looking longing of the exile. To stop with the exile and so to locate Christianity in nostalgia seemed to me to be as limiting as locating its reality elsewhere, as the tourist and traveller do. In short, all three tropes perpetuate the continuation of both Christianity as religion and the religion of Christianity. Such linking of Christianity and religion increasingly seeks a withdrawal from the western, urban, secular world. As modern western tropes of the Christian religion, they increasingly seek forms of withdrawal either into contextual theologies that arise elsewhere, or into forms of sectarian, pietistic retreat and nostalgic longing. In contest to such withdrawals, the *flaneur* seems to offer a way forward past nostalgic longing and the self-limiting lack of hope that marks the exile. What disturbed me about all three initial tropes was the concern that originally set me off on this path of textual discovery, away from a concentration on biblical texts and away from a focus on the history of Christian piety and movement. What became central to me were the issues of location of authenticity in my western, secular modern culture.

The challenge of the *flaneur* was to be found in his determination to find a fleeting authenticity in the *midst* of that viewed by so many in the modern world as the most inauthentic location: the crowds and environment of modern urban experience. As a modern, urban way of being, the *flaneur* as a trope seemed to echo the challenge of Bonhoeffer: where and how is that which is most authentic to be experienced and expressed today? Where and how is the fleeting experience of grace to be found in a world seemingly denied this possibility?

As I became aware of the need to respond to the challenge that was raised in different ways by both the *flaneur* and by Bonhoeffer, I was challenged to find a way forward and not just a way back, to search for an alternative to the turning back of the tourist, traveller or exile. I needed an alternative that did not retreat into biblical texts and the texts of Christian history and piety, but that attempted to express the liminal, fleeting experience of grace in the midst of what is all too often viewed as inauthentic. Here, the challenge of re-reading the self-revelation of the divine name pushed me onwards. The more I read secular texts on tourism, travel and exile, the more it seemed that they were based on either the pursuit of, or the pursuit of the replacement for, the static authenticity of the I AM. That is, they were based on the pursuit of the I AM who was increasingly viewed as I WAS. Such an authenticity was seemingly only really approachable in the authentic otherness of dislocation from where we now are. And such an authenticity was apparently only approachable via two strategies. The first was seen as only physically approachable when you relocate to another culture, a non-western one. The second involved an approach to the Bible which posited the most authentic encounter as back in fabled biblical times or, likewise textually, in the early centuries of Christianity in the works of the desert abbas and ammas. Both approaches viewed authenticity as something irrevocably lost or distant from the modern, secular, urban world of the West. Such claims of inauthenticity face major challenges from the work of Bonhoeffer and the associated work of theologians such as Harvey Cox in *The Secular City* and, more recently, Graham Ward's provocative *Cities of God*. Cox's work from the 1960s was of course contemporaneous with that of the death of God theologians, and so I became interested in why their engagement with late modernity seemed all of a sudden to collapse. I was intrigued to discover that many of them in fact had a neo-orthodox background. Furthermore, their struggles with the issues of the presence and experience of God in *urban* modernity were forced through an encounter and an engagement with not only the work of Bonhoeffer, but also that of Karl Barth. My particular studies of the death of God scene also occurred in a dialectical engagement with the writings and architecture of Adolf Loos and Mies van der Rohe – and indeed the whole religious aspect of modernist architecture, where we can see the emergence over the last few years of a re-engaged modernity. In architecture and its theory, there has been a return of modernity after postmodernity, with modernity experienced *after* postmodern pluralism and relativizing. In making the connection with architecture, I recognized a need to turn again to the questions posed by modern theology: how do we see and seek grace in the location we now live? What is the self-revelation of God in the modern, western, urban, secular world? Such questions remain important because modern life is still experienced architecturally in environments that express the central secular challenges of modernity.

Over the past forty years, it seems that most western theologians have increasingly rejected any real possibility of grace and revelation in the environments that they now live. What I mean by this is a turn away from a modern, western, urban, secular environment. On the one hand there is often the turn to contextual theology which is almost always a turn to those theologies representative of another (increasingly any other) context. These contexts are now viewed as being the location(s) of that which is now authentic. This has of course provided a necessary corrective to the hegemonic imposition of a particular western theology. However, it threatens to become a new hegemony from the other. It can be linked into the subtext of increasingly viewing *another* (increasingly *any* other) context as *more* authentic than the western, urban, modern, secular environment. And I would argue that such a turn is just another manifestation of what in New Zealand is called the cultural cringe: a belief that the real, the authentic and that which is important can never really be experienced here. Rather that it is only somewhere over there that the authentic resides. To experience "it" over there is more real, more important and more authentic than experiencing "it" where you are. In fact "it" can never be really, truly experienced here. To do so, one has to shift to the place of the real, to the location of the authentic.

I would argue that in theology the turn to the cultural cringe has often been done out of all the best post-colonial motives. But, in fact, it involves a form of essentialist, Rousseauean inversion that objectifies the authentic other (whether location, experience or theological claim) by increasingly uncritically rejecting the claims of the theologian's own culture and experience. It involves, in effect, a naïve form of theological essentialist anthropology. In the theologian's case, the view is, it seems, that God and grace are elsewhere and can only be experienced in a form of post-colonial simulacra (which may still be tied to a colonial mind-frame). In terms of my own work, this perception presented a strong challenge to the tropes of tourist, traveller and exile, forcing a radical rethinking of what I was initially attempting to say. In this, the turn to the *flaneur* was, it seemed, the least of my problems! For if I was to claim the necessity and importance of the *flaneur* as a theological trope then I had to wrestle with the question of what it was that he glimpsed in and amongst the crowds (and I admit that the *flaneur* seems to primarily be a masculine identity/activity). In particular, I found myself challenged by the issue of a Christology of and for the *flaneur:* a Christology of and for religionless Christianity.

Positioning this theological approach in relation to a particular context is what makes my work a form of contextual theology. Like many understandings of contextual theology, I see my approach as at the same time provisional and attempting to express the universal nature of Christian theology. On the one hand, I can only write theology out of my particular context, which can only ever provide a partial perspective. On the other hand, the universal claim of Christianity leads much theology into expressions of certain norms. This tension sits at the centre of every attempt to undertake *cross*-cultural theology, for the Christian response is to the cross that includes and transcends all cultures. Yet grace may be encountered in the tension.

My constant wrestling with these issues led me to the trope of the *flaneur*. The possibility offered by the *flaneur* for theology occurs because he travels through the modern, western secular urban environment, more often than not *against* the crowd, glimpsing grace. I have placed the intertextual hermeneutic of this text under the trope of the *flaneur* because in the re-reading strategy he suggests, the entire world is a text, or rather a variety of texts through which, in a logocentric approach, the Logos can potentially be read. The *flaneur* is a challenge in that he reads by glimpsing – and glimpses in his reading, with the aimlessness of the *flaneur*'s wandering that allows the encounter(s) to occur. I realized that my wandering through the texts of tourism, travel, exile and the *flaneur* was itself a type of *flanerie*. For as I read I seemed to be challenged by an elusive sense that these texts could be re-read as variously talking about, referring to and critiquing religion. In short they could be re-read as a form of theological critique.

On the one hand this reading strategy of the *flaneur* echoes the fundamental Marxist critique that "the criticism of religion is the prerequisite of all criticism."[1] Yet it is also part of a wider logocentrism where the Logos hides itself and locates itself in words as presence/absence. The two approaches are connected in their foundational linking of religion and words. My starting point is a re-reading of the prologue of John's gospel: The Logos is that which sits within and behind all logos. This premise is linked into the notion of the *saeculum* in that the encounter with the Logos might be termed secular theology. Crucially, that secular theology is, via the Logos, the basis of religionless Christianity: a Christianity of the modern, western, urban, secular world. This reading strategy of the theological *flaneur* resulted in a work of contextual theology. However, this is a type of contextual theology in which the context is secular texts (primarily) in which and out of which theology is written and grace is glimpsed and potentially experienced. In this approach two experiences inform each other: wandering the streets and wandering the texts of my contemporary western secular, urban environment so as to pursue, indirectly, the possibility of grace.

Central to this approach is the acknowledgment that it only ever involves the possibility of grace. Possibility is the crucial element of this kind of a contextual theology: a possibility that is to be found in a God who is I WILL BE/BECOME, not as I AM with its static locatedness and claims of definite presence. Like the *flaneur*, having wandered into the possibility of grace is only ever recognized in retrospect: after the event, after the encounter, after the challenge or after the glimpse. This is why the *flaneur* responds to what I have termed the Emmaus Christ: the Christ who is not recognized when present – and when he is recognized, disappears. In other words the *flaneur* responds to a Christ of presence/absence. This Christ *flaneurs* through the modern, western, secular, urban world as well as the "more authentic" (to so many) non-western contexts.

As previously mentioned, Gianni Vattimo presented what I would term the central issue of the theological *flaneur*:

> [T]he religious problem seems to be always the recovery of an experience that one has somehow already had. None of us in our western culture – and perhaps not in any culture – begins from zero with the question of religious faith.[2]

Vattimo's claim is that none of us can move in western culture, can read in western culture or can experience life in western culture without actually encountering the challenge of the Judeo-Christian legacy that has shaped and continues to shape that culture. This claim still holds even if the legacy is articulated and expressed in the repudiation of the Judeo-Christian message – either implicitly or explicitly. A problem of the past half century, though, is that too often theology, or more precisely contextual theology, gives up on western culture as the sight and site of an encounter with grace, rejecting western culture as an authentic location in which to undertake theological reflection. Oftentimes, secular society is viewed as a society in which grace is absent, or that God has rejected because that society seems to have rejected God. Such a belief means that theologically it can appear that we not only attempt to begin from zero, but also can only ever achieve zero – that is nothing and nothingness – in our western, urban, secular context. It is crucial, therefore, to remember that the challenge of the death of God movement was the challenge to an age critically *within* that context. Yet the challenge the death of God theologians put forward was largely rejected because it pointed to the demand for a religionless Christianity in western, urban locations and experience. It invited a turn to become theological *flaneurs*: glimpsing, often only in retrospect, the possibility of grace, being open to the paradoxical possibility of presence in absence and absence in presence. It also, perhaps most challengingly, forced the religionless Christian to become other to themselves as Christian, and other to Christianity as religion.

And yet, sitting at the heart of the response of the religionless Christian and sitting at the heart of the approach of the western, urban, secular theological *flaneur* is a theology of the incarnation. Without the incarnation there is no possibility of grace, no possibility of the glimpse of grace and no possibility of the continuation of grace. Yet the theological *flaneur* responds to a God in Christ who moved as humanity amongst humanity, who was primarily not recognized as God in Christ until the moments of his absence. The theological *flaneur* proclaims that the incarnation is the starting point for any religionless Christianity and the starting point for any contextual theology of dislocation and movement, doing so in response to what has been first revealed by God in Christ. For the incarnation was God in Christ experienced as on the move and unrecognized, as only a glimpse of grace. As in Pasolini's film *The Gospel according to St Matthew*, Jesus is continually on the move: always talking, often glimpsed, seldom still and often not recognized. This happens because of Pasolini's reading of the gospel, translating its message of challenge into modernity. Likewise, in the gospels themselves, the response of faith is concerned with God in Christ who is seldom located and recognized. For the Christ of the gospels, as *flaneur*, is glimpsed by those who were not expecting to encounter him. He moves amongst, eats with and associates with those who inhabit transgressive contexts. He refuses to be limited by the expectations and impositions of culture, institutions or context. In response to the Christ who *flaneurs*, the message of Christianity is that every context is open to the encounter with Christ. The universal claim of Christ incarnated and resurrected is that which is revealed as a corrective to every contextual claim. For the universal corrective reminds us that whilst Christ can be encountered in any context he is not the Christ of any particular context over others. And yet we cannot respond contextually without responding via the Christ who includes all contexts within his liminal frontier of grace. The centrality of the incarnation for any attempt to respond contextually is forcibly expressed by Gianni Vattimo:

> Only in the light of the Christian doctrine of the incarnation of the Son of God does it seem possible for philosophy to think of itself as a reading of the signs of the times without this being reduced to a purely passive record of the times...[3]

As I noted in my section on the *flaneur*, the focus on the incarnation has often, it seems, been more on the pre-resurrection incarnation and a downplaying of the post-resurrection challenge. Yet it needs to be remembered that the gospels and the New Testament writings are a response not only to the pre-death incarnation, but primarily, to the post-resurrection experiences. For without the resurrection there is no gospel and there is no Christianity. All we have is yet another good man, yet another guru, yet again a failed messiah. Furthermore, a Christianity that downplays the resurrection is merely the false culture of the Christianity of the I AM as I WAS. What we have is not Christianity but another culture of Baal. This is, of course, often an affront to modern sensibilities, yet as Barth reminds us, "Christology deals with the revelation of God as a mystery. It must first of all be aware of this mystery and acknowledge it as such."[4]

This mystery is, I claim, one that challenges the reduction of God to Baal as is too often evidenced by the location of the misread I AM as "I AM not here now, but I AM over there now" – in short, the reduction of God to a Baal of place. This mystery challenges the way all too many contextual theologians dismiss western, urban, secular society, especially those located *within* that society. We need to be constantly reminded that the mystery of Christology is that the revelation of God continues even when and where we may not wish it to. As Barth further challenges those who seek the authentic other elsewhere:

> the ontological determination of all human beings is that Jesus is present among them as their divine Other, their Neighbour, Companion and Brother...[5]

It was this concern that drove the 1960s death of God theologians, and drives them still today. This was the concern of Bonhoeffer not only in his *Christology*, but also in his call for a religionless Christianity.

The challenge of secular theology arises out of three central concerns. Firstly, the concern is not to dismiss the possibility of an encounter of grace in western, secular, urban society. Secondly, it is not to reduce Christianity into religion. Thirdly, it is not to seek to relocate the mystery of grace as only (or even primarily) to be found elsewhere. As such, secular theology can be seen as a continuation of the biblical message that God continues to reveal Godself where humanity believes God shall not, God should not, and God could not. Secular theology views revelation in ways that challenge the Enlightenment reductionism that relocates Christianity as merely religion. In 1934, discussing the influence of Barth on early twentieth-century modernity, Emil Brunner paid this compliment:

> Today we struggle no longer, as we did fifteen years ago, concerning "religion," but concerning the "word of God"; no longer concerning the *deus in nobis*, but concerning the revelation in Jesus Christ. To put it briefly: no longer concerning the themes of the enlightenment but concerning the theme of the Bible itself.[6]

It is significant that some sixty years later, in a move signalling the return to a discussion of the issues raised by religionless Christianity, Gianni Vattimo proclaimed:

> All of us should claim the right not to be turned away from the truth of the Gospel in the name of a sacrifice of reason demanded only by a naturalistic human, all too human, ultimately unChristian, conception of God's transcendence.[7]

The challenge of the theological *flaneur* in western, secular, urban society is, then, to glimpse grace in the environment that has rejected transcendence, to glimpse grace in the environment that has constructed itself *as* the rejection of transcendence.

Vattimo challenges us to rethink a particular type of Christian pursuit, obsession and demand for the transcendence of God that makes us view our own location as inauthentic. The transcendence of culture revealed in Christ should never be confused with a view of the western, secular, urban culture and context as the *impossible* place for, and of the encounter with, that God we continue to wish to perceive and locate as transcendent. Secular Christianity seeks to respond to God in Christ who is transcendent and yet, by God's self-action, continually incarnated in encounter in the *saeculum*. For secular Christianity this means the challenge of the Emmaus Christ is that of the resurrected Christ who continues to be incarnated. Secular Christianity responds to the central message of the story of Thomas (John 20:24–29) where even those who doubt it experience the physicality of the resurrection. Of central importance for secular Christianity is the recognition that the physicality of the incarnation is continued because the physical resurrection is the rejection of a Gnostic belief in God as purely transcendent. Such recognition follows secular Christianity's insight that incarnation is God in Christ *in this world*, this world of the *saeculum*.

Today, in western urban society, we tend to become theological tourists, travellers or exiles, "believing" by *not believing* in the rejection of transcendence as revealed in the incarnation and the resurrection. We desire transcendence because it fits our religious view of God, and in doing so we reject God in Christ who has rejected transcendence to be with us, to be among us in our here and now. Our problem is that we turn our back on the Emmaus Christ of our own context and go in pursuit of transcendent Christs. We mistakenly pursue the false transcendent Christs of the religion of Baal we believe to be (increasingly) only found elsewhere – either physically in another location, or historically, in the past of traditions and text. In undertaking such a false pursuit, our Bible is misread as a *Baedeker* to elsewhere and in doing so we reject its challenge both of and for our own context.

Barth of course signalled a return to the transcendence of God. But this, I argue, occurred as the only way to signal the rejection of the locatedness, that is the Baal, of Christianity as religion that he found himself confronting in the early twentieth century. Yet, it must also be recognized that central to Barth (and to all those who followed him whether as neo-orthodox theologians, secular theologians, or death of God theologians) is the overcoming of that transcendence by an act of God – but not by any act of humanity. That is, the overcoming of God's transcendence occurs by God's self action in the incarnation. What can occur in the turn towards contextual theologies of other places, other contexts, other cultures or other locations by western, urban Christians is precisely the rejection of these moves. In doing so, they unfortunately reject a move firstly made by God, as well as rejecting an acknowledgment of God's transcendence and self-overcoming as recognized by Barth and those who followed him. For the radical challenge of the reaffirmation of the neo-orthodox position was that God in Christ is incarnated in the here and now, in our western, secular urban here and now. Furthermore, what is crucial is that this incarnation in our here and now is an act of God and so is a challenge to our human claims to incarnate and locate God in Christ as a God or Christ of a particular place or culture. The turn to our here and now means that the *flaneur*, as the quintessential figure of urban, western modernity is, theologically speaking, the one who moves amongst and in the location in which God in Christ is present. The *flaneur* is the response of those who recognize that urban secular western modernity is also a location in which God in Christ has chosen to overcome transcendence by God's self-action.

The absence that so many in western, urban, secular, modernity claim to experience is real, but is caused, I would state, by two things. On the one hand it is an absence because we are seeking transcendence in religion. On the other hand, it is an absence because God in Christ in our location is the Emmaus Christ who rejects any attempt to make him a Baal-Christ of geopiety, a Baal-Christ of I AM (here). As Laurence Paul Hemming notes:

> Self-reflection lies at the heart of faith. Christ is not a style; we live in Christ, and insofar as we do, we are open to the redemption offered us through Christ. I am the place where Christ is revealed to myself, and if I am to be as place of revelation of Christ to the world, I am also what obscures that revelation.[8]

Such self-reflection is central to my interest in the religionless *flaneur* and as such it is central to Bonhoeffer's call for a religionless Christianity. The religionless conviction is that we fail to recognize God in Christ in our modern, western, secular urban society for precisely the same reason as outlined in the Emmaus narrative: God in Christ appears where and as we do not expect him to be. Our failure means that we construct an expectation based, in Bonhoeffer's phrasing, *on religion*. This, I would claim, is a continuation of the misreading resulting in the Baal of I AM. We fail to recognize that God in Christ is God in Christ in the here and now of our modern, western, urban secular environment and, as Bonhoeffer claims, *not* in the *religion* of Christianity in these societies which in fact acts as sectarian location of I AM. In a *Baedeker*-Bible approach, we search for Christ, we search for God and we search for the real and the authentic, *anywhere but here*. Such theological failure means that we pursue what we construct and locate elsewhere – because we reject any possibility of incarnation or presence in our here and now. What the theological tourist, the theological traveller, the theological exile all seek is a *god of religion* and a religion of Christianity that is ultimately the Baal of I AM located amongst and as others who are not me. And often allied to the I AM also is what can be termed the THEY ARE, the THIS IS and the THAT WAS – all of which are ultimately the Baal of religion. Alternatively, the theological *flaneur* is the one who is open to the presence and absence of Christ, the Emmaus Christ glimpsed and yet not contained in this western urban, secular location.

The *flanerie* of the religious Christian occurs in two ways. Firstly, the theological *flaneur* moves in response and not in belief amongst the modern, urban, secular crowd open to the I WILL BE/BECOME. Secondly, the theological *flaneur* undertakes a *flanerie* of all texts because the *Logos* is the logos behind all words. He responds to the Logos in what I term "Emmaus texts" and as such is present/absent and absent/present in them. As Hemming, following Bonhoeffer, reminds us, we should not go looking for God in Christ elsewhere because God in Christ is present in and amongst us, in and amongst our humanity (that is the promise of the incarnation). Yet we do not see this because it is our wilful actions that obscure the revelation of Christ to the world.

The challenge of religionless Christianity is a reminder that to be modern is to be self-reflexive, and to be self-reflexive is to be challenged that *we* are in fact the *Baedeker* to the presence of Christ in the world. The *flaneur*, as the trope of western, urban, secular modernity, is the one who challenges us to be self-reflexive, to move against the crowds, to be open to the glimpse, in ourselves and in others, of the Emmaus Christ present in our here and now. To be a theological tourist, traveller or exile is to use the Bible as a *Baedeker* to religion located elsewhere. Such mis-readings which pursue and privilege another's context and contextual theology over our own location is too often a turn to the Baal of I AM, rejecting the religionless challenge of I WILL BE/BECOME.

The challenge of the *flaneur* is to move *in* our here and now, open to the possibility of grace offered by the Emmaus Christ who does not conform to our expectation or religious beliefs. The Emmaus Christ is the ongoing challenge of the revelation (in self and in others) of I WILL BE/BECOME. So we are confronted by the revelation that the dislocation of religion (that is the rejection of the religion of belief and human expectation and demand) is, in fact, the location of Christianity. To use our Bible as a *Baedeker* to elsewhere is to pursue religion and to reject the incarnation that sits at the heart of God's revelation in Christianity. Yet the universal, secular challenge of Christianity is to each of us in our own particular here and now. The revelation of God in the *saeculum* invites response to God in Christ amongst us. The challenge of the Emmaus Christ and the challenge of the *flanerie* of religionless Christianity are challenges to reject the security of religion.

To be a theological *flaneur*, to undertake a theology of *flanerie*, is to wander in *our* here and now, open to the possibility of glimpsing the I WILL BE/BECOME. The recourse to the *Baedeker*, the retreat to religion which occurs as either Christianity as religion and the religion of Christianity, is too often to seek and privilege the contextual *religion* of elsewhere. Such moves, both theologically and physically, deny the possibility of grace in our here and now and ultimately deny the incarnation. For Christ, if he is to be God with us, is God with us in our here and now. Christ for us in western, urban, secular modernity is not constrained by human belief or expectation and is not to be relocated elsewhere where we can visit or constrain him. Christ for us in western, urban, secular modernity is also not constrained to the memory of the exile who is always determined by what was, and not fully open to what is. For the secular Christian, to *flaneur* is to be open to the Emmaus Christ present yet absent, the Emmaus

Christ unconstrained yet who confronts us in our here and now. For the secular Christian, Christ is freed of religion and glimpsed away from all our attempts to constrain him in religion. Christ himself *flaneurs* away from all our attempts to limit him in and to sectarian locations and experiences. For if Christ is not present in the world of all humanity, in a world that includes our secular, western, urban humanity, then he is not Christ but merely the Baal of religion.

The challenge of the theological tropes of *Baedeker*, tourist, traveller and exile is to confront us with the impossibility of relocating God in Christ as only, as primarily, located and encountered elsewhere. For it is only the response of the *flaneur* of secular Christianity that truly returns our gaze to our here and now. Only the response of the *flaneur* of religionless Christianity challenges our religious reading of the Bible as a *Baedeker*. This occurs because the religionless challenge of the theological *flaneur* in the *saeculum* is that of responding to the Logos Christ who is the Emmaus Christ confronting, challenging and encountering us precisely where we believe he is not present. In conclusion, the religionless challenge is the acknowledgment of the response *that he is*.

Notes

Introduction

1. Karl Marx, "Introduction to A Contribution to the Critique of Hegel's Philosophy of Right," February 1844. In *Marx and Engels on Religion* (New York: Shocken Books, 1974), 141–58; 141.

2. For a thoughtful discussion of the influence of Kierkegaard and Kant on the place or non-place of religion in modernity see Calvin O. Schrag, "The Kierkegaard-effect in the Shaping of the Contours of Modernity," in *Kierkegaard in Post/Modernity*, ed. M. Matustik and M. Westphal (Bloomington: Indiana University Press, 1995), 1–17.

3. For a recent interesting discussion see Jose Ignacio Cabezon, "The Discipline and its Other: The Dialectic of Alterity in the Study of Religion," *Journal of the American Academy of Religion*, 4, no. 1 (March 2006): 21–38.

4. See, for example, the essays by B. Lichtenberg-Ettinger and J. Rancière in *Traveller's Tales: Narratives of Home and Displacement*, ed. G. Robinson et al. (London and New York: Routledge, 1994); A. K. Martin and S. Kryst, "Encountering Mary: Ritualization and Place Contagion in Postmodernity," in *Places Through the Body*, ed. H. J. Nast and S. Pile (London: Routledge, 1998), 207–29; Celeste Olalquiaga in *Megalopolis: Contemporary Cultural Sensibilities* (Minneapolis: University of Minnesota Press, 1992); and Zygmunt Bauman, "From Pilgrim to Tourist – or a Short History of Identity," in *Questions of Cultural Identity*, ed. S. Hall and P. du Gay (London: Sage, 1996), 18–36. There has also been a noticeable rise in the use of the later Derrida and Levinas, in particular in discussions as to the response to be made to the "other." Yet this often seems to occur in a secular mis-reading that fails to reflect that the turn to the other is predicated on a prior response to the ultimate "other" of God – who may no longer be there – and so a form of kenotic other is substituted.

5. There are what I term transitional moves such as G. Aichele, et al. (Bible and Culture Collective)'s *The Postmodern Bible* (New Haven: Yale University Press, 1995) and its complement *The Postmodern Bible Reader*, ed. P. Jobling, T. Pippin and S. Schliefer (Oxford: Blackwell, 2001) as well as *Biblical Studies/Cultural Studies: The Third Sheffield Colloquium*, ed. C. Exum and S. Moore (Sheffield: Sheffield Academic Press, 1998). There have also been attempts to reassess the Bible and post-colonialism in texts such as *Vernacular Hermeneutics*, ed. R. S. Sugirtharajah (Sheffield: Sheffield Academic Press, 1999) and *Interpreting Beyond Borders*, ed. Fernando F. Segovia (Sheffield: Sheffield Academic Press, 2000). These have all been attempts to engage biblical studies with contemporary/popular culture. As for explicitly theological texts, little has really been done that does not posit the theological as the normative base. This text is an attempt to readdress the imbalance – and perhaps pull the intersection of popular culture and Christianity back from primarily the field of Biblical Studies. The cross-culture(s) under review here are the theological and the secular – read from the secular as "normative."

6. Such an environment is readily apparent in New Zealand, which is often referred to (in tandem with Australia) as "the most secular country in the world." It is also a

country where, not surprisingly, the theological endeavour has struggled for acknowledgment and coherency, not least in recent decades, within the churches themselves. For a succinct and incisive appraisal of the current state of religion in New Zealand, and the dominant predisposition for "spirituality" over either religion or theology, see Paul Morris, "A Time for Re-enchantment," in Millennium Essays special supplement, *New Zealand Books* 9, no. 5 (December 1999): 4–5.

7. In this text I want to differentiate between Christ as Logos (Word of God) and text as logos. I proceed on the basis that Logos is Christ as Word of God and logos is word(s) that includes biblical and secular text. Therefore the Bible as logos (word of God) is only so because it is here where we encounter the corrective of Christ as Logos. Furthermore, it is a claim of this text that the priority of Logos behind logos opens the challenge of the possibility of Logos being encountered in secular logos – and in fact the corrective demand that we read secular texts as open to the corrective encounter with Logos. I want to claim that to limit Logos to sacred/biblical text is in fact to seek to limit God and God's corrective encounter with humanity. In effect it reduces God to the explicitly sacred, the explicitly religious, and increasingly to the explicitly "Christian" in a manner that I believe Bonhoeffer came to reject in his call for a religionless Christianity. To make Logos, to make God, to make the corrective encounter with humanity the preserve of a sectarian, explicitly religious humanity is seeking to turn God and logos into a form of tribal fetish and pietistic totem.

8. It is "negative" in two senses. Firstly, insofar as it negates the specificity of the singular incarnation thesis of pre-postmodern theology. Secondly, it is "negative" in negating the historicity of the singular incarnation thesis. Such a "negative" incarnation claims that such an event was only ever textual.

9. The use of the term "underwrites" is a deliberate play on the notion that the Logos underwrites all our logos: all texts potentially act as a location for the encounter of rupture.

10. I am indebted to the expanding oeuvre and challenges of Mark C. Taylor for forcing me to locate theology in such a manner. This is not to claim that such statements would find him in agreement; rather, it is an acknowledgment that he has forced me to continually think in inter-textual new ways.

11. (Hip)gnosis is my term for the forms of contemporary spirituality where "being spiritual" (i.e. postmodern kabbalism, westernized feng shui, shamanism, wicca, western Tibetan Buddhism, lifestyle eco-spirituality and the like) possesses a "street cred" and "hipness/cool factor" because they are seen as embodying an acceptable alternative to a popular (mis)understanding of the Judeo-Christian tradition. As such they establish a dualism between spirituality (seen as gnosis, individualistic, found, acceptable, contemporary) and theology (seen as imposed, communal, given, unacceptable, out-of-date) that in many ways becomes a definition by repudiation.

12. Edward Said, *Representations of the Intellectual* (London: Vintage Books, 1994).

13. Caren Kaplan, *Questions of Travel: Postmodern Discourses of Displacement* (Durham: Duke University Press, 1996).

14. My use of the term "rupture" is a response to how Giorgio Agamben, drawing on Walter Benjamin, positions grace as a rupture, as that which interrupts. I am indebted to Agamben's positioning, *pace* Benjamin, of grace as a type of citation, whereby past and present encounter each other. However, the use of citation in this text, as a form of rupture, was begun long before I encountered Agamben's text. I feel this is an interesting

example as to how rupture within theory can be encountered in the contemporary world. Reading strategies are in themselves possible sites of the rupture that, following Zizek, exists as forms of "short-circuit." See G. Agamben, *The Time That Remains: A Commentary on the Letter to the Romans*, trans. P. Daly (Stanford: Stanford University Press, 2005), 119–39.

15. Said, *Representations*, 36.

16. For the purposes of this inquiry I wish to posit that modernist (as in those attempting to write theology in the present context without taking on the challenges and insights of postmodernism) and orthodox (that is of a more broadly evangelical and traditional understanding) theologians are ultimately engaged in a similar pursuit of the real, as opposed to postmodern theologians who are to be broadly characterized as being concerned with the non-real.

17. See, for example, *God, the Gift, and Postmodernism*, ed. J. D. Caputo and M. J. Scanlon (Bloomington and Indianapolis: Indiana University Press, 1999) in which the inter-textualities are debated.

18. While the difference between an explorer and a traveller in both travel writing and theology will be discussed in greater detail later in this text, it is important to restate (in continuation of the above discussion) that while the traditionalist/orthodox (traveller) seeks to restate and reiterate and the modernist (explorer) seeks to explore and discover new understandings, both are still on the real side of post/non-reality and the modern side of the postmodern.

19. My term for this still-being-worked-out repositioning is "soft modernism," a term appropriated from the world of architecture where there has been a move to re-impose a form of modernist order and aesthetic. Culturally this can be seen as a turn back from the relativizing and pluralism of postmodernity toward a new sense of a reworked order – conceived either in the turn back to religion (as opposed to spirituality) as in de-secularization – or indeed a reaffirmation of secularization over and against both religion and spirituality. Yet it is in this "soft modernism" that a re-encounter with secular Christianity is beginning to reoccur. For a fuller discussion as to what I perceive as "soft modernism" see my *CTheory* article: "Soft Modernism: The World of the Post-Theoretical Designer." http://www.ctheory.net/text_file.asp?pick=418.

20. For example, J. Derrida and G. Vattimo's book on *Religion* (Cambridge: Polity Press, 1998), and the work of Bauman, Derrida, Vattimo and Zizek.

21. This occurred in one of my frequent discussions with Paul Morris, Professor of Religious Studies at Victoria University of Wellington, New Zealand. We were discussing, amongst other things, what I was writing, and I mentioned how, with the *flaneur* I was engaging with, what could be a re-articulation of religionless Christianity – yet noting the difficulties of its original mid-twentieth century, Modernist designation and challenge. In response, Paul mentioned the need, outside of just Christianity, in a world experiencing desecularization, of articulating what he termed, in the wake of Derrida and Vattimo, religionless religion.

22. It is my aim that this text is part of an ongoing engagement with these issues of a resurgent modernity, religionless religion and religionless Christianity. Further texts are planned on a reassessment with Barth's two commentaries on *Romans* when read after postmodernity, and a text rethinking the death of God, revisiting the 1960s debates and critiquing both why their challenge was quickly abandoned and where a re-engagement in our newly nascent soft Modernity may take us.

23. For an essay I have written discussing these issues – as it more specifically played itself out in the pages of *The Christian Century* – see the August 2005 issue of the online *Journal of Cultural and Religious Theory* 6, no. 3. http://www.jcrt.org/

24. This is a text written from the triply marginal location of the city of Christchurch in the South Island of New Zealand – therefore marginal within marginal locations. Yet conversely, the marginality provides a freedom in that such a frontier allows, by necessity, a free-ranging access to a variety of ideas and challenges – and the marginal location in which to be provocative.

25. See my *CTheory* essay on "Soft Modernism", op. cit., for one way of entering this debate.

26. Slavoj Zizek, *The Puppet and the Dwarf: The Perverse Core of Christianity* (Cambridge, MA and London: MIT Press, 2003), "foreword," vii–viii.

27. Charles E. Winquist, "Postmodern Secular Theology," in *Secular Theology: American Radical Theological Thought*, ed. Clayton Crockett (London and New York: Routledge, 2001), 26–36, quotation at 28.

28. Graham Ward, *Cities of God* (London and New York: Routledge, 2000), 188.

29. See Valentine Cunningham's essay "The Rabbins Take It Up One After Another," in V. Cunningham, *In the Reading Goal: Postmodernity, Texts and History* (Oxford and Cambridge, MA: Blackwell, 1994), 363–64. He notes that all our linguistics, critical theory and writing occur under the shadow of the logos.

30. Roberto Calasso, "Introduction: *Chette-Wynde*," in B. Chatwin and R. Calasso, *Winding Paths* (London: Jonathan Cape, 1999), 9–15, quotation at 14.

31. For example, Slavoj Zizek in *On Belief* (London and New York: Routledge, 2001) states: "What characterizes the European civilization is…precisely its *ex-centered* character – the notion that the ultimate pillar of Wisdom, the secret *algama*, the spiritual treasure, the lost object-cause of desire, which we in the west long ago betrayed, could be recuperated out there, in the forbidden, exotic place" (67). While Dean MacCannell notes: "modern man has been condemned to look elsewhere, everywhere, for his authenticity, to see if he can catch a glimpse of it reflected in the simplicity, poverty, chastity or purity of others." D. MacCannell, *The Tourist: A New Theory of the Leisure Class* (London: Macmillan, 1976), 4.

32. While Vahanian has been wrestling with the issue of secularity and Christianity for over forty years, a provocative recent challenge is his chapter "Theology and the Secular," in C. Crockett, ed., *Secular Theology: American Radical Theological Thought* (London and New York: Routledge, 2001), 10–25.

33. Gianni Vattimo, *After Christianity*, trans. Luca D'Isanto (New York: Columbia University Press, 2002), 98.

34. Charles Taylor, *Modern Social Imaginaries* (Durham: Duke University Press, 2004), 185.

35. Cunningham, "The Rabbins Take It Up One After Another," 371–75.

36. Winquist, "Postmodern Secular Theology," 29.

37. Cunningham, "The Rabbins Take It Up One After Another," 402.

38. Vattimo, *After Christianity*, 8.

Chapter 1

1. Dean MacCannell, *The Tourist: A New Theory of the Leisure Class* (London: Macmillam, 1976), 2.

2. This linking of religion and tourism as "primitive" expressions will have echoes in the later discussion of what exists as "unnecessary decoration" amongst modern people as put forward in the work of the critic Adolf Loos. This is discussed in Chapter 4.

3. MacCannell, *The Tourist*, 10.

4. Ibid., 13.

5. This locating of falsity with the act of mechanical reproduction can be traced to Walter Benjamin's essay, "The Work of Art in the Age of Mechanical Reproduction" which was concerned with the issues of aura and authenticity in the attempts to reproduce an "original." Benjamin's text has become an almost clichéd starting point for cultural theory over the past twenty years, and yet its central challenge of delineating the "real" in the reproduction that is a copy but not a fake is something that sits as a question in the commodification of contemporary life and experience. For a re-reading of Benjamin and religion see S. Brent Plate, *Walter Benjamin, Religion, and Aesthetics: Rethinking Religion through the Arts* (London and New York: Routledge, 2005).

6. MacCannell, *The Tourist*, 44–45.

7. Mark C. Taylor on Las Vegas in *About Religion: Economies of Faith in Virtual Culture* (Chicago: University of Chicago Press, 1999).

8. David Lodge, *Paradise News* (London: Viking, 1991).

9. Ibid., 61–64. It is this invoking of Marx that alerts us to the fact that Lodge is attacking MacCannell here, as MacCannell critiques tourism from a Marxist perspective.

10. Nelson H. H. Graburn, "Tourism: The Sacred Journey," in *Hosts and Guests: The Anthropology of Tourism*, 2nd ed., ed. V. L. Smith (Philadelphia: University of Philadelphia Press, 1989), 21–36 (25–26).

11. Mark Twain, *The Innocents Abroad* (New York: Penguin, 2002) [orig. 1869], 384.

12. Ibid., 352.

13. Timothy Larsen, "Thomas Cook, Holy Land Pilgrim, and the Dawn of the Modern Tourist Industry," in *The Holy Land, Holy Lands, and Christian History: Papers Read at the 1998 Summer Meeting and the 1999 Winter Meeting of the Ecclesiastical History Society*, ed. R. N. Swanson (Woodbridge, Suffolk and Rochester, NY: Boyatel & Brewer, 2000), 329–42, at 329, 334.

14. Ibid., 331.

15. See Lester I. Vogel, *To See a Promised Land: Americans and the Holy Land in the Nineteenth Century* (University Park, PA: Pennsylvania State University Press, 1993). This is a thorough discussion of the centrality of the Holy Land to American life in this period.

16. Victor Turner and Edith Turner, *Image and Pilgrimage in Christian Culture: Anthropological Perspectives* (New York: Columbia University Press, 1978), 20.

17. John Casey, "A Place in the Shade" (August 23, 1986) in *Views from Abroad: The Spectator Book of Travel Writing*, ed. P. Marsden-Smedley and J. Klinke (London: Grafton Books, 1988), 40–42, quotation at 42.

18. Lawrence Durrell, *Sicilian Carousel* (London: Faber and Faber, 1977), 55.

19. See Orvar Lofgren, *On Holiday: A History of Vacationing* (Berkeley: University of California Press, 1999), 282.

20. Graburn, "Tourism: The Sacred Journey," 27.

21. I prefer the non-word of "fakeness" to falsity because of what I perceive to be the difference in intention between false and fake. In the discussion of tourism, fakeness signals a deliberate falsity that celebrates its existence as fake. Fakeness" is something that is agreed on by all as being deliberately false" – as part of a "game" perhaps, a complicit agreement that the fake stands in for, and perhaps even transcends, the real.

22. David Brown, "Genuine Fakes," in *The Tourist Image: Myths and Myth Making in Tourism*, ed. T. Selwyn (Chichester: John Wiley and Sons, 1996), 33–47, esp. 45.

23. See Donald Horne, *The Intelligent Tourist* (McMahon's Point, NSW: Margaret Gee, 1992).

24. Ibid., 74.

25. James Buzard, *The Beaten Track: European Tourism, Literature and the Ways to 'Culture'* (Oxford: Clarendon Press, 1993), 266.

26. Ibid.

27. John Julius Norwich, "Introduction," in *A Taste for Travel: An Anthology*, ed. John Julius Norwich (New York: Alfred A. Knopf, 1987), 7.

28. Leonard R. Koos, "(T)here: The Rise of Touristic Culture in the Travel Writings of Jacques Arago," *Literature Interpretation Theory* 7, nos 2–3 (1996): 179.

29. William B. Whitman, "Baedeker's Travels," *Biblio* 4, no. 2 (February 1999): 36.

30. Anthony Weller, "Baedeker Revisited," *Forbes* 152, no. 7 (September 1993): 188.

31. Buzard, *The Beaten Track*, 75.

32. Jas Elsner and Joan-Pau Rubies, "Introduction," in *Voyages and Visions: Towards a Cultural History of Travel*, ed. Elsner and Rubies (London: Reaktion Books, 1999), 16.

33. Alan Sillitoe, *Leading the Blind: A Century of Guide Book Travel 1815–1914* (London: Macmillan, 1995), 186.

34. Bruce Feiler, *Walking the Bible: A Journey by Land through the Five Books of Moses* (New York: William Morrow/HarperCollins, 2001), 57.

35. In what follows the terms *Baedeker* and guidebook will become virtually synonymous. This follows established custom whereby *Baedeker* has become the generic term of guidebooks – the "Ur-text" as it were. I use the italicized *Baedeker* to refer to the guides and the non-italicized Baedeker to refer to the parent company.

36. Buzard, *The Beaten Track*, 67.

37. Edward Mendelson, "Baedeker's Universe," *The Yale Review* (Spring 1985): 387–89.

38. Weller, "Baedeker Revisited," 188.

39. While it is noted that Orthodox Christianity is of course not just located in the Middle East, the primary encounter and suspicion of this type of Christianity for northern European Protestant travellers occurred in their travels in the Levant. Greece was, of course, the other primary location of package tour Protestant encounter with Orthodox Christianity.

40. Of course this mythical creature extends to include tourists from North America – and later, from South Africa, Australia and New Zealand.

41. Esther Allen, "'Money and Little Red Books': Romanticism, Tourism and the Rise of the Guidebook," *Literature Interpretation Theory* 7, nos 2–3 (1996): 224.

42. Ibid.

43. Ibid.

44. Penny Travlou, "Go Athens: A Journey to the Centre of the City," in *Tourism: Between Place and Performance*, ed. S. Coleman and M. Crang (New York and Oxford: Bergahan Books, 2002), 108–127 (110).

45. E. M. Forster, *A Room with a View* (London: Edward Arnold & Co., 1947) [orig. 1908], 25.

46. James Buzard, "Forster's Trespasses: Tourism and Cultural Politics," *Twentieth Century Literature* 34, no. 2 (Summer 1988): 158.

47. Aldous Huxley, *Along the Road: Notes and Essays of a Tourist* (London: Chatto and Windus, 1928), 37.

48. Ibid., 39.

49. Durrell, *Sicilian Carousel*, 101.

50. B. Elissalde, "Guides, mode d'emploi," in *Espaces-Temps, Reflechir les Sciences Sociales: Edition Special 'Voyage au Centre de la Ville'* 33 (1986): 27–30 (27). Quoted in Travlou, "Go Athens," 108.

51. Terry Caesar, *Forgiving the Boundaries: Home as Abroad in American Travel Writing* (Athens and London: University of Georgia Press, 1995), 90.

52. Lydia Wevers, *Country of Writing: Travel Writing and New Zealand 1809–1900* (Auckland: Auckland University Press, 2002), 10.

53. Horne, *The Intelligent Tourist*, 23.

54. Ibid., 52.

55. Travlou, "Go Athens," 109.

56. Lodge, *Paradise News*, 153.

57. Durrell, *Sicilian Carousel*, 73.

58. John Taylor, *A Dream of England: Landscape, Photography and the Tourist's Imagination* (Manchester: Manchester University Press, c. 1994), 240.

59. Ibid., 243.

60. Lucy Lippard, *On the Beaten Track: Tourism, Art and Place* (New York: The New Press, 1999), 5.

61. Buzard, *The Beaten Track*, 4.

62. M. Risse, "White Knee Socks versus Photojournalist Vests: Distinguishing between Travelers and Tourists," in *Travel Culture: Essays on What Makes Us Go*, ed. Carol Traynor Williams (Westport, CT: Praeger, 1998), 41–50 (48).

63. Paul Fussell, "Tourist Tendencies," in *The Norton Book of Travel*, ed. P. Fussell (New York: Norton, 1987), 649–54 (651). Quoted in Buzard, *The Beaten Track*, 3.

64. Daniel Boorstin, *The Image: A Guide to Pseudo-Events in America* (New York: Harper & Row, 1964), 85.

65. Caren Kaplan, *Questions of Travel: Postmodern Discourses of Displacement* (Durham: Duke University Press, 1996), 60–61.

66. Evelyn Waugh, *Labels* (London: Duckworth, 1974) [orig. 1930], 64.

67. Michel Houellebecq, *Platform*, trans. Frank Wynne (London: Vintage, 2003), 105.

68. Michel Houellebecq, *Lanzarotte*, trans. Frank Wynne (London: Vintage, 2004), 2.

69. Houellebecq, *Platform*, 231.

70. For an account of Flaubert's travels in Egypt available in English see *Flaubert in Egypt: A Sensibility on Tour: A Narrative drawn from Gustave Flaubert's Travel Notes and Letters*, trans. and ed. Francis Steegmuller (London: Michael Haag, 1983) [orig. London: Bodley Head, 1972].

71. Julian Barnes, "Hate and Hedonism," *The New Yorker* (July 7, 2003), 72–75 (74).

72. Edward Bruner, "Transformation of the Self in Tourism," *Annals of Tourism Research* 18 (1991): 238–50 (241–42).

73. Boorstin, *The Image*, 106.

74. Bruner, "Transformation of the Self in Tourism," 241.

75. Jonathan Culler, "The Semiotics of Tourism," in idem, *Framing the Sign: Criticism and its Institutions* (Oxford: Basil Blackwell, 1988), 153–67 (153).

76. Ibid., 160.

77. Jim Butcher, *The Moralisation of Tourism: Sun, Sand...and Saving the World?* (London and New York: Routledge, 2003), 1.

78. Ibid., 8.

79. Houellebecq, *Lanzarotte*, 35.

80. McKenzie Wark, *Dispositions* (Applecross, WA and Cambridge, UK: Salt Publishing, 2002), April 28, 2001 9:42 AM WET.

81. Georges van den Abbeele, "Sightseers: The Tourist as Theorist," *Diacritics* 10, no. 4 (Winter 1980): 2–14 (13).

82. Twain, *The Innocents Abroad*, 91.

83. Claudia Bell and John Lyall, *The Accelerated Sublime: Landscape, Tourism and Identity* (Westport, CN and London: Praeger, 2002), 25.

84. Ibid., 26.

85. Twain, *The Innocents Abroad*, 136.

86. Ibid.

87. Ibid., 137.

88. John Urry, *The Tourist Gaze*, 2nd ed. (London: Sage, 2002), 1.

89. Ibid., 149.

90. Ibid., 79.

91. Ibid., 12.

92. Tom Gunning, "The Whole World within Reach: Travel Images without Borders," in *Travel Culture: Essays on What Makes Us Go*, ed. Carol Traynor Williams (Westport, CN: Praeger, 1998), 25–37 (26).

93. Ibid., 27.

94. Geoff Dyer, *Yoga for People who Can't be Bothered to Do it* (London: Abacus, 2003), 37.

95. Bell and Lyall, *The Accelerated Sublime*, 36.

96. *Travel Photography* (New York: Time-Life Books, 1972), 202.

97. Peter Osborne, *Travelling Light: Photography, Travel and Visual Culture* (Manchester: Manchester University Press, 2000), 72.

98. Maxine Feifer, *Going Places: The Ways of the Tourist from Imperial Rome to the Present Day* (London: Macmillan, 1985), 1.

99. Angus Wilson, *Reflections in a Writer's Eye* (London: Penguin Books, 1987), 175.

100. Lippard, *On the Beaten Track*, 2.

101. This is my reading taken in discussion with what Osborne puts forward in *Travelling Light*, 34.

102. Ibid., 34.

103. Lippard, *On the Beaten Track*, 37.

104. Dyer, *Yoga for People who Can't be Bothered to Do it*, 35.

105. Zygmunt Bauman, "From Pilgrim to Tourist – or a Short History of Identity," in *Questions of Cultural Identity*, ed. Stuart Hall and Paul du Gay (London: Sage, 1996), 18–36 (29–30).

106. John H. Richardson, "The Long Way Home," *Esquire* 136, no. 5 (November 2001), http://www.esquire.com.

107. Butcher, *The Moralisation of Tourism*, 29–30.

108. Fred Inglis, *The Delicious History of the Holiday* (London and New York: Routledge, 2000), 75.

109. Osborne, *Travelling Light*, 84.

110. Taylor, *A Dream of England*, 243.

111. Ibid.

112. Kaplan, *Questions of Travel*, 64.

113. The types of tourist that theorists delineate take different forms. For example, E. Cohen, "Towards a Sociology of International Tourism," *Social Research*, 39 (1972): 164–82; idem, "Who is a Tourist? A Conceptual Clarification," *Sociological Review*, 22 (1974): 527–55 [critiqued in Eugenia Wickens, "The Sacred and the Profane: A Tourist Typography," *Annals of Tourism Research* 29, no. 3 (July 2002): 834–51]) has: the drifter, the explorer, the individual mass and the communal mass. Wickens reflects a more pop-cultural turn with the categories of: the Cultural Heritage, the Raver, the Shirley Valentine (older woman in search of romance – from the 1989 film of the same name), the Heliolatrous (sun worshippers) and the Lord Byron. Perhaps more apposite for this investigation are Smith's five types who all reflect (unwittingly) current forms of piety and theological movements: ethnic, cultural, historical, environmental and recreational (of course the last is more a form of piety than theology!) See Valene L. Smith, "Introduction," in *Hosts and Guests: The Anthropology of Tourism*, 2nd ed., ed. Smith (Philadelphia: University of Philadelphia Press, 1989).

114. See note 16 of the Introduction for the differences and similarities of the Orthodox and Modernist theologians.

115. Paul Fussell, *Abroad: British Literary Travelling Between the Wars* (New York: Oxford University Press, 1980), 39.

116. In this case works of popular theology such as the books of John Spong are the theological equivalent to the *Lonely Planet Guide* series for backpackers.

117. Bauman, "From Pilgrim to Tourist."

118. Ibid., 23.

119. See n. 115 above.

120. Ibid., 38, 39.

121. Waugh, *Labels*, 44.

122. Ibid., 44–45. Also, writing in *American Vogue* in 1935 Waugh notes "tourist" is a term of contempt compared to those who self-style themselves "travellers and cosmopolitans." All travellers, he observes, define themselves versus others who either seem not to "do it" correctly or do not possess the right attitude. See Evelyn Waugh, "The Tourists' Manual," *Vogue* (NY), July 1, 1935, in *The Essays, Articles and Reviews of Evelyn Waugh*, ed. Donat Gallagher (Boston and Toronto: Little, Brown & Co., 1984), 170.

123. Huxley, *Along the Road*, 9–10.

124. Risse, "White Knee Socks versus Photojournalist Vests," 41.

125. Culler, "The Semiotics of Tourism," 156.

126. Jan Morris, *Travels* (London: Faber & Faber, 1976), 40.

Chapter 2

1. My use of the terms "modernist" and "orthodox" with reference to theology are those I set out in the Introduction. It must be noted that orthodox in this schema refers to theology that is recognized as orthodox belief by Christianity, not orthodox as practised by the variety of orthodox Churches (Russian, Serbian, Greek, for instance).

2. The distinction is that texts on travel are those discussing the trope of travel and the art of travel writing, while travel texts are those recording a journey. Of course, the inter-textual nature of both genres results in close links and similarities.

3. Holland attributes this to Benjamin as cited in Floyd Wayne Whitson, Jr., "Style and the Critique of Metaphysics: The Letter as Form in Bonhoeffer and Adorno," in *Theology and the Practice of Responsibility: Essays on Dietrich Bonhoeffer*, ed. Floyd Wayne Whitson, Jr. and Charles Marsh (Valley Forge, PA: Trinity Press International, 1994), 239–51.

4. Scott Holland, "First We Take Manhattan, Then We Take Berlin: Bonhoeffer's New York," *Crosscurrents* 50, no. 3 (Fall 2000): 2.

5. Frederic Bartkowski, *Travellers, Immigrants, Inmates: Essays in Estrangement* (Minneapolis and London: University of Minnesota Press, 1995), 21.

6. Jacques Rancière, "Discovering New Worlds: Politics of Travel and Metaphors of Space," in *Travellers' Tales: Narratives of Home and Displacement*, ed. George Robertson et al. (London and New York: Routledge, 1994), 29–37 (30).

7. Siegfried Kracauer, "Travel and Dance," in idem, *The Mass Ornament: Weimar Essays*, trans. and ed. Thomas Y. Levin (Cambridge, MA and London: Harvard University Press, 1995), 65–73 (71–73).

8. Kracauer, "Travel and Dance," 72.

9. Ibid., 73.

10. Ihab Hassan, "Travel as Metaphor: Unmargined Realities," in *Dissent and Marginality: Essays on the Borders of Literature and Religion*, ed. K. Tsuchiya (London: Macmillan; New York: St Martin's Press, 1997), 163–78 (178). Hassan notes the location of radical theology in doubt and that of radical literature in recreating "the forms of poetic belief" (ibid.).

11. Ibid., 178.

12. Simon Raven, "Travel: A Moral Primer" (August 9, 1968), in *Views From Abroad: The Spectator Book of Travel Writing*, ed. P. Marsden-Smedley and J. Klinke (London: Grafton Books, 1988), 18–21 (18).

13. Pico Iyer, *Sun After Dark: Flights into the Foreign* (New York: Alfred A. Knopf, 2004), 7.

14. Ibid., 10.

15. Billie Melman, "The Middle East of Arabia: 'The Cradle of Islam'," in *The Cambridge Companion to Travel Writing*, ed. P. Hulme and T. Youngs (Cambridge: Cambridge University Press, 2002), 105–21 (115).

16. Bauman, "From Pilgrim to Tourist," 21, 22.

17. Trinh T. Minh-ha, "Other than Myself/My Other Self," in *Travellers' Tales: Narratives of Home and Displacement*, ed. George Robertson et al. (London and New York: Routledge, 1994), 9–26 (23).

18. Robert Dessaix, "Busting Out," *Sydney Morning Herald*, September 17, 2004, http://www.smh.com.au/articles/2004/09/17/1095320946227.html

19. Ibid.

20. Yet as Steve Clark warns us: "The travel narrative is addressed to the home culture; by its very nature, however, that to which it refers cannot be verified, hence the ready and habitual equation of traveler and liar." Steve Clark, "Introduction," in idem, ed., *Travel Writing and Empire: Postcolonial Theory in Transit* (New York and London: Zed Books, 1999), 1.

21. Mark Cocker, *Loneliness and Time: British Travel Writing in the Twentieth Century* (London: Secker & Warburg, 1992), 18.

22. Chris Rojek, "Indexing, Dragging and the Social Construction of Tourist Sights," in *Touring Culture*, ed. C. Rojek and R. Urry (London and New York: Routledge, 1992), 53.

23. That is, in both writing and rewriting "the self."

24. Faction is that branch of literature which combines elements of the factual and the imaginative.

25. Paul Fussell, *Abroad: British Literary Travelling Between the Wars* (New York: Oxford University Press, 1980), 30.

26. Geoffrey Moorhouse, *The Fearful Void* (London: Hodder & Stoughton, 1974), 37–38.

27. Wark quotes here from Adorno, *Minima moralia*, 39.

28. McKenzie Wark, *Dispositions* (Applecross, WA and Cambridge, UK: Salt Publishing, 2002), January 29, 2001 3:55 PM EST.

29. For a stringent critique of the intellectual appropriation of "nomad" see Dick Pels, *The Intellectual as Stranger: Studies in Spokespersonship* (London and New York: Routledge, 2000), 177–89. He is critical of what he terms "nomad narcissism" (184) and the associated use of dislocated and relocating metaphors by sedentary intellectuals who use them without recognition of their privileged position (189). Pels' is a valid critique, but I still want to make use of the terms of exile and dislocation in Chapter 3, because I argue that theological-intellectual exile is, indeed, a valid form of exile – perhaps inescapable in the modern/postmodern world.

30. Bruce Chatwin, *Anatomy of Restlessness: Uncollected Writings*, ed. J. Borm and M. Graves (London: Jonathan Cape, 1996), 106.

31. Ibid.

32. In Marinetti's Futurist Manifesto: "The New Religion – Morality of Speed," speed is the new location and expression of divinity. Marinetti, viewing the Great War as one that is "liberating," expresses a futurist morality that: "will defend man from the decay caused by slowness, by memory, by analysis, by repose and habit. Human energy centupled by speed will master time and space." This creates a new secular religious response: "If prayer means communication with the divinity, running at high speed is a prayer. Holiness of wheels and rails. One must kneel on the tracks to pray to the divine velocity." This also means that "one must persecute, lash, torture all those who sin against speed." Filippo Marinetti, *The New Religion-Morality of Speed* (Futurist Manifesto, first number of *L'Futalia Futirista*, May 11, 1916), in *Marinetti: Selected Writings*, ed. R.W. Flint, trans. R. W. Flint and Arthur A. Coppotelli (New York: Farrar, Straus and Giroux, 1972), 94–96 (94).

33. Jack Kerouac, *On the Road* (New York: Penguin, 1991), 133, original emphasis.

34. See note 32 above.

35. Pico Iyer, *The Global Soul* (New York: Alfred A. Knopf, 2000), 12.

36. William Dalrymple, *From the Holy Mountain: A Journey in the Shadow of Byzantium* (London: HarperCollins, 1997), 13–14. In fact, this is increasingly the case

with religious communities and leaders. The late Pope John Paul II was the most travelled Pope in history, globe-trotting and available to be encountered seemingly almost everywhere. I have heard the Dalai Lama talk to a sell-out audience in Dunedin, New Zealand and conversed with Tibetan monks in the common room of a Presbyterian Theological College in the same city. I also recall attending a lecture in the same theological college where a visiting Iranian Mullah lectured us on Islam and the Iranian Revolution. More recently I have met His Holiness Pope Shenouda III, of the Egyptian Coptic Church and organized a public lecture for him and his travelling retinue of Bishops in a lecture hall at Canterbury University in Christchurch. Here a secular lecture hall was converted into an exotic "non-space" with Coptic sounds, smells, talk and people while we received a frankly un-orthodox mythology of the centrality of Egypt for Christianity as digressed through the recounting of Coptic legends as to the exile of the holy family in Egypt, here presented as undisputed fact.

37. Iyer, *The Global Soul*, 159.

38. Jason Cowley, "Still Life in Mobile Homes," *New Statesman*, November 19, 2001, 49–51 (49).

39. Fred Inglis, *The Delicious History of the Holiday* (London and New York: Routledge, 2000), 82.

40. Michel de Certeau, *The Practice of Everyday Life*, trans. Steven F. Rendall (Berkeley: University of California Press, 1984), 106–7.

41. Chatwin, *Anatomy of Restlessness*, 82; letter from Chatwin to Tom Maschler, February 24, 1969. A version of this is expressed in Richard Grant, *Ghost Riders: Travels with American Nomads* (London: Little, Brown, 2003) in which he recounts "a nomad's creed" as part of the American psyche: 'that freedom is impossible and meaningless within the confines of the sedentary society, that the only true freedom is the freedom to roam across the land, beholden to no one' (12).

42. Gilles Deleuze and Felix Guattari, *A Thousand Plateaus: Capitalism and Schizophrenia*, trans. Brian Massumi (London: The Althone Press, 1988 [orig. 1980]), 380.

43. Ibid.

44. Ibid., 381.

45. Ibid., 382, original emphasis.

46. Ibid.

47. Ibid., 383.

48. Ibid., 383.

49. A fascinating evangelical Christian reading of this claim (yet explicitly counter to the claims of Deleuze and Guatarri) is that offered by Philip Yancey, editor at large for *Christianity Today*: "As I travel, I have observed a pattern, a strange historical phenomenon of God 'moving' geographically from the Middle East, to Europe, to North America to the developing world. My theory is this: God goes where he's wanted." Source: Philip Jenkins, *The Next Christendom: The Coming of Global Christianity* (Oxford: Oxford University Press, 2002), 15. (Orig. Philip Yancey, *Christianity Today* 45, no. 2 [February 5, 2001]: 136.)

This view of a "needy God" tied to evangelical institutions and missions, in effect arriving with missions and departing with evangelists, is, in the nomadic view, a God tied to place and institution. In the Bonhoefferian sense, this is a God of Religion. This text is, under Yancey's schema, an attempt to grapple with the issue of God for those where God has "moved on."

50. Slavoj Zizeck, *The Puppet and the Dwarf: The Perverse Core of Christianity* (Cambridge, MA and London: MIT Press, 2003) 3.

51. Richard Sennett, *The Conscience of the Eye: The Design and Social Life of Cities* (London: Faber & Faber, 1993), 6. Quoted in Zygmunt Bauman, "From Pilgrim to Tourist – or a Short History of Identity," in *Questions of Cultural Identity*, ed. Stuart Hall and Paul du Gay (London: Sage, 1996), 18–36 (20).

52. Edmond Jabes, *The Little Book of Unsuspected Subversions*, trans. Rosmarie Waldrop (Stanford: Stanford University Press, 1996), 81.

53. I am indebted to Bracha Lichtenberg-Ettinger for reminding me of this in Bracha Lichtenberg-Ettinger, "The Becoming Threshold of Mattrixial Borderlines," in *Travellers' Tales: Narratives of Home and Displacement*, ed. George Robertson et al. (London and New York: Routledge, 1994), 38–62 (39).

54. See Donald E. Cowan, *Theology in Exodus: Biblical Theology in the Form of a Commentary* (Louisville: Westminster John Knox Press, 1994), 80–85, for a considered discussion as to the possibilities of this self-expression of the name of God. Cowan concludes that the name of God/Yahweh has no definition, but it has an evident link with the verb "to be."

I want to follow such a reading, raising the issue of how, if we read the divine self-revelation as "to be/become," it challenges what is often our "religious capture" of "I AM."

Rabbi W. Gunter Plaut, in his commentary on Exodus, notes the difficulty of the self-declaration, but also the link to "to be." He notes that most Jewish commentators have decided on the future tense and a meaning along the lines of "I will be what tomorrow demands" – that is, God responds to human need. He also notes what is termed a "philosophical meaning" by S. R. Hirsh of "I will be what I *want* to be." Plaut also states: "it is an aspect of God's freedom to conceal his essence, and hence Ehyeh-Asher-Ehyeh must remain elusive." He believes it is therefore best to "convey it, untranslated and inexplicable, as Ehyeh-Asher-Ehyeh." See W. Gunter Plaut, ed., *The Torah: A Modern Commentary* (New York: Union of American Hebrew Congregations, 1981), 405–6.

55. Lichtenberg-Ettinger, "The Becoming Threshold of Mattrixial Borderlines," 40.

56. Patrick Leigh Fermor in Robert D. Kaplan, *Mediterranean Winter: The Pleasures of History and Landscape in Tunisia, Sicily, Dalmatia and Greece* (New York: Random House, 2004), 232–33.

57. Gary Krist, "Ironic Journeys: Travel Writing in the Age of Tourism," *The Hudson Review* XLV:4 (Winter 1993): 593–601 (598).

58. Paul Theroux, "Travel Writing: The Point of It," in idem, *Fresh-Air Fiend: Travel Writings 1985–2000* (London: Hamish Hamilton, 2000), 40.

59. Ibid., 38.

60. Thomas Swick, "On the Road without a Pulitzer," *The American Scholar* 66, no. 3 (Summer 1997): 423–29. Swick refers to Theroux's *The Great Railway Bazaar* (1975).

61. This is a reference to Patrick Holland and Graham Huggan, *Tourists with Typewriters: Critical Reflections on Contemporary Travel Writing* (Ann Arbor: University of Michigan Press, 1998).

62. Marc Auge, *Non-Places: Introduction to an Anthropology of Supermodernity*, trans. John Howe (New York and London: Verso, 1995 [Orig. 1992]), 85–86.

63. Jonathan Raban, *For Love and Money. Writing. Reading. Traveling. 1968–1987* (London: Picador/Pan, 1988), 246. As he states: "there is a convention of guileless

immediacy about literary travel books, a long established pretence that the traveling and the writing are part and parcel of each other" (247).

64. Ibid., 247.

65. Lawrence Durrell, *Sicilian Carousel* (London: Faber & Faber, 1977), 216.

66. Sallie Tisdale, "Never Let the Locals See Your Map," *Harpers* 291:1774 (September 1995), http://proquest.umi.com.ezproxy.canterbury.ac.nz/pqdlink?did=6755750&Fmt=7&clientId=13346&RQT=309&VName=PQD.

67. Susan Rubin Suleiman, "Introduction," in *Exile and Creativity: Signposts, Travelers, Outsiders, Backward Glances*, ed. Susan Rubin Suleiman (Durham: Duke University Press, 1998), 1–6 (3). As she comments: "one can be an outsider in one's hometown, as members of minority groups know" (3).

68. Clark, "Introduction," 1.

69. Lydia Wevers, *Country of Writing: Travel Writing and New Zealand 1809–1900* (Auckland: Auckland University Press, 2002), 10.

70. Hassan, "Travel as Metaphor," 166.

71. Wevers, *Country of Writing*, 159.

72. Hassan, "Travel as Metaphor," 166, original emphasis.

73. Ibid., 165.

74. Jan Morris, "Travel Lit's Novel Pursuit," *The Nation* 265:10 (October 6, 1997): 37.

75. Colin Thubron, "Both Seer and Seen: The Travel Writer as Left Over Amateur," *Times Literary Supplement* 5026 (July 30, 1999): 13.

76. Wevers, *Country of Writing*, 5.

77. Peter Bishop, *The Myth of Shangri-La: Tibet, Travel Writing and the Western Creation of Sacred Landscape* (Berkeley and Los Angeles: University of California Press, 1989), 4.

78. Nicholas Howe, "Reading Places," *The Yale Review* 81, no. 3 (July 1993): 60–73 (68).

79. Jas Elsner and Joan-Pau Rubies, "Introduction," in *Voyages and Visions: Towards a Cultural History of Travel*, ed. Elsner and Rubies (London: Reaktion Books, 1999), 5.

80. Ibid., 6.

81. Robert Byron, "The Problems of Modern Travel" (orig. *Vogue*, August 21, 1929), in *Travel in Vogue* (London: Macdonald Futura, 1981), 254.

82. Evelyn Waugh, "Desert and Forest" (orig. *The Spectator*, September 28, 1934) in *The Essays, Articles and Reviews of Evelyn Waugh*, ed. Donat Gallagher (Boston and Toronto: Little, Brown and Co., 1984), 139.

83. Helen Carr, "Modernism and Travel (1880–1940)," in *The Cambridge Companion to Travel Writing*, ed. Peter Hulme and Tim Youngs (Cambridge: Cambridge University Press, 2002), 70–86 (81).

84. Graham Dann, "Writing out the Tourist in Space and Time," *Annals of Tourism Research* 26, no. 1 (1999): 159–87 (167).

85. Ibid., 168.

86. Clive James, *Flying Visits: Postcards from the Observer 1976–1983* (London: Jonathan Cape, 1984), 1.

87. Carr, "Modernism and Travel (1880–1940)," 80.

88. Victoria Mather, "Travelling Bookfully," *Encounter* LXXIV:4 (May 1990): 38–43 (38).

89. Cowley, "Still Life in Mobile Homes," 49.

90. Esther Allen, "'Money and Little Red Books': Romanticism, Tourism and the Rise of the Guidebook," *Literature Interpretation Theory* 7, nos 2–3 (1996): 213–26 (214).

91. Ibid.

92. Robin Magowan, "Writing Travel," *Southwest Review* (Spring–Summer 2001): 174–86 (174).

93. James Duncan and Derek Gregory, *Writes of Passage: Reading Travel Writing* (London: Routledge, 1999), 7.

94. Karl Barth, *Karl Barth: Theologian of Freedom. Selected Writings*, ed. Clifford Green (London: Collins, 1989), 207. (Orig. Karl Barth, *Church Dogmatics*, IV/I 18b.)

95. Zizeck, *The Puppet and the Dwarf*, 24.

96. In the Eden narrative, the expulsion from the garden occurs because God fears that having eaten of the fruit of the tree of knowledge of good and evil, humanity may now eat of the tree of life and live for ever (Genesis 3:22). The expulsion is not just for disobedience but also to separate humanity from the possibility of becoming like God – for what appears to now make God and humanity different is that God "lives for ever." The expulsion is a safeguarding of this difference, by God. And yet the enforcement of death by this move is that which maintains the relationship between God and humanity.

97. Laurence Paul Hemming, "Introduction," in idem, ed., *Radical Orthodoxy? A Catholic Enquiry* (Aldershot: Ashgate, 2000), 19.

98. As Holland and Huggan note, travel writing is often "seeking solace for a troubled present in nostalgic cultural myths." Holland and Huggan, *Tourists with Typewriters*, xi.

99. Dennis Porter, *Haunted Journeys: Desire and Transgression in European Travel Writing* (Princeton: Princeton University Press, 1991), 15.

100. In Protestant theology this can be seen in the debates between those who follow(ed) in the tradition of Schleiermacher's *Religion, Speeches to its Cultured Despisers* (1799) and those barking the neo-orthodox *"nein"* of the twentieth century.

101. Anthony Powell, *What's Become of Waring?* (London: Heinemann, 1964 [orig. 1939]). For detailed discussion on the themes and content of the novel see Robert K. Morris, *The Novels of Anthony Powell* (Pittsburg: University of Pittsburg Press, 1974), 85–100; and Neil McEwan, *Anthony Powell* (New York: St Martins Press, 1991), 35–39.

102. Jan Morris notes that "Waring" was taken from Robert Browning's poem, whose model was the poet Alfred Domett (1811–1877) who "gave us all the slip" to become, later, Premier of New Zealand (1862–63). Jan Morris, *Trieste and the Meaning of Nowhere* (London: Faber and Faber, 2001), 74. Michael Barber, in his biography of Anthony Powell, notes that the title of the draft was actually "What's Become of Stokes." He then mentions a theory (noting he has forgotten who told him) that whoever inherited Powell's desk from his time at the publishing house Duckworth discovered that "the 'Waring' was missing from the 'Waring and Gillow' trademark." As Barber goes on to surmise: "Since the novel implies that publishing is, at best, a pretty ramshackle trade, I like to think that Powell's desk deserves the credit rather than Browning." Michael Barber, *Anthony Powell: A Life* (London and Woodstock, NY: Duckworth Overlook, 2004), 117.

103. This is a tradition that reaches back to the celebrated travelogue *The Book of Sir John Mandeville* of c. 1325. Mandeville's travels to far-away lands were read for many hundreds of years as a truthful (admittedly embellished) form of pilgrim's travelogue, that, in reality, was created in a plagiaristic compendium of other texts. For an interesting "unmasking" of Mandeville see Giles Milton, *The Riddle and the Knight: In Search of Sir John Mandeville* (London: Allison and Busby, 1997).

104. Powell, *What's Become of Waring?*, 156.

105. Ibid., 178.

106. This is the non-existent god analogous to the navigational Point of Aries, not the non-existent god of the heretic Arius.

107. The "popular theologian" is not so oxymoronic a state as it might first appear. The theological equivalent of a Bill Bryson or Paul Theroux, their approach is to make the exotic or other domesticated and approachable through the personal journeying of the author. Good storytellers, their audience is the armchair traveller (theologian) who, in the act of reading, feels they have "been there" and so now "knows about it." The aimed-for result is a reader left with the satisfaction that while "there" might be "interesting," in the end "there is no place like home."

108. Edwin Dobb, "Where the Good Begins: Notes on the Art of Modern Travel," *Harpers* (July 1998): 59–66 (59).

109. Cocker, *Loneliness and Time*, 253.

110. In this form of travel writing the doyen would surely be the English writer Patrick Leigh Fermor.

111. As noted, the British travel writer Bruce Chatwin (1940–1989) wrote lyrical books of travel faction which relate a searching after a sense that nomad culture still possesses a knowledge that the industrialized West had lost.

112. The term "back to the future" is taken from the films of that name from the 1980s starring Michael J. Fox and Christopher Lloyd as time travellers who venture into the past to correct the present and, in doing so, result in an alternate future.

113. For a thoughtful discussion of the challenge laid down to a dialectic of Enlightenment and theology in a continuing "Modern Project" see Helmeut Peukert, "Enlightenment and Theology as Unfinished Projects," in *The Frankfurt School on Religion*, ed. Eduardo Mendieta (London and New York: Routledge, 2005), 351–70.

114. Philip Marsden, "Como Conversazione: On Travel and Travel Writing," *The Paris Review* 40, no. 147 (Summer 1998): 218–38. http://proquest.umi.com.ezproxy. canterbury.ac.nz/pqdweb?did=34784607&sid=1&Fmt=4&clientId=13346&RQT= 309&VName=PQD.

115. Howe, "Reading Places," 61–62.

116. Bishop, *The Myth of Shangri-La*, 3.

117. Michael Jacobs, *Between Hopes and Memories: A Spanish Journey* (London: Picador, 1994), 95.

118. John Julius Norwich, ed., *A Taste for Travel: An Anthology* (New York: Alfred A. Knopf, 1987), 3.

119. Marsden, "Como Conversazione."

Chapter 3

1. Gianni Vattimo, "The Age of Interpretation," in Richard Rorty and Gianni Vattimo, *The Future of Religion*, ed. Santiago Zabala (New York: Columbia University Press, 2005), 43–54 (47).

2. Ibid., 52.

3. Ibid., 50–53.

4. This is Waitemata harbour in Auckland in New Zealand's North Island. New Zealand's largest city, Auckland, sprawls along an isthmus between two large harbours, the Manukau in the west and the Waitemata in the east.

5. Lesley Max, "Having It All: The Kibbutznik and the Powhiri," in *Pakeha: The Quest for Identity in New Zealand*, ed. Michael King (Auckland: Penguin, 1991), 79–91 (89).

6. R. Radhakrishnan, *Diasporic Meditations: Between Home and Location* (Minneapolis and London: University of Minnesota Press, 1996), xiii.

7. Nikos Papastergiadis, *Modernity as Exile: The Stranger in John Berger's Writing* (Manchester and New York: Manchester University Press, 1993), 10.

8. Radhakrishnan, *Diasporic Meditations*, xiii.

9. R. B. Kitaj, *First Diasporist Manifesto* (London: Thames and Hudson, 1989), 19.

10. Ibid., 29.

11. Ibid., 35.

12. Pico Iyer, *The Global Soul* (New York: Alfred A. Knopf, 2000), 23.

13. Ibid., 140.

14. Ibid., 121.

15. Ibid., 140.

16. Kitaj, *First Diasporist Manifesto*, 37.

17. Ibid., 29–30.

18. Ibid., 71–72.

19. John Berger, *And Our Faces, My Heart, Brief as Photos* (New York: Pantheon Books, 1984), 67.

20. Ibid., 57.

21. Agnes Heller, *A Philosophy of History in Fragments* (Oxford: Blackwell, 1993), viii.

22. Lloyd S. Kramer, *Threshold of a New World: Intellectuals and the Exile Experience in Paris 1830–1848* (Ithaca and London: Cornell University Press, 1988), 2.

23. Ibid.

24. Nicholas Lash, *Theology on Dover Beach* (New York: Paulist Press, 1979), 12.

25. C. K. Stead, "Without," in idem, *The Red Tram* (Auckland: Auckland University Press, 2004), 52–53 (53).

26. James K. Baxter, "Recent Trends in New Zealand Poetry 1951," in *James K. Baxter as Critic*, ed. Frank McKay (Auckland: Heinemann Educational Books, 1978), 11.

27. Mark Williams cited in Stuart Murray, "Writing an Island's Story: The 1930s Poetry of Allen Curnow," *The Journal of Commonwealth Literature* 309, no. 2 (1995): 25–44 (31) (orig. from M. Williams, "Selected Poems 1940–1989," unpublished review).

28. See Jean-Luc Nancy, *The Inoperative Community*, ed. Peter Connor, trans. Peter Connor et al.; Foreword Christopher Fynsk (Minneapolis, MN: University of Minnesota Press, c. 1990). Nancy posits the idea that the absence of God becomes the basis for community. His critique is established in the claim that the basis of community was that it defined and orientated itself towards and before God. Now, when God dies/retreats/declines/removes/dissolves, the community acts *as if it is* God. What this means is God cannot return. Nor can the community effect the return of God because only in the withdrawal of God does the community become aware of its self-definition and orientation. If God is there or here, then God is immanent: there is no need then for singular locations for the community to encounter God. In other words, the community creates places to take the place of the absent God. This means our encounter with the

divine is actually the experience of the desertion of the divine; no longer is it a God of the desert but a God who has deserted.

Nancy goes on to discuss four western notions of community: The first is the lost community that is to be regained or reconstituted. This is an essentialist view; it is the ideal against which the contemporary can be judged. The second is the view of community as communion, based on the Christian notion of communion in the mystical body of Christ. This lost community is part of the death of God. Thus calls for community are often then a call for a return to or replacement for the "divine"/the "sacred" to fill the loss of unity at the heart of existence. The third view is of community as a totalitarian death wish. Here the aim is for absolute immanence where we dissolve the worked-for community in the ideal of a pure immanent community. This pursues self-sacrifice as leading to the realization of total pure community. So we subsume our self in the search for either the "community to come" or to realize the return of the lost community. To stand against the aimed-for community is (to stand against the idea(l) of "self" itself. Finally, there is the view of aiming for communication – not communion. Here communication has replaced communion as the basis for community.

Nancy's central point is that community now occupies the place of the sacred. This occupation results in community being experienced as/is the sacred – but it is a sacred that is stripped of "the sacred." In other words, community takes on the role/position/recipient of beliefs and arbitrator of values – but it is not sacred. Community is thus nothing more than the incomplete sharing in community; that is, the community acts as resistance to claims of immanence. Now a situation arises where myth and community are defined by each other. Community writes myths that articulate, justify and explain community. But, as Nancy notes, myth is self-communicating – it does not contain a knowledge that can be verified from outside; myth thus acts as the myth of a communion.

29. A "cultivated garden amongst mountains" in T. H. Scott's phrase in T. H. Scott, "South Island Journal," *Landfall* (December 16, 1950): 289–301.

30. James K. Baxter, "Aspects of Poetry in New Zealand" (Victoria University of Wellington, 1967) in *James K. Baxter as Critic*, ed. McKay, 79.

31. That is, myths that boosted, i.e. overly promoted, the attractions and opportunities of New Zealand to potential colonists in Britain.

32. It is a common New Zealand colloquialism to refer to New Zealand as "godzone," that is, as "god's own country." This is a referral to its paradisal qualities of scenery, temperate climate and egalitarian society.

33. Peter Simpson, "'The Trick of Standing Upright'; Allen Curnow and James K. Baxter," *World Literature Written in English* 26, no. 2 (Autumn 1986): 369–78.

34. Ibid., 373.

35. Allen Curnow to Joseph Heenan, May 7, 1945, cited in Stuart Murray, *Never a Soul at Home: New Zealand Literary Nationalism and the 1930s* (Wellington: Victoria University Press, 1998), 243, 277, n. 56.

36. Allen Curnow, "Introduction," in idem, ed., *A Book of New Zealand Verse 1923–50* (Christchurch: Caxton Press, 1951), 18.

37. Ibid., 20.

38. Ibid.

39. Ibid., 26.

40. Mark C. Taylor, *Erring: A Postmodern A/Theology* (Chicago: University of Chicago Press, 1984), 5.

41. Ibid., 6.

42. Kramer, *Threshold of a New World*, 7.

43. Ibid., 9.

44. Ibid., 231.

45. Henry Miller, *Tropic of Cancer* (New York: Grove Press, reprint 1961 [orig. 1934]), 153, in J. Gerald Kennedy, *Imagining Paris: Exile, Writing and American Identity* (New Haven and London: Yale University Press, 1993), 26.

46. Kennedy, *Imagining Paris*, 26.

47. Kramer, *Threshold of a New World*, 9.

48. Zygmunt Bauman, "Assimilation into Exile," in *Exile and Creativity: Signposts, Travelers, Outsiders, Backward Glances*, ed. Susan Rubin Suleiman (Durham and London: Duke University Press, 1998), 321–52 (351).

49. Marc Robinson, "Introduction," in idem, ed., *Altogether Elsewhere: Writers on Exile* (San Diego, New York and London: A Harvest Book/Harcourt Brace and Co., 1994), xi–xxii (xv).

50. Kasia Body notes the crucial experience of being an expatriate (a self-chosen exile) for modernists like Pond and Stein: "it enabled the writer to step outside the borders of his or her own cultural and national identity in order to create language and literature afresh." Kasia Body, "The European Journey in Postwar American Fiction and Film," in *Voyages and Visions: Towards a Cultural History of Travel*, ed. J. Elsner and J.-P. Rubies (London: Reaktion Books, 1999), 232–51 (250).

51. The expatriate exile is for those who do not come to the attention of "the authorities" and so are not officially deported or for those who find the present location and context/ethos intolerable. Critically closely associated with a Modernist sense of autonomous self, the expatriate feels forced into Exile in order to "truly be."

52. Caren Kaplan, *Questions of Travel: Postmodern Discourses of Displacement* (Durham and London: Duke University Press, 1996), 69.

53. Kennedy, *Imagining Paris*, 190.

54. Malcolm Cowley, *Exile's Return: A Literary Odyssey of the 1920s* (New York: Penguin, 1976), 9.

55. By "literal periodization" I mean the attempts (explicit and implicit) to make Exile itself only able to be read as either modernist or postmodernist. Rather, I want to use descriptions and discussions of and on Exile as that which can be re-read as the basis for articulating an Exilic theology.

56. Ian Buruma, "The Romance of Exile – Real Wounds, Unreal Wounds," *The New Republic*, February 12, 2001, 33.

57. Christopher Sawyer-Laucanno, *The Continual Pilgrimage: American Writers in Paris, 1944–1960* (New York: Grove Press, 1992), 91. I refer here to the discussion regarding the experience of the writer Richard Wright who had chosen Exile in 1946, but later, having returned to America, was Exiled in 1953 and so "lost the premier existential value: choice."

58. Jan Morris, *Trieste and the Meaning of Nowhere* (London: Faber and Faber, 2001), 74.

59. Mark C. Taylor and Carl Raschke, "About *About Religion*," *Journal of Cultural and Religious Theory* 2, no. 2 (http://www.jcrt.org/archives/02.2/taylor_raschke.shtml).

60. Dietrich Bonhoeffer, *Letters and Papers from Prison*, ed. Eberhard Bethge, trans. Reginald H. Fuller (London: SCM Press, 1953/1954), 164 (July 16, 1944).

61. The challenge between thinking theology and doing theology is a contentious one. On the one hand, the privileging of thinking "god-talk" is of course different from undertaking action out of that thinking: "the doing" of theology. And yet to think is itself a form of action and may be "the doing" that has the greatest impact. Too often the doing of theology (action) is piety or a form of Pelagianism that disparages the work of thinking. I would want to argue that to "do theology" is to do the thinking, which results in action – that is, the doing. What that thinking involves – and how the doing is expressed – is perhaps the most challenging issue thrown up by Bonhoeffer. To do theology outside of – or more so against – religion will perhaps lead to what is, from the religious standpoint, non-Christian action.

62. Eberhard Bethge, *Bonhoeffer: Exile and Martyr*, ed. John W. De Gruchy (London: Collins, 1975), 103.

63. Ibid., 104.

64. Ibid.

65. Ibid.

66. As Bethge comments: "has it not once again been demonstrated in the history of the church that it is more committed to 'settledness' than it is to showing any solidarity with the uprooted wanderer?" Bethge, *Bonhoeffer*, 102.

67. Ibid., 102.

68. See E. M. Brunner and K. Barth, *Natural Theology: Comprising "Nature and Grace" by Professor Dr. Emil Brunner and the Reply "No" by Dr. Karl Barth*, trans. Peter Fraenkel (London: Geoffrey Bles, 1946). I realize that my use of Barth and Brunner's argument in this way takes it out of its context and, in arguing with Barth against Brunner's Baal, I would most probably (most certainly?!) not find Barth agreeing with me. So, I posit this position in the expectation of a "*nein*" from the past.

What I want to argue, with Barth, is against any capacity for natural revelation, against any capacity for natural theology as such a position, in populist forms of ecotheology and theologies of place, does indeed locate the I AM in "nature and homeland." The I WILL BE/BECOME that I wish to argue for is what challenges us from the other side of the death of God, the death of the I AM, the death of the God of religion.

69. Bethge, *Bonhoeffer*, 155.

70. Ibid., 105.

71. Bonhoeffer, *Letters and Papers from Prison*, 167 (July 18, 1944).

72. Ibid., 123 (April 30, 1944).

73. Ibid.

74. Dietrich Bonhoeffer, *Christology*, trans. John Bowden (London: Collins, 1966), 61–62. (Taken from a series of lectures 1933.)

75. Slavoj Zizek, *On Belief* (London and New York: Routledge, 2001), 145.

76. Ibid.

77. Ibid.

78. Bonhoeffer, *Letters and Papers from Prison*, 164 (July 16, 1944).

79. Zizek, *On Belief*, 146.

80. Salvoj Zizek, *The Puppet and the Dwarf: The Perverse Core of Christianity* (Cambridge, MA and London: MIT Press, 2003), 91.

81. Robinson, "Introduction," in idem, ed., *Altogether Elsewhere*, xxii.

82. Ibid.

83. This is where the ahistorical position of modern theology poses special problems. For postmodern theologians to recant and return to orthodoxy, they must concur with a

form of ahistorical modernity which, paradoxically, most probably forced their Exile in the first place. It is often their experience within secular modernity that made them postmodernists in the first place. Here there is actually a double Exile, from theology and modernity, that makes any return especially problematic.

84. Dick Pels, *The Intellectual as Stranger: Studies in Spokespersonship* (London and New York: Routledge, 2000), 192.

85. Abdul R. JanMohamed, "Worldliness – without World, Homelessness-as-Home: Toward a Definition of the Specular Border Intellectual," in *Edward Said: A Critical Reader*, ed. Michael Sprinker (Oxford and Cambridge, MA: Blackwell, 1992), 96–120 (103).

86. Ibid.

87. Ibid., 97.

88. Trinh Minh-ha, "An Acoustic Journey," in *Rethinking Borders*, ed. J. C. Welchman (London: Macmillan, 1996), 1–17 (12).

89. Ibid., 1.

90. Such a postmodern reading of God arises out of deconstructionist thinking where God is both textual and sign – and yet also existing as a form of negative mysticism. In this understanding, God is a liminal presence that is also an intuitive perception and experience in a non-real manner. As such the postmodern God is beyond the limitations of a modernist realism and is thus a referent trope rather than an actual entity or, even, concrete experience or perception. God is, therefore, the "other other," the "real nonreal," the liminal encounter and the liminal itself. As is readily apparent, such an understanding and experience of that which is called God is therefore beyond the realms of concrete coherence, but rather is alluded to in non-realist referencing and textual re-readings.

91. Hubert Aquin in Anthony Purdy, "Shattered Voices: The Poetics of Exile in Quebec Literature," in *Literature and Exile*, ed. David Bevan (Amsterdam and Atlanta: Rodopi, 1990), 24.

92. John Glad, "Introduction," in idem, ed., *Literature and Exile* (Durham: Duke University Press, 1990), ix.

93. Fernando Alegria, "One True Sentence," in *Altogether Elsewhere*, ed. Robinson, 193–98 (195).

94. Edward Said, *Representations of the Intellectual: The 1993 Reith Lectures* (London: Vintage, 1994), 39.

95. Ibid., 47.

96. Yet postmodern theory is actually far more accommodating of theology that seeks postmodern expression than traditional theology is of any encounter with postmodern theory. In large part this is due to the postmodern recognition of language games whereby theology becomes just another form of articulation and expression. For traditional theology, such a proposal cuts to the core against its statement that what it is engaged in is a real encounter with absolute truth.

97. Mary McCarthy traces Exile back to the story of Adam and Eve, with their exile being "a punishment decreed from above" (Mary McCarthy, "A Guide to Exiles, Expatriates, and Inner Emigrés," in *Altogether Elsewhere*, ed. Robinson, 49–58 [50]). In a sense the postmodern theologian is in Exile as a reversal of this story, in that the recognition of "no above" has forced them into Exile.

98. George Santayana, "The Philosophy of Travel," in *Altogether Elsewhere*, ed. Robinson, 41–48 (44).

99. J. Stevenson, ed., *A New Eusebius: Documents Illustrating the History of the Church to AD 337*, new ed., rev. W. H. C. Frend (London: SPCK, 1987 [orig, 1957]), 167.

100. Paris is taken here as a symbolic home of postmodern thought.

101. Andrew Gurr, *Writers in Exile: The Creative Use of Home in Modern Literature* (Sussex: Harvester Press, 1981), 153.

102. Gabriella Ibieta, "Transcending the Culture of Exile," in *Literature and Exile*, ed. David Beaven (Amsterdam and Atlanta, GA: Rodopi, 1990), 69.

103. For an interesting discussion of religion, postmodernity and kitsch, see Celeste Olalquiaga, *Megalopolis: Contemporary Cultural Sensibilities* (Minneapolis: University of Minnesota Press, 1992), Chapter 3: "Holy Kitschen: Collecting Religious Junk from the Street."

104. Gurr, *Writers in Exile*, 15.

105. Jan Vladislav, "Exile, Responsibility, Destiny," in *Literature in Exile*, ed. Glad, 15.

106. Nikos Papastergiadis, *Dialogues in the Diasporas: Essays and Conversations on Cultural Activity* (London and New York: Rivers Oram Press, 1998), 5.

107. Kennedy, *Imagining Paris*, 28.

108. Berger, *And Our Faces, My Heart, Brief as Photos*, 64.

109. McKenzie Wark, *Dispositions* (Applecross, WA and Cambridge, UK: Salt Publishing, 2002), March 14, 2001 4.45pm EST.

110. Trinh T. Minh-ha: "Other than Myself/My Other Self," in *Travellers' Tales: Narratives of Home and Displacement*, ed. Robertson et al. (London and New York: Routledge, 1994), 9–26 (14–15).

111. Papastergiadis, *Dialogues in the Diasporas*, xi.

112. Kennedy, *Imagining Paris*, xii.

113. Peter Calder, *Travels With My Mother* (Auckland: Tandem Press, 2003), 70.

114. Ibid., 17.

115. Ibid.

116. Ibid., 140.

117. Ibid., 143.

118. Ibid., 178–79.

119. Ibid., 198.

120. E. M. Cioran, *Tears and Saints*, trans. Ilanca Zarifopol Johnston (London and Chicago: University of Chicago Press, 1995 [orig. 1937]), 68.

121. Ibid., 74.

122. Michel de Certeau, *The Practice of Everyday Life*, trans. Steven F. Rendall (Berkeley: University of California Press, 1984), 104–105.

123. Roberto Calasso, "Introduction: *Chette-Wynde*," in Bruce Chatwin and Roberto Calasso, *Winding Paths*. Photographs Bruce Chatwin, Introduction Roberto Calasso (London: Jonathan Cape, 1999), 9–15 (13).

124. *The Last Temptation of Christ*, director Martin Scorsese, producer Barbara de Fina, screenplay Paul Schrader, Universal Pictures and Cineplex Odean Films, 1988.

125. David E. Klemm, "Foreword," in David Jasper, *The Sacred Desert: Religion, Literature, Art and Culture* (Malden, MA and Oxford: Blackwell, 2004), xi–xiv (xii–xiii).

126. Ibid., vi.

127. Jasper, *The Sacred Desert*, 162.

128. Richard Kearney, "Desire of God," in *God, the Gift, and Postmodernism*, ed. John D. Caputo and Michael J. Scanlon (Bloomington and Indianapolis: Indiana University

Press, 1999), 112–45 (128). "Desertification" refers to: "those wandering prophets and anchorite desert fathers who desired a God without being, beyond being, otherwise than being."

129. Ibid.

130. Derrida's comment in Kearney, "Desire of God," 133.

131. Mark C. Taylor, *Disfiguring: Art, Architecture, Religion* (Chicago: University of Chicago Press, c. 1992), 319.

132. Vicki Karamis, Review Essay of *Dispositions*, McKenzie Wark, *borderlands* 3, no. 2 (2004), http://www.borderlandsejournal.adelaide.edu.au/vol3no2_2004/karaminas_dispositions.htm

133. Pico Iyer, *The Global Soul* (New York: Alfred A. Knopf, 2000), 44.

Chapter 4

1. See Gabriel Vahanian, "Theology and the Secular," in *Secular Theology: American Radical Theological Thought*, ed. Clayton Crockett (London and New York: Routledge, 2001), 10–25.

2. Taken from A. Betsky, *Violated Perfection: Architecture and the Fragmentation of the Modern* (New York: Rizzoli, 1990), 29.

3. Lewis Mumford in D. L. Miller, "Introduction," section 2 in *The Lewis Mumford Reader*, ed. Miller (Athens, GA and London: University of Georgia Press, 1995), 43. Source: Lewis Mumford, "Random Notes" 1934 LM MSS.

4. Blake describes *beaux arts* in terms of subscription to the principles of the original *École* in Paris: traditional styles, plans and methods of presentation. Peter Blake, *No Place Like Utopia: Modern Architecture and the Company We Kept* (New York: Alfred Knopf, 1993), 28.

5. See D. Gartman, "Why Modern Architecture Emerged in Europe, not America: The New Class and the Aesthetics of Technology," *Theory, Culture & Society* 17, no. 5 (2000): 75–96.

6. Panayotis Tournikiotis, *Adolf Loos* (New York: Princeton Architectural Press, 1994 [orig. Paris: Editions Macula, 1991]), 23.

7. Ibid.

8. It seems that, while Mies certainly coined the German statement *"beinahe Nichts"* (almost nothing) it is less sure if he coined "less is more." V. E. Savi and J. M. Montaner, eds, *Less is More: Minimalism in Architecture and the Other Arts* (Barcelona: Col. Legi d'Arquitectes de Catalunya y ACTAR, 1996), 12.

9. See Ayn Rand's *The Fountainhead* (1943) for reference to the architect as the Nietzschean über-man.

10. Mark C. Taylor, *About Religion: Economies of Faith in Virtual Culture* (Chicago: University of Chicago Press, 1999), 117.

11. Adolf Loos, "Architecture" (1910) in *The Architecture of Adolf Loos*, ed. Y. Safran and W. Wang (An Arts Council Exhibition; Arts Council of Great Britain, 1985), 108.

12. Tournikiotis, *Adolf Loos*, 108. Orig. Loos, "Règles pour celui qui construe dans les montages" (1913).

13. Alexandre Kostka, "Architecture and the 'New Man': Nietszche, Kessler, Beuys," in *Nietzsche and "An Architecture of Our Minds"*, ed. A. Kostka and I. Wohlfarth (Los Angeles: Getty Research Institute for the History of Art and the Humanities, c. 1999), 199–231 (199).

14. Fritz Neumeyer, *The Artless Word: Mies van der Rohe on the Building Art*, trans. Mark Jarzombek (Cambridge, MA: MIT Press, c. 1991), xviii.

15. Ibid.

16. For an overview of this period, see my essay: "Did God Die in the *Christian Century*?" *Journal for Cultural & Religious Theory* 6, no. 3 (Fall 2005), http://www.jcrt.org/archives/06.3/

17. A similar experience has recently occurred here in New Zealand where Lloyd Geering, formerly Professor of Old Testament, a past Principal of the Theological Hall, Knox College for the Presbyterian Church of New Zealand, and then Professor of Religious Studies, Victoria University of Wellington, New Zealand now, in an antipodean secularization of *Honest to God*, attacks academic theology as "gobblegook." See L. Geering, *Christianity Without God* (Wellington: Bridget Williams Books; Santa Rosa, CA: Polebridge Press, 2002), 15. My review essay can be found in ...*Push. Occasional Papers in Theology & Religion* 1, no. 4 (March 2003), 152–66. ISSN 1175-7744.

18. T. J. J. Altizer and W. Hamilton, *Radical Theology and the Death of God* (Indianapolis: Bobbs- Merrill Co., 1966).

19. Ibid., "Preface."

20. T. J. J. Altizer, *The Gospel of Christian Atheism* (Philadelphia: Westminster Press, 1966), 22.

21. T. Buddenseig, "Architecture as Empty Form: Nietzsche and the Art of Building," in *Nietzsche and "An Architecture of Our Minds,"* ed. Kostka and Wohlfarth, 259–84 (264, 266). The reference is to Nietzsche's *The Gay Science*.

22. Zizek, *The Puppet and the Dwarf*, 3.

23. N. Berdyaev, *The Bourgeois Mind* (London: Sheed & Ward, 1934), 28. Tom Wolfe makes a similar comment in his critique of Seagram Building (1954–58) of Mies and Johnson: "At the heart of Functional, as everyone knew, was not *function* but the spiritual quality known as *nonbourgeois*." Tom Wolfe, *From Bauhaus to Our House* (New York: Farrar Straus Giroux, 1981), 76.

24. Neumeyer, *The Artless Word*, 55; orig. J. J. P. Oud, "Uber die Zukkungtige Baukunst und ihre architektonischen Moglichkeiten," *Fruhlicht* 1, no. 4 (1922): 199.

25. Theo van Doesburg in Neumeyer, *The Artless Word*, 56; orig. van Doesburg, "Der Wille zum Still" in *Bachler and Letsch De Stijl*, 173.

26. Le Corbusier, "The Decorative Art of Today," in *Raumplan versus Plan Libre: Adolf Loos and Le Corbusier 1919–1930*, ed. M. Risselada (Delf: Delf University Press, 1988), 142–45 (142), original emphasis.

27. Walter Gropius, *The New Architecture and the Bauhaus*, trans. P. M. Shand (New York: Museum of Modern Art, 1937), 62.

28. Gropius, *The New Architecture and the Bauhaus*, 17–18.

29. Ibid., 24–28. As setting free will enable the fruits of civilization to be extended to all and also end unnecessary competition.

30. Ibid., 60.

31. Ibid., 19–20.

32. Ibid., 20.

33. Adolf Loos, "Culture" (1908) in *The Architecture of Adolf Loos*, ed. Safran and Wang, 97.

34. Gropius, *The New Architecture and the Bauhaus*, 49.

35. Joseph Hudnut, "Preface," in Gropius, *The New Architecture and the Bauhaus*, 9–10.

36. R. Padovan, "Machine a Metier," in *Mies van der Rohe: Architect as Educator*, ed. R. Achilles, K. Harrington and C. Myhrum; catalogue for exhibition 6 June through 12 July 1986, Mies van der Rohe Centennial Project (Chicago: Illinois Institute of Technology, 1986), 25.

37. Mertins speculates that the Dutch "van der" was added with reference to the De Stijl school, while Rohe is his mother's name. D. Mertins, "Introduction," in *The Presence of Mies*, ed. D. Mertins (Princeton: Princeton Architectural Press, 1994), 21. Quite why he decided to keep Mies which means "rotting or foul" in German is unclear – unless, like Le Corbusier's assumption of the mantle "the Black Crow," such an epithet signals a determination to confront the constrictions and "good taste" of a repudiated past.

38. Paul Rudolph notes: "Mies usually thought of the free-standing, complete-within-itself, beautifully detailed building, unconnected to any means of transportation or to other buildings. Indeed, it is an element placed in space, pure, free, a temple. It may be eighty stories high, but, nevertheless, conceptually a temple." John W. Cook and Heinrich Klotz, *Conversations with Architects* (London: Lund Humphries, 1973), 109.

39. Robert Hughes has described the Seagram Building as "the eloquence of the Void, and architecture of ineloquence and absolute renunciation." R. Hughes, *The Shock of the New*, 2nd ed. (New York: McGraw-Hill, 1991 [orig. 1980]), 194. Mark C. Taylor refers to the forecourt separating the building into "a world apart" so that "insofar as Mies' architecture captures the moment, its attraction is spiritual or even religious as well as aesthetic." Mark C. Taylor, *The Moment of Complexity: Emerging Network Culture* (Chicago: University of Chicago Press, 2001), 32.

40. In 1959 Philip Johnson (in typically revisionist manner) made this link between the International Style and "Religion": "The subject of religious feeling never got expressed in the older modern period. I don't know what you were meant to have instead of religious feeling. In the last thirty years Puritanism took over to a degree. Simplicity was emphasized in much the same way it was in Puritan America. Both Modern architecture and Early American used white paint and clear windows; the white meeting house was almost as anti-religious as modern buildings. We are so used to seeing a 'lovely' eighteenth church that we forget how anti-religious the atmosphere is in those bare white rooms with the glaring windows..."

P. Johnson, "Whither Away-Non-Miesian Directions," Speech to Yale University, February 5, 1959 (previously unpublished), in P. Johnson, *Writings* (New York: Oxford University Press, 1979), 237.

41. Theo van Doesburg, "Vers la peinture blanche," *Art Concret* 1, no. 1 (1930): 11–12. Source: M. Wigley, *White Walls, Designer Dresses: The Fashioning of Modern Architecture* (Cambridge, MA: MIT Press, 1995), 239.

42. L. Grant, *When I Lived in Modern Times* (London: Granta, 2000), 72.

43. Le Corbusier, "The Decorative Art of Today," *L'Espirit Nouveau* (1925): 142–45. Source: M. Risselada, ed., *Raumplan versus Plan Libre*, 144.

44. As Hitchcock and Johnson stated, at the heart of the International Style lay an emphasis on volume not mass: "The effect of mass, of static solidity, hitherto the prime quality of architecture, has all but disappeared; in its place there is the effect of volume, or more accurately, of the plane surfaces bounding a volume. The prime architectural symbol is no longer the dense brick but the open box. Indeed, the great majority of buildings are in reality, as well as in effect, mere planes surrounding a volume." H. R. Hitchcock and P. Johnson, *The International Style* (New York: W.W. Norton & Co., 1966), 41; originally published as *The International Style: Architecture Since 1922* (1932).

45. Le Corbusier, *Precisions on the Present State of Architecture and City Planning: With an American Prologue, a Brazilian Corollary followed by the Temperature of Paris and the Atmosphere of Moscow*, trans. Edith Schreiber Aujame (Cambridge, MA: MIT Press, c. 1991), 106.

46. Wigley, *White Walls, Designer Dresses*, xviii.

47. Ibid., 30.

48. F. Neumeyer, "Mies as Self-educator," in *Mies van der Rohe: Architect as Educator*, ed. Achilles, Harrington and Myhrum, 36 n. 8.

49. Ibid., 30; orig. Mies, "bauen" G. Nv., September 2, 1923, 1.

50. J. Peter, *The Oral History of Modern Architecture: Interviews with the Greatest Architects of the Twentieth Century* (New York: Harry N. Abrams, Inc., 1994), 158.

51. Padovan, "Machine a Metier," 17. Padovan sources Mies' mistranslation to Peter Carter in *Architectural Design* (March 1961): 97.

52. W. Gropius in *Internationale Architektur* (1925) in H.-U. Khan, *International Style: Modernist Architecture from 1925-1965* (Koln: Taschen, 1998), 13.

53. Wolfe, *From Bauhaus to Our House*, 43.

54. The term "Chippendale" is one commonly used because affixed to the top of a conventional square glass tower is the "unnecessary ornamentation" of a decorative extension similar to that found on the famous furniture made by Thomas Chippendale (1718–1779).

55. Now the Sony Building, 550 Madison Avenue (between 55th and 56 Streets), New York.

56. P. Johnson, "Whither Away," *Writings*, 228. Johnson states the style lasted from 1923–1959 and refers to: "the International style with its credo of simplicity, structural clarity, and functionalism – both structural and social."

57. Rem Koolhass, "Miestakes," in *Mies in America*, ed. P. Lambert (Montreal: Canadian Centre for Architecture; New York: Whitney Museum of American Art; New York: Harry N. Abrams Inc., 2001), 716–43 (723).

58. Neumeyer, *The Artless Word*, 236. Source: Mies van der Rohe, miscellaneous notes to lectures.

59. Franz Schulze, *Mies van der Rohe: A Critical Biography* (Chicago: University of Chicago Press, 1985), 324.

60. Neumeyer, *The Artless Word*, xii. Source: Mies, manuscript for a lecture, in Library of Congress.

61. Hughes, *Shock of the New*, 180.

62. Mies, "Baukunst und Zeitwille!" (Building Art and the Will of the Epoch), *Der Querschnitt* 4, no. 1 (1924): 31–32, in Neumeyer, *The Artless Word*, 8.

63. Jean Baudrillard, *Simulations*, trans P. Foss, P. Patton and P. Beitchman (New York: Semiotext(e), 1983), 8–9.

64. See Louis Sullivan, "Ornament in Architecture" (1892) in *Louis Sullivan: The Public Papers*, ed. R. Twombly (Chicago: University of Chicago Press, 1988).

65. The same claim could be made for the difference between a crucifix and a cross. The cross, unadorned, is the ultimate symbol of absent presence; the crucifix, adorned by the "necessary ornamentation" of the crucified Christ, negotiates a recognition that this cross is like no other. The crucifix is an acknowledgment that a transition is occurring from universal death-instrument to universal Christian symbol. The secular space is that which occurs between the body of Christ and the underlying cross. With the Protestant turn to the empty cross, that cross has truly entered secular space as a symbol of immanent presence. It is now read as only the Christian cross; it is ornament in and by itself.

66. The issue of Christology from below is that the cultural Christ so articulated seems more the Christ of that particular humanity of that particular time and space than the incarnated Christ who includes all humanity, in all time and space within the reconciliation of the incarnation. The vernacular Christ is in this way very similar to vernacular architecture: on the one hand, it is the expression of local interests and concerns, and yet, always privileging the context and the particular history of that context over all others. Thus, it becomes open to the "Barthian-Bonhoefferian critique" that it is a religion that stands against the universalistic revelation. Or, if we re-read ornamentation as religion, it is that which obscures, that which unnecessarily decorates the Christianity that lies beneath it.

67. J. D. Caputo, *On Religion* (London: Routledge, 2001), 46–47.

68. Schulze, *Mies van der Rohe*, 214. Source: letter from Mies, January 31, 1938 to Carl O. Scniewind, Curator of Prints and Drawings at the Arts Institute of Chicago.

69. A. H. Barr, "Introduction," in Hitchcock and Johnson, *The International Style*, 13. Or as the Fords stated: "Modern architecture then seeks not style but substance, not ornament or ostentation but rational simplicity, not standard plans and façade but proficiency in exposition...not imitation but creation." J. Ford and K. M. Ford, *Classic Modern Homes of the Thirties* (New York: Dover Publications, Inc., 1989), republication of *The Modern House in America* (New York: Architectural Book Publishing Co., 1940), 11.

70. Lewis Mumford in D. L. Miller, "Introduction," section 2 in *The Lewis Mumford Reader*, 43. Source: Mumford, "Random notes" 1934 LM MSS.

71. Peter, *The Oral History of Modern Architecture*, 99.

72. Ibid., 290 (Saarinen, 1958).

73. Charles Jencks, *The Language of Post-Modern Architecture*, 6th enlarged ed. (London: Academy Editions, 1991), 23.

74. Robert Venturi, *Complexity and Contradiction in Architecture*, 2nd ed. (New York: Museum of Modern Art, 1977 [orig. 1966]), 16, 17.

75. Wolfe provides a most prescient analogy in *From Bauhaus to Our House*, 108: "This, then, was the genius of Venturi. He brought modernism into its scholastic age. Scholasticism in the Dark Ages was theology to test the subtlety of other theologians. Scholasticism in the twentieth century was architecture to test the subtlety of other architects."

76. Loos, "Culture" (1908) in *The Architecture of Adolf Loos*, ed. Safran and Wang, 97.

77. As the one-time Miesian disciple, Philip Johnson, commented: "Mies never got anything from anybody else. He was adamant; he was *sui generic*. He was a success because of what he did for the American steel fabrication system. For him, that was no

accident because *bauen* [to build] means the technique of our time, the technological expression of our day." Cook and Klotz, *Conversations with Architects*, 28.

78. Johnson made the cover of *TIME*, January 7, 1979. Franz Schulze remarks: "He [Johnson] was photographed looking slightly down on the viewer, while holding an effigy of the façade of the building. The metaphor was clear: Moses and the tablets of the Law." Schulze also states that the lead article on Johnson, written by Robert Hughes, whilst noting others who had been working longer, with greater commitment and with more originality than Johnson in the postmodernist movement, positioned Johnson (due to the size of this building and his client, as well as Johnson's fame and close proximity to architectural changes over the past half century) as the one who "more than anyone had legitimated the postmodernist movement." F. Schulze, *Philip Johnson: Life and Work* (New York: Alfred A. Knopf, 1994), 344, 345.

79. For a good overview see Altizer and Hamilton, *Radical Theology and the Death of God*. For an intellectual history see Thomas J. J. Altizer, ed., *Toward a New Christianity: Readings in the Death of God Theology* (New York: Harcourt, Brace & World, Inc., 1967). For an account of the death of God movement in the 1960s and the response to it, see Grimshaw, "Did God Die in the *Christian Century*?" http://www.jcrt.org/archives/06.3/.

80. In the 1960s Peter Berger was at the forefront of what was known as secularization theory which broadly posited that western society would be secular by the end of the twentieth century. With the rise of fundamentalism, the New Age and the revival of Pentecostal Christianity, Berger was forced to recant his thesis. See P. Berger, ed., *The Desecularization of the World: Resurgent Religion and World Politics* (Washington DC: Ethics & Public Policy Centre, 1999).

81. The image and reference to the retreat of The Sea of Faith as expressed in Matthew Arnold's great poem "Dover Beach" (1867) and which, in turn, became title of a highly influential book by Don Cupitt (1984). Building on the influence of the book and its attendant BBC documentary series, it also became the name of a global network of post-Christians attempting to engage with the ideas and work of Don Cupitt, and latterly, also Lloyd Geering.

82. For an "on the ground" critique of the Bonaventure hotel and Jameson's fetishizing of it in *Post-modernism* see John Needham's chapter "A Brief Excursion into Hotel-Theory," in his *The Departure Lounge: Travel and Literature in the Post-Modern World* (Manchester: Carcarnet, 1999).

83. I have deliberately used lower case for soft modernism as it is more of a period that we are transitioning into. The capitalization of Modernism and Postmodernism signify the state of communal agreement that these periods actually occurred – and continue to occur as perhaps ways of experiencing Modernity. By comparison, soft modernism is a term that arose out of architecture and is only gradually seeping into a wider frame of use – and one that I myself am encouraging the use of.

84. As such it has entered the realm of lifestyle magazines with *Home & Entertaining (New Zealand)* stating in a recent editorial: "And if any design style fits comfortably with the way we live today, it must be the dual-natured 'soft modernism.' Mixing elements of mid-century architecture-sleek, clean lines, natural materials and transparent barriers – with modern accents of luxury to soften the edges…" (April/May 2002).

85. Architects such as Cass Calder Smith in San Francisco exemplify this trend.

86. As Philip Johnson stated, "the modern way of being modern is to hook into regionalism," orig. P. Goldberger, "The New Age of Philip Johnson," *The New York Times Magazine*, May 14, 1978, 14. Quoted in Schulze, *Philip Johnson*, 352.

87. Many still triumph the continuation of either modernity (often as high or late modernity) or the universalization of postmodernity. My articulation of soft modernism, admittedly provisional, is taken as recognizing a type of return to the ideals of modernism – yet as a variant "run through" postmodernism. Now in the twenty-first century, all three types – modernism, postmodernism and soft modernism – are, I would argue, running alongside each other, in vernacular representations.

88. H. Pearman, *Contemporary World Architecture* (London: Phaidon Press, 1999), 238.

89. M. Sorkin, "Frozen Light," in *Gehry Talks: Architecture + Process*, ed. M. Friedman, with an essay by M. Sorkin and commentaries by F. O. Geary (London: Thames & Hudson, 2003), 30.

90. Ibid., 31.

91. Charles Jencks, *Ecstatic Architecture* (Chichester: Academy Editions, 1999), 14, 167.

92. Ibid., 14.

93. Ibid., 169.

94. Ibid., 170.

95. H. Ibelings, *Supermodernism: Architecture in the Age of Globalization* (Rotterdam: Nai Publishers, 1998), 51.

96. Taylor, *The Moment of Complexity.*

97. Ibid., 14, 44.

98. Ibid., 41.

99. Pico Iyer, *The Global Soul* (New York: Alfred A. Knopf, 2000), 144.

100. I italicize *flaneur* to signify its discordant, disruptive position in any attempt to read our contemporary context. Just as to *italicize* is to force a noticing of difference in the text, the *flaneur* as an identity and an activity is in himself the noticing of difference in contemporary life.

101. Walter Benjamin, *The Arcades Project*, trans. Howard Eiland and Kevin McLaughlin, prepared on the basis of the German volume, ed. Rolf Tiedemann (1982) (Cambridge, MA and London: Belknapp Press/Harvard University Press, 1999/2002), 11. From *Paris, the Capital of the 19th Century <expose of 1935> 3-13; v. Baudelaire, or the streets of Paris.*

102. Jonathan Raban, *Soft City* (London: Collins Harvill, 1988 [orig. 1974]), 10.

103. Ibid., 70.

104. S. Brent Plate, *Walter Benjamin, Religion, and Aesthetics: Rethinking Religion through the Arts* (London and New York: Routledge, 2005), 131.

105. Benjamin, *The Arcades Project*, "the Flaneur," 416–455, 417 [M1, 4].

106. Ibid., 420 [M2, 8].

107. The distinction here is deliberate between the city of religion and city of God. The city of religion is not necessarily the city of God, but rather that experience of popular and institutional piety and religion that religionless Christianity is in opposition to.

108. Benjamin, *The Arcades Project*, "the Flaneur," 419 [M 2, 4].

109. Ibid., 425 [M 4 a, 1]. Benjamin contrasts the doubt of the *flaneur* with the "waiting of the impassive thinker."

110. Graham Ward, *Cities of God* (London and New York: Routledge, 2000), 2.

111. Ibid.

112. Ibid., 32–33.

113. Harvey Cox, *The Secular City: Secularization and Urbanization in Theological Perspective* (London: SCM Press, 1965), 61.

114. Ibid.

115. Ibid., 62.

116. Ibid., 56.

117. Ibid.

118. Ibid., 58.

119. Ibid.

120. Anke Gleber, *The Art of Taking a Walk: Flanerie, Literature, and Film in Weimar Germany* (Princeton: Princeton University Press, 1999), 58–59.

121. Michel de Certeau, *The Practice of Everyday Life*, trans. Steven F. Rendall (Berkeley: University of California Press, 1984), 103.

122. Joachim Schlor, *Nights in the Big City: Paris. Berlin. London. 1840–1930*, trans. Pierre Gottfried Imhof and Dafydd Rees Roberts (London: Reaktion Books, 1998 [orig. 1991]), 244.

123. Ward, *Cities of God*, 4.

124. Gleber, *The Art of Taking a Walk*, 312.

125. Schlor, *Nights in the Big City*, 17.

126. Keith Tester, "Introduction," in *The Flaneur*, ed. Tester (London and New York: Routledge, 1994), 1–21 (7).

127. Zygmunt Bauman, "Desert Spectacular," in *The Flaneur*, ed. Tester, 138–57 (138).

128. Ibid.

129. Ibid.

130. Schlor, *Nights in the Big City*, 17.

Chapter 5

1. Rowan Williams, "Introducing the Debate: Theology and the Political," in *Theology and the Political: The New Debate*, ed. C. Davis, J. Milbank and S. Zizek (Durham and London: Duke University Press, 2005), 1–13 (1).

2. Ibid., 1–2.

3. *Volkgeist* means variously, the spirit of the people, the folk spirit, the national spirit, and arises out of the Romanticist thought of Johann Gottfried Herder (1744–1803). In the twentieth century, and into the twenty-first century, *Volkgeist* occurs as claims of cultural essentialism and organic national and cultural identity. In Christianity, *Volkgeist* often gets expressed in a syncretic mixing of culture and Christianity that becomes viewed as culturally organic and particular. As such it is in opposition to the universalism of both Christianity and the Enlightenment. For a powerful critique of *Volkgeist* and need for the defence of Enlightenment ideals see Alain Finkielkraut, *The Defeat of the Mind*, trans and intro. Judith Friedlander (New York: Columbia University Press, 1995 [orig. 1987]).

4. J.-F. Lyotard, *The Postmodern Condition: A Report on Knowledge* (Minneapolis: University of Minnesota Press, 1984), 79.

5. Eduardo Mendieta, "Introduction," in *The Frankfurt School on Religion*, ed. E. Mendieta (New York and London: Routledge, 2005), 1–17 (10).

6. Max Horkheimer, "Theism and Atheism," in *The Frankfurt School on Religion*, 213–23 (214).

7. Helmut Peukert, "Enlightenment and Theology as Unfinished Projects," in *The Frankfurt School on Religion*, 351–70 (352).

8. Ibid., 353.

9. See Alain Badiou, *Saint Paul: The Foundation of Universalism*, trans. Ray Brassier (Stanford: Stanford University Press, 2003 [orig. 1997]).

10. See Slavoj Zizek, *The Fragile Absolute – or, Why is the Christian Legacy Worth Fighting For?* (London and New York: Verso, 2000); or Zizek, *The Puppet and the Dwarf*.

11. John Milbank, "Materialism and Transcendence," in *Theology and the Political: The New Debate*, 393–426 (400).

12. This is what I term "soft modernism" as discussed in Chapter 4. For a fuller discussion of what I mean by this see my *CTheory* article: "Soft Modernism: The World of the Post-Theoretical Designer," *CTheory*, 4/8/2004, http://www.ctheory.net/text_file.asp?pick=418.

13. The term "post-secular" is a variant on what is also termed de-secularization. Post-secular society is viewed as the return of public religion into the public square. It is the attempt to overcome the traditional western separation of church and state. Post-secular society occurs when religious beliefs and cultures attempt to express and impose particular religious beliefs as binding or normative within the public square. Often this occurs in the name of cultural beliefs and religious commands within that particular belief. The discussion on post-secular society in the West is particularly concerned with the rise of Islamic demands, a resurgent Catholic identity under Pope Benedict XVI and the continued rise of fundamentalist and pentecostal Christianity. It can also be encountered in post-colonial countries when minority cultures express a particular cultural practice and beliefs as "culture," when they also include beliefs, often of a syncretic nature.

14. Milbank, "Materialism and Transcendence," 400.

15. Ibid., 401.

16. Timothy Gorringe, "Culture and Barbarism: Barth amongst the Students of Culture," in *Conversing with Barth*, ed. J. McDowell and M. Higton (Aldershot and Burlington, VA: Ashgate, 2004), 40–52 (40).

17. Ibid., 40.

18. Karl Barth, "Church and Culture," in idem, *Theology and Church: Shorter Writings 1920–1928*, trans. Louise Pettibone Smith (London: SCM Press, 1962 [orig. 1926]), 334–54 (337).

19. Ibid., 338.

20. Ibid., 339.

21. Ibid., 351.

22. Ibid., 347.

23. Peter Bishop, *The Myth of Shangri-La: Tibet, Travel Writing and the Western Creation of Sacred Landscape* (Berkeley and Los Angeles: University of California Press, 1989), 10.

24. Ibid.

25. Charles Taylor, *Modern Social Imaginaries* (Durham and London: Duke University Press, 2004), 185.

26. In Clayton Crockett, "Introduction," in *Secular Theology: American Radical Theological Thought*, ed. Clayton Crockett (London and New York: Routledge, 2001), 1–9 (1).

27. Gabriel Vahanian, "Theology and the Secular," in *Secular Theology*, ed. Crockett, 10–25 (11).

28. Gianni Vattimo, *Belief*, trans. Luca D'Isanto and David Webb (Stanford: Stanford University Press, 1999), 21.

29. Burke O. Long, *Imagining the Holy Land: Maps, Models and Fantasy Travels* (Bloomington and Indianapolis: Indiana University Press, 2003), 1; orig. John Kirkland Wright, *Human Nature in Geography* (Cambridge, MA: Harvard University Press, 1966).

30. Roberto Calasso, "Introduction: *Chette-Wynde*," in Bruce Chatwin and Roberto Calasso, *Winding Paths* (London: Jonathan Cape, 1999), 9–15 (14).

31. Ibid.

32. McKenzie Wark, *Dispositions* (Applecross, WA and Cambridge, UK: Salt Publishing, 2002), April 20, 2001 11:18 EST.

33. Stephen Turner, "In Derrida's Wake: Why I Can't Think Where I Am," in *Derrida Down Under*, ed. Laurence Simmons and Heather Worth (Palmerston North: Dunmore Press, 2001), 69–85 (70).

34. Wark is Australian and Turner a New Zealander. Both are post-colonial scholars in the interstices of literature, culture and theory. My argument is such scholastic marginality combined with a history of geographical marginality forces in itself a type of *flaneur* knowledge. Antipodean scholars are forced to wander both textually and physically and often assume liminal positions by choice.

35. Dietrich Bonhoeffer, *Christology*, trans. John Bowden (London: Collins, 1966), 61–62.

36. Karl Barth, *Karl Barth: Theologian of Freedom. Selected Writings*, ed. Clifford Green (London: Collins, 1989), 58.

37. Bonhoeffer, *Christology*, 46.

38. Ibid., 88.

39. Graham Ward, "Bodies: The Displaced Body of Jesus Christ," in *Radical Orthodoxy: A New Theology*, ed. John Milbank, Catherine Pickstock and Graham Ward (London and New York: Routledge, 1999), 176.

40. Bonhoeffer, *Christology*, 47.

41. My reference here is to Charles E. Winquist's claim that a postmodern secular theology is textual and situated in existing discourses. Charles E. Winquist, "Postmodern Secular Theology," in *Secular Theology*, ed. Crockett, 26–36. I acknowledge the textual nature and that it is a series of discourses, but I want to widen the notion of texts to include humanity and the *saeculum* in which we exist.

42. Gianni Vattimo, "The Age of Interpretation," in *The Future of Religion*, ed. Santiago Zabala (New York: Columbia University Press, 2005), 43–54 (47).

43. Ibid., 53.

44. Ibid., 50.

45. Ibid., 52.

46, W. Benjamin, "The Work of Art in the Age of Mechanical Reproduction," section 2 (orig. 1936); source: The International Museum of Collage, Assemblage and Construction, http://www.ipdg.org/museum/collage/benjamin.htm

47. Ibid., section 2.

48. Ibid., section 2.

49. Mark C. Taylor, "Reframing Postmodernisms," in *Shadow of Spirit: Postmodernism and Religion*, ed. P. Berry and A. Wernick (London and New York: Routledge, 1992), 25.

50. Bonhoeffer, *Christology*, 61–62.

51. Luke 24:13–22.

Conclusion

1. Karl Marx, "Introduction to A Contribution to the Critique of Hegel's Philosophy of Right," February 1844, in *Marx and Engels on Religion*, Introduction Reinhold Neibuhr (New York: Shocken Books, 1974), 141–58 (141).

2. Gianni Vattimo, *Belief*, trans. Luca D'Isanto and David Webb (Stanford: Stanford University Press, 1999), 21.

3. Gianni Vattimo, "The Trace of the Trace," in *Religion*, ed. Jacques Derrida and Gianni Vattimo (Cambridge: Cambridge University Press, 1998), 79–94 (92).

4. Karl Barth, *Church Dogmatics. Vol.1: The Doctrine of the Word of God*, ed. G. W. Bromiley and T. F. Torrance (Edinburgh: T&T Clark, 1956), 131.

5. Karl Barth, *Karl Barth: Theologian of Freedom. Selected Writings*, ed. Clifford Green (London: Collins, 1989), 230.

6. Emil Brunner and Karl Barth, *Natural Theology: Comprising "Nature and Grace" by Professor Dr. Emil Brunner and the Reply "No" by Dr. Karl Barth*, trans. Peter Fraenkel (London: Geoffrey Bles, 1946), 17.

7. Vattimo, *Belief*, 55.

8. Laurence Paul Hemming, "Introduction," in *Radical Orthodoxy: A New Theology*, ed. John Milbank, Catherine Pickstock and Graham Ward (London and New York: Routledge, 1999), 19.

Bibliography

Achilles, R., Harrington, K., and Myhrum, C., eds. *Mies van der Rohe: Architect as Educator*. Catalogue for Exhibition 6 June through 12 July 1986, Mies van der Rohe Centennial Project. Chicago: Illinois Institute of Technology, 1986.

Agamben, G. *The Time That Remains: A Commentary on the Letter to the Romans*, trans. P. Daly. Stanford: Stanford University Press, 2005.

Aichele, G., et al. (Bible and Culture Collective). *The Postmodern Bible*. New Haven: Yale University Press, 1995.

Alegria, F. "One True Sentence." In *Altogether Elsewhere: Writers on Exile*, ed. M. Robinson, 193–98. San Diego, New York and London: A Harvest Book/Harcourt Brace and Co., 1994.

Allen, E. "'Money and Little Red Books': Romanticism, Tourism and the Rise of the Guidebook." *Literature Interpretation Theory* 7, nos 2–3 (1996): 213–26.

Altizer, T. J. J. *The Gospel of Christian Atheism*. Philadelphia: Westminster Press, 1966.

Altizer, T. J. J., and Hamilton, W. *Radical Theology and the Death of God*. Indianapolis: Bobbs-Merrill Co., 1966.

Altizer, T. J. J., ed. *Toward a New Christianity: Readings in the Death of God Theology*. New York: Harcourt, Brace and World, Inc., 1967.

Auge, M. *Non-Places: Introduction to an Anthropology of Supermodernity*. Trans. J. Howe. New York and London: Verso, 1995 (orig. 1992).

Badiou, A. *Saint Paul: The Foundation of Universalism*. Trans. R. Brassier. Stanford: Stanford University Press, 2003 (orig. 1997).

Barber, M. *Anthony Powell: A Life*. London and Woodstock, NY: Duckworth Overlook, 2004.

Barnes, J. "Hate and Hedonism." *The New Yorker*, July 7, 2003, 72–75.

Barth, K. *Church Dogmatics. Vol.1: The Doctrine of the Word of God*. Ed. G. W. Bromiley and T. F. Torrance. Edinburgh: T&T Clark, 1956.

——— "Church and Culture." In idem, *Theology and Church: Shorter Writings 1920–1928*, trans. L. Pettibone Smith. London: SCM Press, 1962.

——— *Karl Barth: Theologian of Freedom. Selected Writing*. Ed. C. Green. London: Collins, 1989.

Bartkowski, F. *Travellers, Immigrants, Inmates: Essays in Estrangement*. Minneapolis and London: University of Minnesota Press, 1995.

Baudrillard, J. *Simulations*. Trans. P. Foss, P. Patton and P. Beitchman. New York: Semiotext(e), 1983.

Bauman, Z. "Desert Spectacular." In *The Flaneur*, ed. K. Tester, 138–57. London and New York: Routledge, 1994.

——— "From Pilgrim to Tourist – or a Short History of Identity." In *Questions of Cultural Identity*, ed. S. Hall and P. du Gay, 18–36. London: Sage, 1996.

——— "Assimilation into Exile." In *Exile and Creativity: Signposts, Travellers, Outsiders, Backward Glances*, ed. S. R. Suleiman, 321–52. Durham and London: Duke University Press, 1998.

Baxter, J. K. "Recent Trends in New Zealand Poetry 1951." In *James K. Baxter as Critic*, ed. F. McKay. Auckland: Heinemann Educational Books, 1978.

——— "Aspects of Poetry in New Zealand" (Victoria University of Wellington, 1967). In *James K. Baxter as Critic*, ed. F. McKay. Auckland: Heinemann Educational Books, 1978.

Bell, C., and Lyall, J. *The Accelerated Sublime: Landscape, Tourism and Identity*. Westport, CN and London: Praeger, 2002.

Benjamin, W. "The Work of Art in the Age of Mechanical Reproduction." Section 2 (orig. 1936). The International Museum of Collage, Assemblage and Construction. http://www.ipdg.org/museum/collage/benjamin.htm

——— *The Arcades Project*. Trans. H. Eiland and K. McLaughlin. Prepared on the basis of the German volume, ed. R. Tiedemann (1982). Cambridge, MA and London: Belknapp Press/Harvard University Press, 1999/2002.

Berdyaev, N. *The Bourgeois Mind*. London: Sheed & Ward, 1934.

Berger, J. *And Our Faces, My Heart, Brief as Photos*. New York: Pantheon Books, 1984.

Berger, P., ed. *The Desecularization of the World: Resurgent Religion and World Politics*. Washington DC: Ethics & Public Policy Centre, 1999.

Bethge, E. *Bonhoeffer: Exile and Martyr*. Ed. J. W. DeGruchy. London: Collins, 1975.

Betsky, A. *Violated Perfection: Architecture and the Fragmentation of the Modern*. New York: Rizzoli, 1990.

Bevan, D., ed. *Literature and Exile*. Amsterdam-Atlanta: Rodopi, 1990.

Bishop, P. *The Myth of Shangri-La: Tibet, Travel Writing and the Western Creation of Sacred Landscape*. Berkeley and Los Angeles: University of California Press, 1989.

Blake, P. *No Place Like Utopia: Modern Architecture and the Company We Kept*. New York: Alfred Knopf, 1993.

Body, K. "The European Journey in Postwar American Fiction and Film." In *Voyages and Visions: Towards a Cultural History of Travel*, ed. J. Elsner and J.-P. Rubies, 232–51. London: Reaktion Books, 1999.

Bonhoeffer, D. *Letters and Papers from Prison*. Ed. E. Bethge. Trans. R.H. Fuller. London: SCM Press, 1953/1954.

——— *Christology*. Trans. J. Bowden. London: Collins, 1966.

Boorstin, D. *The Image: A Guide to Pseudo-Events in America*. New York: Harper & Row, 1964.

Brown, D. "Genuine Fakes." In *The Tourist Image: Myths and Myth Making in Tourism*, ed. T. Selwyn, 33–47. Chichester: John Wiley and Sons, 1996.

Bruner, E. "Transformation of the Self in Tourism." *Annals of Tourism Research* 18 (1991): 238–50.

Brunner, E. M., and Barth, K. *Natural Theology: Comprising "Nature and Grace" by Professor Dr. Emil Brunner and the Reply "No" by Dr. Karl Barth*. Trans. P. Fraenkel. London: Geoffrey Bles, 1946.

Buddenseig, T. "Architecture as Empty Form: Nietzsche and the Art of Building." In *Nietzsche and "An Architecture of Our Minds"* Ed. A. Kostka and I. Wohlfarth, 259–84. Los Angeles: Getty Research Institute for the History of Art and the Humanities, c.1999.

Buruma, I. "The Romance of Exile – Real Wounds, Unreal Wounds." *The New Republic*, February 12, 2001, 33.

Butcher, J. *The Moralisation of Tourism: Sun, Sand… and Saving the World?* London and New York: Routledge, 2003.

Buzard, J. "Forster's Trespasses: Tourism and Cultural Politics." *Twentieth Century Literature* 34, no. 2 (Summer 1988): 157–79.

——— *The Beaten Track: European Tourism, Literature and the Ways to 'Culture'.* Oxford: Clarendon Press, 1993.

Byron, R. "The Problems of Modern Travel." (Orig. *Vogue*, August 21, 1929). In *Travel in Vogue*, 254. London: Macdonald Futura, 1981.

Cabezon, J.L. "The Discipline and its Other: The Dialectic of Alterity in the Study of Religion," *Journal of the American Academy of Religion*, 4, no. 1 (March 2006): 21–38.

Caesar, T. *Forgiving the Boundaries: Home as Abroad in American Travel Writing.* Athens and London: University of Georgia Press, 1995.

Calasso, R. "Introduction: *Chette-Wynde*." In B. Chatwin and R. Calasso, *Winding Paths*, 9–15. Photographs Bruce Chatwin. Introduction Roberto Calasso. London: Jonathan Cape, 1999.

Calder, P. *Travels With My Mother.* Auckland: Tandem Press, 2003.

Caputo, J. D., and Scanlon, M. J., eds. *God, the Gift, and Postmodernism.* Bloomington and Indianapolis: Indiana University Press, 1999.

Caputo, J. *On Religion.* London: Routledge, 2001.

Carr, H. "Modernism and Travel (1880–1940)." In *The Cambridge Companion to Travel Writing*, ed. P. Hulme and T. Youngs, 70–86. Cambridge: Cambridge University Press, 2002.

Casey, J. "A Place in the Shade" (August 23, 1986). In *Views from Abroad: The Spectator Book of Travel Writing*, ed. P. Marsden-Smedley and J. Klinke, 40–42. London: Grafton Books, 1988.

de Certeau, M. *The Practice of Everyday Life.* Trans. S. F. Rendall. Berkeley: University of California Press, 1984.

Chatwin, B. *Anatomy of Restlessness: Uncollected Writings.* Ed. J. Borm and M. Graves. London: Jonathan Cape, 1996.

Chatwin, B. and Calasso, R. *Winding Paths.* Photographs Bruce Chatwin. Introduction Roberto Calasso. London: Jonathan Cape, 1999.

Cioran, E. M. *Tears and Saints.* Trans. I. Z. Johnston. London and Chicago: University of Chicago Press, 1995 (orig. 1937).

Clark, S., ed. *Travel Writing and Empire: Postcolonial Theory in Transit.* New York and London: Zed books, 1999.

Cocker, M. *Loneliness and Time: British Travel Writing in the Twentieth Century.* London: Secker & Warburg, 1992.

Cohen, E. "Towards a Sociology of International Tourism." *Social Research*, 39 (1972): 164–82.

——— "Who is a Tourist? A Conceptual Clarification." *Sociological Review*, 22 (1974): 527–55.

Coleman, S., and Crang, M., eds. *Tourism: Between Place and Performance.* New York and Oxford: Bergahan Books, 2002.

Cook, J. W., and Klotz, H. *Conversations with Architects.* London: Lund Humphries, 1973.

Cowan, D. E. *Theology in Exodus: Biblical Theology in the Form of a Commentary*. Louisville: Westminster John Knox Press, 1994.

Cowley, J. "Still Life in Mobile Homes." *New Statesman*, November 19, 2001, 49–51.

Cowley, M. *Exile's Return: A Literary Odyssey of the 1920s*. New York: Penguin, 1976.

Cox, H. *The Secular City: Secularization and Urbanization in Theological Perspective*. London: SCM Press, 1965.

Crockett, C., ed. *Secular Theology: American Radical Theological Thought*. London and New York: Routledge, 2001.

Culler, J. "The Semiotics of Tourism." In idem, *Framing the Sign: Criticism and its Institutions*, 153–67. Oxford: Basil Blackwell, 1988.

Cunningham, V. "The Rabbins Take It Up One After Another." In V. Cunningham, *In the Reading Goal: Postmodernity, Texts and History*, 363–64. Oxford and Cambridge, MA: Blackwell, 1994.

Curnow, A., ed. *A Book of New Zealand Verse 1923–50*. Christchurch: Caxton Press, 1951.

Dalrymple, W. *From the Holy Mountain: A Journey in the Shadow of Byzantium*. London: HarperCollins, 1997.

Dann, G. "Writing Out the Tourist in Space and Time." *Annals of Tourism Research* 26, no. 1 (1999): 159–87.

Davis, C., Milbank, J., and Zizek, S., eds. *Theology and the Political: The New Debate*. Durham and London: Duke University Press, 2005.

Deleuze, G., and Guattari, F. *A Thousand Plateaus: Capitalism and Schizophrenia*. Trans. B. Massumi. London: Althone Press, 1988 (orig. 1980).

Derrida, J., and Vattimo, G., eds. *Religion*. Cambridge: Polity Press, 1998.

Dessaix, R. "Busting Out." *Sydney Morning Herald*, September 17, 2004. http://www.smh.com.au/articles/2004/09/17/1095320946227.html

Dobb, E. "Where the Good Begins: Notes on the Art of Modern Travel." *Harpers* (July 1998): 59–66.

van Doesburg, T. "Vers la peinture blanche." *Art concret* 1, no. 1 (1930): 11–12.

Duncan, J., and Gregory, D. *Writes of Passage: Reading Travel Writing*. London: Routledge, 1999.

Durkheim, E. *The Elementary Forms of the Religious Life*. London: Allen and Unwin, 1976 [orig. 1912].

Durrell, L. *Sicilian Carousel*. London: Faber and Faber, 1977.

Dyer, G. *Yoga for People Who Can't be Bothered to Do It*. London: Abacus, 2003.

Elsner, J., and Rubies, J.-P., eds. *Voyages and Visions: Towards a Cultural History of Travel*. London: Reaktion Books, 1999.

Exum, C., and Moore, S., eds. *Biblical Studies/Cultural Studies: The Third Sheffield Colloquium*. Sheffield: Sheffield Academic Press, 1998.

Feifer, M. *Going Places: The Ways of the Tourist from Imperial Rome to the Present Day*. London: Macmillan, 1985.

Feiler, B. *Walking the Bible: A Journey by Land through the Five Books of Moses*. New York: William Morrow/Harper Collins, 2001.

Finkielkraut, A. *The Defeat of the Mind*. Trans and intro. J. Friedlander. New York: Columbia University Press, 1995 (orig. 1987).

Flaubert, G. *Flaubert in Egypt: A Sensibility on Tour: A Narrative drawn from Gustave Flaubert's Travel Notes and Letters*. Trans. and ed. F. Steegmuller. London: Michael Haag, 1983. (Orig. London: Bodley Head, 1972.)

Ford, J., and Ford, K. M. *Classic Modern Homes of the Thirties*. New York: Dover Publications, Inc., 1989. (Republication of *The Modern House in America*. New York: Architectural Book Publishing Co., 1940.)

Forster, E. M. *A Room with a View*. London: Edward Arnold and Co., 1947 (orig. 1908).

Fussell, P. *Abroad: British Literary Travelling Between the Wars*. New York: Oxford University Press, 1980.

Fussell, P., ed. *The Norton Book of Travel*. New York: Norton, 1987.

Gallagher, D., ed. *The Essays, Articles and Reviews of Evelyn Waugh*. Boston and Toronto: Little, Brown and Co., 1984.

Gartman, D. "Why Modern Architecture Emerged in Europe, not America: The New Class and the Aesthetics of Technology." *Theory, Culture & Society* 17, no. 5 (2000): 75–96.

Geering, L. *Christianity Without God*. Wellington: Bridget Williams Books; Santa Rosa, CA: Polebridge Press, 2002.

Glad, J., ed. *Literature and Exile*. Durham: Duke University Press, 1990.

Gleber, A. *The Art of Taking a Walk: Flanerie, Literature, and Film in Weimar Germany*. Princeton: Princeton University Press, 1999.

Gorringe, T. "Culture and Barbarism: Barth amongst the Students of Culture." In *Conversing with Barth*, ed. J. McDowell and M. Higton, 40–52. Aldershot and Burlington, VA: Ashgate, 2004.

Graburn, N. H. H. "Tourism: The Sacred Journey." In *Hosts and Guests: The Anthropology of Tourism*, 2nd ed., ed. V. L. Smith, 21–36. Philadelphia: University of Philadelphia Press, 1989.

Grant, L. *When I Lived in Modern Times*. London: Granta, 2000.

Grant, R. *Ghost Riders: Travels with American Nomads*. London: Little, Brown, 2003.

Grimshaw, Mike, "Soft Modernism: The World of the Post-Theoretical Designer." http://www.ctheory.net/text_file.asp?pick=418

———— "Did God Die in the *Christian Century*?" *Journal for Cultural and Religious Theory* 6, no. 3 (Fall 2005) http://www.jcrt.org/archives/06.3/

Gropius, W. *The New Architecture and the Bauhaus*. Trans. P. M. Shand. New York: Museum of Modern Art, 1937.

Gunning, T. "The Whole World within Reach: Travel Images without Borders." In *Travel Culture: Essays on What Makes Us Go*, ed. C. T. Williams, 25–37. Westport, CN: Praeger, 1998.

Gurr, A. *Writers in Exile: The Creative Use of Home in Modern Literature*. Sussex: Harvester Press, 1981.

Hassan, I. "Travel as Metaphor: Unmargined Realities." In *Dissent and Marginality: Essays on the Borders of Literature and Religion*, ed. K. Tsuchiya, 163–78. London: Macmillan and New York: St Martin's Press, 1997.

Heller, A. *A Philosophy of History in Fragments*. Oxford: Blackwell, 1993.

Hemming, L. P., ed. *Radical Orthodoxy? A Catholic Enquiry*. Aldershot: Ashgate, 2000.

Hitchcock, H. R. and Johnson, P. *The International Style*. New York: W.W. Norton and Co., 1966. (Originally published as *The International Style: Architecture Since 1922* [1932].)

Holland, P., and Huggan, G. *Tourists with Typewriters: Critical Reflections on Contemporary Travel Writing*. Ann Arbor: University of Michigan Press, 1998.

Holland, S. "First We Take Manhattan, Then We Take Berlin: Bonhoeffer's New York." *Crosscurrents* 50, no. 3 (Fall 2000): 1–11.

Home & Entertaining (New Zealand). April/May 2002.

Horkheimer, M. "Theism and Atheism." In *The Frankfurt School on Religion*, ed. E. Mendieta, 213–23. London and New York: Routledge, 2005.

Horne, D. *The Intelligent Tourist*. McMahon's Point, NSW: Margaret Gee, 1992.

Houellebecq, M. *Platform*. Trans. F. Wynne. London: Vintage, 2003.

——— *Lanzarotte*. Trans. F. Wynne. London: Vintage, 2004.

Howe, N. "Reading Places." *The Yale Review* 81, no. 3 (July 1993): 60–73.

Hughes, R. *The Shock of the New*. 2nd ed. New York: McGraw-Hill, 1991 (orig. 1980).

Hulme, P., and Youngs, T., eds. *The Cambridge Companion to Travel Writing*. Cambridge: Cambridge University Press, 2002.

Huxley, A. *Along the Road: Notes and Essays of a Tourist*. London: Chatto and Windus, 1928.

Ibelings, H. *Supermodernism: Architecture in the Age of Globalization*. Rotterdam: Nai Publishers, 1998.

Ibieta, G. "Transcending the Culture of Exile." In *Literature and Exile*, ed. D. Beaven. Amsterdam and Atlanta, GA: Rodopi, 1990.

Inglis, F. *The Delicious History of the Holiday*. London and New York: Routledge, 2000.

Iyer, P. *The Global Soul*. New York: Alfred A. Knopf, 2000.

——— *Sun After Dark: Flights into the Foreign*. New York: Alfred A. Knopf, 2004.

Jabes, E. *The Little Book of Unsuspected Subversions*. Trans. R. Waldrop. Stanford: Stanford University Press, 1996.

Jack, I., ed. *The Granta Book of Travel*. London: Granta Books, 1998.

Jacobs, M. *Between Hopes and Memories: A Spanish Journey*. London: Picador, 1994.

James, C. *Flying Visits: Postcards from the Observer 1976–1983*. London: Jonathan Cape, 1984.

JanMohamed, A. R. "Worldliness – without World, Homelessness-as-Home: Toward a Definition of the Specular Border Intellectual." In *Edward Said: A Critical Reader*, ed. M. Sprinker, 96–120. Oxford and Cambridge, MA: Blackwell, 1992.

Jasper, D. *The Sacred Desert: Religion, Literature, Art and Culture*. Malden, MA and Oxford: Blackwell, 2004.

Jencks, C. *The Language of Post-Modern Architecture*. Revised enlarged, 6th ed. London: Academy Editions, 1991.

——— *Ecstatic Architecture*. Chichester: Academy Editions, 1999.

Jenkins, P. *The Next Christendom: The Coming of Global Christianity*. Oxford: Oxford University Press, 2002.

Jobling, P., Pippin, T. and Schliefer, S., eds. *The Postmodern Bible Reader*. Oxford: Blackwell, 2001.

Johnson, P. "Whither Away – Non-Miesian Directions." Speech to Yale University February 5, 1959 (previously unpublished). In P. Johnson, *Writings*, 237. New York: Oxford University Press, 1979.

——— *Writings*. New York: Oxford University Press, 1979.

Kaplan, C. *Questions of Travel: Postmodern Discourses of Displacement*. Durham: Duke University Press, 1996.

Kaplan, R. D. *Mediterranean Winter: The Pleasures of History and Landscape in Tunisia, Sicily, Dalmatia and Greece*. New York: Random House, 2004.

Karamis, V. Review Essay of *Dispositions*, McKenzie Wark, *borderlands* 3, no. 2 (2004). http://www.borderlandsejournal.adelaide.edu.au/vol3no2_2004/karaminas_dis positions.htm

Kearney, R. "Desire of God." In *God, the Gift, and Postmodernism*, ed. J. D. Caputo and M. J. Scanlon, 112–45. Bloomington and Indianapolis: Indiana University Press, 1999.

Kennedy, J. G. *Imagining Paris: Exile, Writing and American Identity*. New Haven and London: Yale University Press, 1993.

Kerouac, J. *On the Road*. New York: Penguin, 1991.

Khan, H.-U. *International Style: Modernist Architecture from 1925–1965*. Koln: Taschen, 1998.

King, M., ed. *Pakeha: The Quest for Identity in New Zealand*. Auckland: Penguin, 1991.

Kitaj, R. B. *First Diasporist Manifesto*. London: Thames and Hudson, 1989.

Koolhass, R. "Miestakes." In *Mies in America*, ed. P. Lambert, 716–43. Montreal: Canadian Centre for Architecture; New York: Whitney Museum of American Art; New York: Harry N. Abrams Inc. Publishers, 2001.

Koos, L. R. "(T)here: The Rise of Touristic Culture in the Travel Writings of Jacques Arago." *Literature Interpretation Theory* 7, nos 2–3 (1996): 179–86.

Kostka, A. "Architecture and the 'New Man': Nietzsche, Kessler, Beuys." In *Nietzsche and "An Architecture of Our Minds."* Ed. A.

Kostka and I. Wohlfarth, 199–231. Los Angeles: Getty Research Institute for the History of Art and the Humanities, c.1999.

Kostka, A., and Wohlfarth, I., eds. *Nietzsche and "An Architecture of Our Minds."* Los Angeles: Getty Research Institute for the History of Art and the Humanities, c.1999.

Kracauer, S. *The Mass Ornament: Weimar Essays*. Trans. and ed. T. Y. Levin. Cambridge, MA and London: Harvard University Press, 1995.

Kramer, L. S. *Threshold of a New World: Intellectuals and the Exile Experience in Paris 1830–1848*. Ithaca and London: Cornell University Press, 1988.

Krist, G. "Ironic Journeys: Travel Writing in the Age of Tourism." *The Hudson Review* XLV:4 (Winter 1993): 593–601.

Lambert, P., ed. *Mies in America*. Montreal: Canadian Centre for Architecture; New York: Whitney Museum of American Art; New York: Harry N. Abrams Inc., 2001.

Larsen, T. "Thomas Cook, Holy Land Pilgrim, and the Dawn of the Modern Tourist Industry." In *The Holy Land, Holy Lands, and Christian History: Papers Read at the 1998 Summer Meeting and the 1999 Winter Meeting of the Ecclesiastical History Society*, ed. R. N. Swanson, 329–42. (Published for the Ecclesiastical History Society by the Boyatel Press.) Woodbridge, Suffolk and Rochester, NY: Boyatel and Brewer, 2000.

Lash, N. *Theology on Dover Beach*. New York: Paulist Press, 1979.

Le Corbusier, "The Decorative Art of Today." *L'Espirit Nouveau* (1925): 142–45. In *Raumplan versus Plan Libre: Adolf Loos and Le Corbusier 1919–1930*, ed. M. Risselada, 142–45. Delf: Delf University Press, 1988.

———— *Precisions on the Present State of Architecture and City Planning: With an American Prologue, a Brazilian Corollary followed by the Temperature of Paris and the Atmosphere of Moscow*. Trans. E. Aujame. Cambridge, MA: MIT Press, c.1991.

Lichtenberg-Ettinger, B. "The Becoming Threshold of Mattrixial Borderlines." In *Travellers' Tales: Narratives of Home and Displacement*, ed. G. Robertson et al., 38–62. London and New York: Routledge, 1994.

Lippard, L. *On the Beaten Track: Tourism, Art and Place*. New York: The New Press, 1999.

Lodge, D. *Paradise News*. London: Viking, 1991.

Lofgren, O. *On Holiday: A History of Vacationing*. Berkeley: University of California Press, 1999.

Long, B. O. *Imagining the Holy Land: Maps, Models and Fantasy Travels*. Bloomington and Indianapolis: Indiana University Press, 2003.

Loos, A. "Culture" (1908). In *The Architecture of Adolf Loos*, ed. Y. Safran and W. Wang, 97. (An Arts Council Exhibition). Arts Council of Great Britain, 1985.

———— "Architecture" (1910). In *The Architecture of Adolf Loos*, ed. Y. Safran and W. Wang, 108. (An Arts Council Exhibition). Arts Council of Great Britain, 1985.

Lyotard. J.-F. *The Postmodern Condition: A Report on Knowledge*. Minneapolis: University of Minnesota Press, 1984.

MacCannell, D. *The Tourist: A New Theory of the Leisure Class*. London: Macmillan, 1976.

———— *Empty Meeting Grounds: The Tourist Papers*. London and New York: Routledge, 1992.

Martin, A. K. and Kryst, S. "Encountering Mary: Ritualization and Place Contagion in Postmodernity." In *Places Through the Body*, ed. H. J. Nast and S. Pile, 207–29. London: Routledge, 1998.

McCarthy, M. "A Guide to Exiles, Expatriates, and Inner Emigrés." In *Altogether Elsewhere: Writers on Exile*, ed. M. Robinson, 49–58. San Diego, New York and London: A Harvest Book/Harcourt Brace and Co., 1994.

McEwan, N. *Anthony Powell*. New York: St Martins Press, 1991.

McKay, F., ed. *James K. Baxter as Critic*. Auckland: Heinemann Educational Books, 1978.

Magowan, R. "Writing Travel." *Southwest Review* (Spring–Summer 2001): 174–86.

Marinetti, F. *The New Religion – Morality of Speed* (Futurist Manifesto, first number of *L'Futalia Futurista*, May 11, 1916). In *Marinetti: Selected Writings*, ed. R. W. Flint, trans. R. W. Flint and A. A. Coppotelli, 94–96. New York: Farrar, Straus and Giroux, 1972.

Marsden, P. "Como Conversazione: On Travel and Travel Writing." *The Paris Review* 40, no. 147 (Summer 1998): 218–38.

Marsden-Smedley, P., and Klinke, J., eds. *Views from Abroad: The Spectator Book of Travel Writing*. London: Grafton Books, 1988.

Marx, K. "Introduction to A Contribution to the Critique of Hegel's Philosophy of Right." February 1844. In *Marx and Engels on Religion*. New York: Shocken Books, 1974.

Mather, V. "Travelling Bookfully." *Encounter* LXXIV:4 (May 1990): 38–43.

Max, L. "Having It All: The Kibbutznik and the Powhiri." In *Pakeha: The Quest for Identity in New Zealand*, ed. M. King, 79–91. Auckland: Penguin, 1991.

Melman, B. "The Middle East of Arabia: 'The Cradle of Islam'." In *The Cambridge Companion to Travel Writing*, ed. P. Hulme and T. Youngs, 105–21. Cambridge: Cambridge University Press, 2002.

Mendelson, E. "Baedeker's Universe." *The Yale Review* (Spring 1985): 387–89.

Mendieta, E. ed., *The Frankfurt School on Religion*. London and New York: Routledge, 2005.

Mertins, D., ed. *The Presence of Mies*. Princeton: Princeton Architectural Press, 1994.

Milbank, J., Pickstock, C., and Ward, G., eds. *Radical Orthodoxy: A New Theology*. New York and London: Routledge, 1999.

Milbank, J. "Materialism and Transcendence". In *Theology and the Political: The New Debate*, ed. C. Davis, J. Milbank and S. Zizek, 393–426. Durham and London: Duke University Press, 2005.

Miller, D. L., ed. *The Lewis Mumford Reader*. Athens, GA and London: University of Georgia Press, 1995.

Milton, G. *The Riddle and the Knight: In Search of Sir John Mandeville*. London: Allison and Busby, 1997.

Minh-ha, T. T. "Other than Myself/My Other Self." In *Travellers' Tales: Narratives of Home and Displacement*, ed. G. Robertson et al., 9–26. London and New York: Routledge, 1994.

——— "An Acoustic Journey." In *Rethinking Borders*, ed. J. C. Welchman, 1–17. London: Macmillan, 1996.

Moorhouse, G. *The Fearful Void*. London: Hodder and Stoughton, 1974.

Morris, J. *Travels*. London: Faber and Faber, 1976.

——— "Travel Lit's Novel Pursuit." *The Nation* 265:10 (October 6, 1997): 37.

——— *Trieste and the Meaning of Nowhere*. London: Faber and Faber, 2001.

Morris, P. "A Time for Re-enchantment." In Millennium Essays special supplement, *New Zealand Books* 9, no. 5 (December 1999): 4–5.

Morris, R. K. *The Novels of Anthony Powell*. Pittsburg: University of Pittsburg Press,

Murray, S. "Writing an Island's Story: The 1930s Poetry of Allen Curnow." *The Journal of Commonwealth Literature* 309, no. 2 (1995): 25–44.

——— *Never a Soul at Home: New Zealand Literary Nationalism and the 1930s*. Wellington: Victoria University Press, 1998.

Nancy, J.-L. *The Inoperative Community*. Ed. P. Connor, trans. P. Connor et al.; foreword C. Fynsk. Minneapolis, MN: University of Minnesota Press, c.1990.

Needham, J. *The Departure Lounge: Travel and Literature in the Post-modern World*. Manchester: Carcarnet, 1999.

Neumeyer, F. *The Artless Word: Mies van der Rohe on the Building Art*. Trans. M. Jarzombek. Cambridge, MA: MIT Press, c.1991.

——— "Mies as Self-educator." In *Mies van der Rohe: Architect as Educator*, ed. R. Achilles, K. Harrington and C. Myhrum. Catalogue for Exhibition June 6 through July 12, 1986, Mies van der Rohe Centennial Project. Chicago: Illinois Institute of Technology, 1986.

Norwich, J. J., ed. *A Taste for Travel: An Anthology*. New York: Alfred A. Knopf, 1987.

Olalquiaga, C. *Megalopolis: Contemporary Cultural Sensibilities*. Minneapolis: University of Minnesota Press, 1992.

Osborne, P. *Travelling Light: Photography, Travel and Visual Culture*. Manchester: Manchester University Press, 2000.

Padovan, R. "Machine a Metier." In *Mies van der Rohe: Architect as Educator*, ed. R. Achilles, K. Harrington and C. Myhrum. Catalogue for exhibition June 6 through July 12, 1986, Mies van der Rohe Centennial Project. Chicago: Illinois Institute of Technology, 1986.

Papastergiadis, N. *Modernity as Exile: The Stranger in John Berger's Writing*. Manchester and New York: Manchester University Press, 1993.

————— *Dialogues in the Diasporas: Essays and Conversations on Cultural Activity*. London and New York: Rivers Oram Press, 1998.

Pearman, H. *Contemporary World Architecture*. London: Phaidon Press, 1999.

Pels, D. *The Intellectual as Stranger: Studies in Spokespersonship*. London and New York: Routledge, 2000.

Peter, J. *The Oral History of Modern Architecture. Interviews with the Greatest Architects of the Twentieth Century*. New York: Harry N. Abrams, Inc., 1994.

Peukert, H. "Enlightenment and Theology as Unfinished Projects." In *The Frankfurt School on Religion*, ed. E. Mendieta, 351–70. London and New York: Routledge, 2005.

Plate, S. B. *Walter Benjamin, Religion, and Aesthetics: Rethinking Religion through the Arts*. London and New York: Routledge, 2005.

Plaut, W. G., ed. *The Torah: A Modern Commentary*. New York: Union of American Hebrew Congregations, 1981.

Porter, D. *Haunted Journeys: Desire and Transgression in European Travel Writing*. Princeton: Princeton University Press, 1991.

Powell, A. *What's Become of Waring?* London: Heinemann, 1964 (orig. 1939).

Purdy, A. "Shattered Voices: The Poetics of Exile in Quebec Literature." In *Literature and Exile*, ed. D. Bevan. Amsterdam and Atlanta: Rodopi, 1990.

Raban, J. *Soft City*. London: Collins Harvill, 1988 (orig. 1974).

————— *For Love and Money: Writing. Reading. Travelling. 1968–1987*. London: Picador/Pan, 1988.

Radhakrishnan, R. *Diasporic Meditations: Between Home and Location*. Minneapolis and London: University of Minnesota Press, 1996.

Rancière, J. "Discovering New Worlds: Politics of Travel and Metaphors of Space." In *Travellers' Tales: Narratives of Home and Displacement*, ed. G. Robertson et al. London and New York: Routledge, 1994.

Raven, S. "Travel: A Moral Primer" (August 9, 1968). In *Views from Abroad: The Spectator Book of Travel Writing*, ed. P. Marsden-Smedley and J. Klinke. London: Grafton Books, 1988.

Richardson, J. H. "The Long Way Home." *Esquire* 136, no. 5 (November 2001). http://www.esquire.com

Risse, M. "White Knee Socks versus Photojournalist Vests: Distinguishing between Travelers and Tourists." In *Travel Culture: Essays on What Makes Us Go*, ed. C. T. Williams, 41–50. Westport, CN: Praeger, 1998.

Risselada, M., ed. *Raumplan versus Plan Libre: Adolf Loos and Le Corbusier 1919–1930*. Delf: Delf University Press, 1988.

Robertson, G., et al., eds. *Travellers' Tales: Narratives of Home and Displacement*. London and New York: Routledge, 1994.

Robinson, M., ed. *Altogether Elsewhere: Writers on Exile*. San Diego, New York and London: A Harvest Book/Harcourt Brace and Co., 1994.

van der Rohe, M. "Bauukunst und Zeitwille!" (Building Art and the Will of the Epoch). *Der Querschnitt* 4, no. 1 (1924): 31–32. In F. Neumeyer, *The Artless Word: Mies van der Rohe on the Building Art*. Trans. M. Jarzombek. Cambridge, MA: MIT Press, c.1991.

Rojek, C., and Urry, J., eds. *Touring Culture*. London and New York: Routledge, 1992.

Said, E. *Representations of the Intellectual: The 1993 Reith Lectures*. London: Vintage, 1994.

Santayana, G. "The Philosophy of Travel." In *Altogether Elsewhere: Writers on Exile*, ed. M. Robinson, 41–48. San Diego, New York and London: A Harvest Book/Harcourt Brace and Co., 1994.

Savi, V. E., and Montaner, J. M., eds. *Less is More: Minimalism in Architecture and the Other Arts*. Barcelona: Col. Legi d'Arquitectes de Catalunya y ACTAR, 1996.

Sawyer-Laucanno, C. *The Continual Pilgrimage: American Writers in Paris, 1944–1960*. New York: Grove Press, 1992.

Schlor, J. *Nights in the Big City. Paris. Berlin. London. 1840–1930*. Trans. P. G. Imhof and D. R. Roberts. London: Reaktion Books, 1998 (orig. 1991).

Schrag, C. O. "The Kierkegaard-effect in the Shaping of the Contours of Modernity." In *Kierkegaard in Post/Modernity*, ed. M. Matustik and M. Westphal, 1–17. Bloomington: Indiana University Press, 1995.

Schulze, F. *Mies van der Rohe: A Critical Biography*. Chicago: University of Chicago Press, 1985.

——— *Philip Johnson: Life and Work*. New York: Alfred A. Knopf, 1994.

Scott, T. H. "South Island Journal." *Landfall* (December 16, 1950): 289–301.

Segovia, F. F., ed. *Interpreting Beyond Borders*. Sheffield: Sheffield Academic Press, 2000.

Selwyn, T., ed. *The Tourist Image: Myths and Myth Making in Tourism*. Chichester: John Wiley and Sons, 1996.

Sennet, R. *The Conscience of the Eye: The Design and Social Life of Cities*. London: Faber and Faber, 1993.

Sillitoe, A. *Leading the Blind: A Century of Guide Book Travel 1815–1914*. London: Macmillan, 1995.

Simmons, L., and Worth, H., eds. *Derrida Down Under*. Palmerston North: Dunmore Press, 2001.

Simpson, P. "'The Trick of Standing Upright': Allen Curnow and James K. Baxter." *World Literature Written in English* 26, no. 2 (Autumn 1986): 369–78.

Smith, V. L., ed. *Hosts and Guests: The Anthropology of Tourism*. 2nd ed. Philadelphia: University of Philadelphia Press, 1989.

Sorkin, M. "Frozen Light." In *Gehry Talks: Architecture + Process*, ed. M. Friedman. With an essay by M. Sorkin and commentaries by F. O. Geary. London: Thames & Hudson, 2003.

Sprinker, M., ed. *Edward Said: A Critical Reader*. Oxford and Cambridge, MA: Blackwell, 1992.

Stead, C. K. "Without." In idem, *The Red Tram*, 52–53. Auckland: Auckland University Press, 2004.

Stevenson, J., ed. *A New Eusebius: Documents Illustrating the History of the Church to AD 337*. New ed. Rev. W. H. C. Frend. London: SPCK, 1987 (orig. 1957).

Sugirtharajah, R. S., ed. *Vernacular Hermeneutics*. Sheffield: Sheffield Academic Press, 1999.

Suleiman, S. R., ed. *Exile and Creativity: Signposts, Travelers, Outsiders, Backward Glances*. Durham and London: Duke University Press, 1998.

Sullivan, L. "Ornament in Architecture" (1892). In *Louis Sullivan: The Public Papers*, ed. R. Twombly. Chicago: University of Chicago Press, 1988.

Swanson, R. N., ed. *The Holy Land, Holy Lands, and Christian History: Papers Read at the 1998 Summer Meeting and the 1999 Winter Meeting of the Ecclesiastical History*

Society (Published for the Ecclesiastical History Society by Boyatel Press). Woodbridge, Suffolk and Rochester, NY: Boyatel and Brewer, 2000.

Swick, T. "On the Road without a Pulitzer." *The American Scholar* 66, no. 3 (Summer 1997): 423–29.

Taylor, C. *Modern Social Imaginaries.* Durham and London: Duke University Press, 2004.

Taylor, J. *A Dream of England: Landscape, Photography and the Tourist's Imagination.* Manchester: Manchester University Press, c.1994.

Taylor, M. C. *Erring: A Postmodern A/Theology.* Chicago: University of Chicago Press, 1984.

—— "Reframing Postmodernisms." In *Shadow of Spirit: Postmodernism and Religion*, ed. P. Berry and A. Wernick. London and New York: Routledge, 1992.

—— *Disfiguring: Art, Architecture, Religion.* Chicago: University of Chicago Press, c.1992.

—— *About Religion: Economies of Faith in Virtual Culture.* Chicago: University of Chicago Press, 1999.

—— *The Moment of Complexity: Emerging Network Culture.* Chicago: University of Chicago Press, 2001.

Taylor, M. C. and Raschke, C. "About *About Religion*: A Conversation with Mark C. Taylor." *Journal of Cultural and Religious Theory* 2, no. 2 http://www.jcrt.org/archives/02.2/taylor_raschke.shtml

Tester, K., ed. *The Flaneur.* London and New York: Routledge, 1994.

Theroux, P. *Fresh-Air Fiend. Travel Writings 1985–2000.* London: Hamish Hamilton, 2000.

Thubron, C. "Both Seer and Seen: The Travel Writer as Left Over Amateur." *Times Literary Supplement* 5026 (July 30, 1999): 12–13.

Tisdale, S. "Never Let the Locals See Your Map." *Harpers* 291 (September 1995): 66–74.

Tournikiotis, P. *Adolf Loos.* New York: Princeton Architectural Press. 1994. (Orig. Paris: Editions Macula, 1991.)

Travel in Vogue. London: Macdonald Futura Publishers, 1981.

Travel Photography. New York: Time-Life Books, 1972.

Travlou, P. "Go Athens: A Journey to the Centre of the City." In *Tourism: Between Place and Performance*, ed. S. Coleman and M. Crang, 108–27. New York and Oxford: Bergahan Books, 2002.

Tsuchiya, T., ed. *Dissent and Marginality: Essays on the Borders of Literature and Religion.* London: Macmillan and New York: St Martin's Press, 1997.

Turner, S. "In Derrida's Wake: Why I Can't Think Where I Am." In *Derrida Down Under*, ed. L. Simmons and H. Worth, 69–85. Palmerston North: Dunmore Press, 2001.

Turner, V., and Turner, E. *Image and Pilgrimage in Christian Culture: Anthropological Perspectives.* New York: Columbia University Press, 1978.

Twain, M. *The Innocents Abroad.* New York: Penguin, 2002 (orig. 1869).

Twombly, R., ed. *Louis Sullivan: The Public Papers.* Chicago: University of Chicago Press, 1988.

Urry, J. *The Tourist Gaze.* 2nd ed. London: Sage, 2002.

Vahanian, G. "Theology and the Secular." In *Secular Theology: American Radical Theological Thought*, ed. C. Crockett, 10–25. London and New York: Routledge, 2001.

Van den Abbeele, G. "Sightseers: The Tourist as Theorist." *Diacritics* 10, no. 4 (Winter 1980): 2–14.

Vattimo, G. "The Trace of the Trace." In *Religion*, ed. J. Derrida and G. Vattimo, 79–94. Cambridge: Cambridge University Press, 1998.

——— *Belief*. Trans. L. D'Isanto and D. Webb. Stanford: Stanford University Press, 1999.

——— *After Christianity*. Trans. L. D'Isanto. New York: Columbia University Press, 2002.

_____ "The Age of Interpretation." In R. Rorty and G. Vattimo, *The Future of Religion*, ed. Santiago Zabala, 43–54. New York: Columbia University Press, 2005.

Venturi, R. *Complexity and Contradiction in Architecture*. 2nd ed. New York: Museum of Modern Art, 1977 (orig. 1966).

Vladislav, J. "Exile, Responsibility, Destiny." In *Literature and Exile*, ed. J. Glad. Durham: Duke University Press, 1990.

Vogel, L. I. *To See a Promised Land: Americans and the Holy Land in the Nineteenth Century*. University Park, PA: Pennsylvania State University Press, 1993.

Ward, G. "Bodies: The Displaced Body of Jesus Christ." In *Radical Orthodoxy: A New Theology*, ed. J. Milbank, C. Pickstock and G. Ward. London and New York: Routledge, 1999.

——— *Cities of God*. London and New York: Routledge, 2000.

Wark, M. *Dispositions*. Applecross, WA and Cambridge, UK: Salt Publishing, 2002.

Waugh, E. *Labels*. London: Duckworth, 1974 (orig. 1930).

——— "Desert and Forest." (Orig. *The Spectator*, September 28, 1934). In *The Essays, Articles and Reviews of Evelyn Waugh*, ed. D. Gallagher, 139. Boston and Toronto: Little, Brown and Co., 1984.

——— "The Tourists' Manual" (orig. *Vogue* (NY) July 1, 1935). In *The Essays, Articles and Reviews of Evelyn Waugh*, ed. D. Gallagher, 170. Boston and Toronto: Little, Brown and Co., 1984.

Welchman, J. C., ed. *Rethinking Borders*. London: Macmillan, 1996.

Weller, A. "Baedeker Revisited." *Forbes* 152, no. 7 (September 1993): 188.

Wevers, L. *Country of Writing: Travel Writing and New Zealand 1809–1900*. Auckland: Auckland University Press, 2002.

Whitman, W. B. "Baedeker's Travels." *Biblio* 4, no. 2 (February 1999): 36.

Whitson, F. W. Jr., "Style and the Critique of Metaphysics: The Letter as Form in Bonhoeffer and Adorno." In *Theology and the Practice of Responsibility: Essays on Dietrich Bonhoeffer*, ed. F. W. Whitson and C. Marsh, 239–51. Valley Forge, PA: Trinity Press International, 1994.

Wickens, E. "The Sacred and the Profane: A Tourist Typography." *Annals of Tourism Research* 29, no. 3 (July 2002): 834–51.

Wigley, M. *White Walls, Designer Dresses: The Fashioning of Modern Architecture*. Cambridge, MA: MIT Press, 1995.

Williams, R. "Introducing the Debate: Theology and the Political." In *Theology and the Political: The New Debate*, ed. C. Davis, J. Milbank and S. Zizek, 1–13. Durham and London: Duke University Press, 2005.

Wilson, A. *Reflections in a Writer's Eye*. London: Penguin Books, 1987.

Winquist, C. E. "Postmodern Secular Theology." In *Secular Theology: American Radical Theological Thought*, ed. C. Crockett, 26–36. London and New York: Routledge, 2001.

Wolfe, T. *From Bauhaus to Our House*. New York: Farrar Straus Giroux, 1981.

Zizek, S. *The Fragile Absolute – or, Why is the Christian Legacy Worth Fighting For?* London and New York: Verso, 2000.

——— *On Belief*. London and New York: Routledge, 2001.

——— *The Puppet and the Dwarf: The Perverse Core of Christianity*. Cambridge, MA and London: MIT Press, 2003.

Index of Authors

Index of Subjects

Printed in the United States
125709LV00002B/4-6/P